Relationships, residence and the individual

Relationships, residence and the individual
A rural Panamanian community

Stephen Gudeman

Department of Anthropology,
University of Minnesota

University of Minnesota Press

Minneapolis

First published in 1976
by Routledge & Kegan Paul Ltd
39 Store Street,
London WC1E 7DD
Broadway House,
Newtown Road,
Henley-on-Thames,
Oxon RG9 1EN
Published in the United
States of America by
the University of
Minnesota Press, Minneapolis,
Minnesota 55414
Set in IBM Press Roman
and printed in Great Britain by
Unwin Bros Ltd
Library of Congress Catalog Card Number 75 34875
ISBN 0 8166 0785 0

Contents

Preface   xi

1   The country, people and problem   1

The countryside   4
The community   4
The problem   9

2   Village life and ties to the larger society   16

Governmental and political institutions   16
Santiago and the larger society   21
Social life in the community   23

3   Economic organization   26

The setting   26
Land history and ecology   27
Productive activities   30
Organization of labour   33
Sources and disposal of goods   34
Household units   36
The economy and its social implications   41

4   God, the devil and the saints   43

God and man: destiny and faith   43
The devil and man   47
Women, snakes and fruit trees   51
The saints and man   58

5   The individual   64

Classes of persons: the individual within the larger society   64

Classes of persons: the individual within the
community   68
Classes within the person: the individual divided   74
The total person: respect and shame   77
The individual within the society and community   85

6   **The household**   86

Houses   87
The household in relation to the person   90
The household in relation to other domains   94

7   **The household and the elementary family**   97

Males, females and the conjugal relationship   99
The conjugal relationship   101
Sexual relations and conjugal unions   104
Parents and children   107
Siblings   115

8   **From natal to conjugal household**   117

The co-residential couples prohibition   118
Adolescence   119
Courtship   122
Moving into conjugal unions   123
The household and the co-residential couples
prohibition   128

9   **Forms of conjugal relations**   131

Common-law, civil and church unions   134
The three compared   136
Polygyny, extra-residential liaisons and prostitutes   146

10 **Conjugal instability**   155

Conjugal instability   156
Children, money and property   162
Household re-formation   163

11 **Extra-domestic kinship and affinity**   175

Parents and grown children   175

Affinal relationships 176
Keeping up sibling ties 177
The problem of the aged and the single 181
Kinfolk beyond the nuclear family 182
The kinship network and locality 183

12 **Forming the 'compadrazgo'** 190

From birth to baptism 192
Baptism 194
Confirmation 198
Church marriage 198
Rice 'compadres' 199
'Compadrazgo' rites and the spiritual person 199

13 **The structure of 'compadrazgo'** 206

The godparent-godchild bond 206
The 'compadre'-'compadre' relationship 210
Elaborations 215
The rules of choosing godparent/'compadres' 217
The 'compadrazgo' in relation to the individual, the family and the household 224

14 **Relationships, residence, religion and the individual** 232

Appendix: household and population statistics 237

Notes 248

Bibliography 262

Index 270

Illustrations

Plates   *between pages 114-5 and 146-7*

1   House site
2   Mud-and-tile home
3   Harvesting sugar cane
4   Relaxing after bringing lunch to the fields
5   Listening to lottery results at midday
6   Sweeping the patio
7   Sorting and cleaning rice
8   Bringing home provisions from Santiago
9   Making one's own leather sandals
10 Washing clothes at a brook
11 Near an old-style fireplace at grandmother's house

Figures

1   Sources and uses of household goods   36
2   Kinship and affinal links among nine adults   125
3   Step-parenthood, raising and the household   169
4   Types of sibling bond   171
5   The kinship network and locality   185

Maps

1   Republic of Panama   2
2   Los Boquerones   5

Tables

1   Costs and harvests for one hectare in swidden agriculture   31
2   Major assets of fifteen households   39
3   Five customs in rewritten form   56
4   Work tasks and the household   93
5   Types of co-residential monogamous union by age   137
6   Types of co-residential monogamous union by age   137
7   Types of co-residential monogamous union by duration of union   138
8   Types of co-residential monogamous union by duration of union   138
9   Forms of heterosexual relationship   152
10 Types of godparent-godchild relationship   207

Preface

When I first went to Panama in 1965 my intention was to study economic change and problems of development among a rural people. Veraguas Province was then (and still now is) one of the least developed areas of the country. By 1965, however, a number of national and supranational agencies had begun the effort to revitalize the area, and I hoped to study some of these efforts and their effects. Eventually I chose to study in detail the community of Los Boquerones because it was poised between subsistence and cash-crop farming, and because a small 'pre-cooperative' had been formed in the village. In the course of the study, however, my aims began to shift as I realized that any analysis of change would first require a sound understanding of village social organization. This book is the result — and I hope the fruit — of that diversion. I intend to return to the earlier research on economics, but the midcourse shift left me with a problem: how appropriate for a study of kinship and residence was a community which had been selected for other purposes? 'A village' perhaps was not even the appropriate research unit. Before and after local fieldwork, I travelled throughout central Panama, from large villages in the Pacific savanna to dispersed, isolated settlements in the Atlantic rain forest. As the re-sources and topography change throughout this area of Panama, one finds subtle shifts in the underlying economic scheme, but the basic culture is remarkably uniform, and I am fully satisfied that Los Bo-querones was, if not 'average', at least a good place to observe the essentials of countryman culture.

Much has changed in Panama since my original eighteen months of fieldwork in 1966-7. The current revolutionary government has taken a new interest in the economically depressed areas of the nation. On a brief return visit to Panama in 1974 I found that the economic base of Los Boquerones had been transformed. A land area that once consisted of savanna, forest and subsistence crops is now completely devoted to the raising of sugar cane — a crop financed and milled by a government-sponsored co-operative. Despite this change, I have written this study in the ethnographic present, as if 1966-7 were today. But this is not simply an anthropological fiction, since much of what I describe about rural domestic life in the 1960s is still true, not only of Los Boquerones but of vast areas of the central Panamanian provinces.

A word about terminology may be appropriate here. Los Boquerones is the true name of the village I describe, but the names of the people living there have been disguised. The reader will soon find that I avoid using the term 'peasants' to describe the people, preferring instead the Spanish *campesinos* or countrymen. The latter term is commonly employed by all Panamanians, hence it is ethnographically correct. Use of it also serves to emphasize that this way of life is recognized as a distinctive one by Panamanians themselves. Perhaps as important, much discussion has focused on the 'proper' definition of peasant, and one is somewhat cautious to give the label to a group of people who do not fit many of the existing definitions. In at least one important respect the villagers — indeed, nearly all the rural folk of Panama — differ from some of their cultural cognates in Mexico, Central America and Colombia. They do not now possess, and have never possessed, legal title to the land they work; yet, their relation with the dominant landowners is not a feudal one and the rent they pay is comparatively small. The countrymen are squatters, a fact of some importance for understanding their social organization. Whether the people of Los Boquerones should or should not be included in the category 'peasant' is not, it seems to me, an issue of paramount importance for this study.

The book is longer than I should desire, but its length is not the result of an antiquarian desire to record all the details for posterity. Rather, I have wished at each stage to substantiate, to support empirically, my assertions and generalizations. This does not make for quick reading, but at least the reader is in a better position to judge the argument for himself.

During the course of research one incurs many debts, and mine are numerous. I owe more than I can repay to the people of Los Boquerones, whose conversation and humour I always enjoyed. Professor George C. Lodge, Archbishop Marcos McGrath, and Harvey and Susan Williams all provided different forms of assistance during fieldwork. Professor Sir Edmund Leach not only taught me anthropology but has been a good friend as well. The investigation was supported in part by a Public Health Service fellowship (1-F1-MH-35,467-01) from the

National Institute of Mental Health. I am also grateful to the University of Minnesota (Office of International Programs; Single Quarter Leave). The Royal Anthropological Institute has permitted me to use in chapter 13 some material which first appeared in the *Proceedings of the Royal Anthropological Institute for 1971.* My family have seen it all through with equanimity and have provided immeasurable support. My wife, Roxane, took the photographs.

Stephen Gudeman

Minneapolis,
Minnesota

1   The country, people and problem

The Republic of Panama, a small nation in area and population, occupies the strip of land linking the five Central American countries with the South American continent. The location is strategic and the state has had a turbulent history. Prior to the arrival of the Spanish, Panama was occupied by both tropical forest and savanna-dwelling Indians. Columbus first landed on the north coast in 1502 and was immediately excited by the prospect of gold in the Veragua area; his attempt to found a colony at Belén in early 1503, however, was unsuccessful. Seven years later Balboa was able to establish a colonial foothold further down the coast. For most of the following three centuries the area served mainly as an *entrepôt;* the treasure and merchandise from the Pacific Coast of the Spanish possessions were brought to the southern side of the Isthmus and then shipped to Spain from the northern shore. Panama itself contributed little to the flow of goods but, owing to the concentration of treasure, it was the frequent target of pirates. Panama declared its independence from Spain in 1821 and shortly thereafter formed a union with Colombia (which then comprised both the current country and Venezuela). The present Republic declared its independence from Colombia in 1903, and almost immediately afterwards granted a special concession to the United States permitting it to construct the Panama Canal and to institute special military control in the Canal Zone and adjacent areas.

The two major cities of the present state, Panama City and Colón, located at either end of the Canal, are cosmopolitan urban areas which are successors to similar trading ports of earlier centuries (see Map 1). In contrast to the continuing international character of the transit area, the central provinces of the country have remained relatively isolated and detached since the first half of the seventeenth century. In the early 1500s the Spanish made several expeditions into the interior.[1] Much of the indigenous population, organized under local chiefs, was decimated by the Spanish, while the survivors were pressed into labour

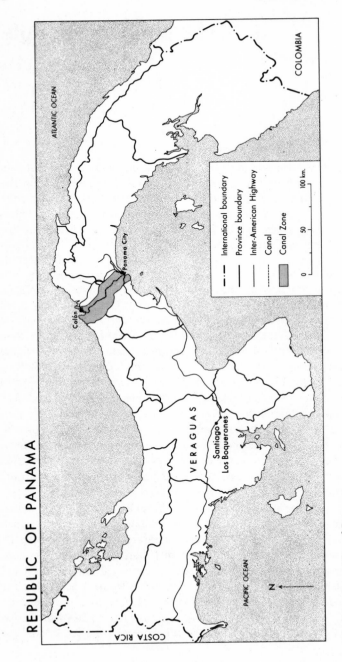

MAP 1   *Republic of Panama*

service of the conquerors. Due to disease and hard working conditions, the remaining Indians suffered greatly and their numbers dwindled. Throughout the sixteenth century, therefore, Negro slaves were imported to the area.

In 1537 the 'Duchy of Veragua' along with the title *Duque de Veragua* were granted to Luis Columbus, grandson of the sailor, in partial settlement of promises made by the Spanish Crown to the explorer. The area given included all of present-day Veraguas and portions of the neighbouring provinces.[2] By 1556, however, the Columbus descendant had to renounce his rights to the land, although the title *Duque de Veragua* is still extant today (Lothrop, 1950: 10).

Gold in the mountainous northern part of what is now Veraguas Province attracted Spanish settlers in the latter part of the 1500s. Santiago, now the central town of the interior and the present capital of Veraguas, was established sometime between 1620 and 1640; it is located on the traditional east-west path from the Isthmus toward Central America.

In the north of Veraguas the mines did not produce a lucrative return for long. Also, many of the slaves fled, and by the first half of the 1600s the native population, in theory, was liberated. With the cessation of the mining the urban Spanish colonists maintained little interest in the interior. The populace in the countryside turned its attention to the lowland savanna areas, and by this time there was also an increasing genetic mixing of the Negroes, Indians and Spanish (Castillero C., A., 1967: 109-10). The pure Spanish who remained in the interior turned primarily to cattle raising, while agriculture became the job of the mixed bloods, who, despite the dominant impact of the Spanish, adopted aboriginal farming techniques. The interior population was not large and has only grown markedly since the turn of this century.[3]

The impact of these historical changes and continuities is evident today. The current rural population is physically mixed. The culture of the people derives primarily from that of colonial Spain.[4] A few African influences are to be found, while only some economic and material traits derive from the original Indian cultures. At the same time, modern industrial life has not yet had a large impact upon much of the rural area.[5]

The countryside

The current state is divided into nine provinces plus the *comarca* of San Blas, a special area set aside for the San Blas Cuna. The three central provinces are known collectively to Panamanians as the 'interior'. Of the three the largest in land area is Veraguas.

Roughly, the present-day inhabitants of Veraguas may be divided into three categories. Some (2.5 per cent) are Indians, such as the Guaymí, most of whom have lived in the more remote mountainous areas since early colonial times.[6] The principal inhabitants of the interior, however, are the rural folk and the town dwellers. The rural people sometimes refer to themselves as 'agriculturalists' or simply as 'the people'; but the most common word applied to them by all sectors of the society is *campesino* or countryman. The distinction between countryman and town dweller is not easy to draw, and it is perhaps best to envisage each as lying at the opposite poles of a continuum. Town dwellers generally reside in the larger towns of the province, although some own large, mechanized farms or cattle ranches. For his part the *campesino* is basically a farmer who utilizes hand methods of production.[7] The countrymen live in a variety of settlement patterns. Some are the peripheral residents of the larger provincial towns; others live in well-settled rural towns of 1,000-1,500 persons. Most commonly the *campesino* lives in a village containing 50-150 households; the homes may be grouped about a plain or slightly spread out. In the less transited areas of the province a countryman community may consist mainly of a large number of homes spread over the countryside. Despite the lack of a clear social distinction between town and rural dweller, however, the *campesinos* do have a distinctive culture. Adams, who has provided the most thorough survey of the countryside, terms it the 'Basic Countryman Culture' and suggests that it extends throughout the entire central part of the country (1957: 109), a point confirmed by my own investigations.

The community

The community of Los Boquerones lies approximately ten miles east of Santiago, the provincial centre (see Map 2). It occupies something less than 2,600 hectares of land and is located on both sides of the two-lane Inter-American Highway which connects Santiago to Panama City. This link in the road system was finished in the late 1950s, while the westward section joining Santiago to Costa Rica was completed in

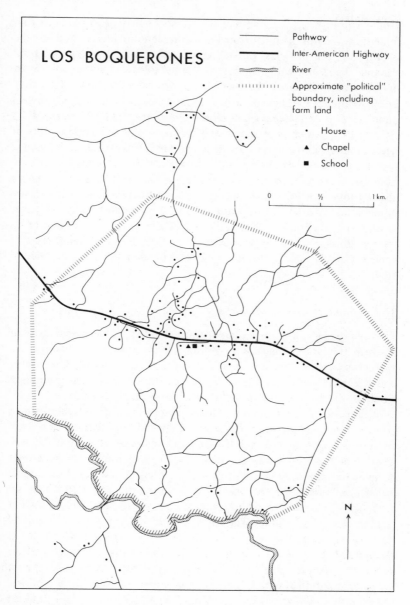

LOS BOQUERONES

Pathway
Inter-American Highway
River
Approximate "political" boundary, including farm land

• House
▲ Chapel
■ School

0   ½   1 km.

N

MAP 2 *Los Boquerones*

1967. Although Los Boquerones is only some fifty years old – its first inhabitant did not die until after I had completed fieldwork and left the country – the village's general characteristics are typical of rural Panama. The community contains 91 households and 350 people. Most of the people are agriculturalists but do not hold title to the land they work. Within the village are a four-room school, a small chapel, several hand water-pumps, four small stores which are parts of homes, and a *cantina* (bar) which is operated only on *fiesta* days. The houses are not agglomerated about a central site. Most are located near the highway, but a number are spread around the extremities of the village. House-hold groups vary in size from one to ten persons and have an average of slightly less than four. The kinship system is bilateral, and although the composition of houses varies, the core of the group is usually a nuclear family. The essentially Spanish roots of the people are exhibited in nearly all aspects of their culture from their Roman Catholicism to their system of godparenthood to certain of their secular value orienta-tions.

The community as a group in the countryside

As a group the community is an ill-defined entity. It has no surveyed or discrete boundaries, and at its borders there is some ambiguity con-cerning who does and does not live in the village. In fact, Los Boque-rones is not a single group of people but several different groupings, none of which is congruent but all of which partially overlap.

The most precise grouping is based upon the political-legal divisions of the state. Each province of Panama is divided into districts, and these in turn are divided into subdistricts (*corregimientos*). Within the sub-district or directly within the district a smaller grouping is sometimes recognized: the *regimiento* (smaller subdistrict). Legally Los Boque-rones is a *regimiento*. The boundaries of provinces and districts are set nationally, while those of a *corregimiento* are defined by the district administration. The boundaries of a *regimiento,* however, are specified in rough terms by the mayor of the larger district and are interpreted as desired by the persons who live in the area of the *regimiento*. Effec-tively the people residing at the edge of a *regimiento* may choose whether they live within one or the other of two local political communities; and they even may change their affiliations over time. At a particular time, then, Los Boquerones as a *regimiento* is a precisely defined unit since everyone must live in one or another legal group, but through time it is not, since individuals may change their affiliations without physically moving.

Geographically the countryside is divided by the *campesinos* into a patchwork of localities. Each locality, which may be as small as 20 hectares, bears a distinctive name. Such names are drawn primarily from the environment itself, such as 'green tree', or 'pretty spring'. For the immediate Los Boquerones area I recorded more than thirty such named geographical subdivisions. Four of these named areas refer to sites on which clusters of houses are found; the rest primarily denote work areas. Of the four named locales with houses one bears the name of the community itself: Los Boquerones refers both to the entire community and to an area within it. The other three occupied locales lie on the borders of the community and actually extend into neighbouring named settlements. The people residing within one of these locales may live either within Los Boquerones as a *regimiento* or in a neighbouring village. In terms of geography, then, the countryside is divided by the people into localities but these do not coincide with any other recognized groupings.

Groupings established by the census bureau provide a third way of defining the community. The smallest unit into which the census bureau groups the people is the *caserío* (hamlet, small settlement). This entity is primarily a statistical abstraction, although it is based upon settlement patterns. To define a *caserío*, each decade the bureau takes a regional map, plots clusters of houses on the map, and shades in these clusters. The island of houses is then said to constitute a *caserío*. Theoretically, a *caserío* also has a name, though as I have just described, every geographic area is already named. This method of defining *caseríos* may be useful for census purposes but it is little more than a statistical device. Homes normally are not agglomerated but are spread over a large area of land. Moreover, house sites, house clusters, and the names of these clusters all change over time. Thus, Los Boquerones as a census unit has been defined differently in each of the last three censuses, making it quite impossible to compare the statistics.[8]

Organizations and institutions located in Los Boquerones itself do not provide unambiguous markers of the community. The school can draw children from other settlements. The parents of these children attend meetings for the school parents but do not consider themselves to be part of the community. Similarly the chapel committee sometimes receives aid from people of different hamlets. Land rights do not provide a basis for defining the community. Title to nearly all the land in the community is presently held by the Panamanian government; however, the area which the state owns extends beyond the borders of the political village and includes parts of three other political communities. A small piece of land owned by a town dweller also juts into the settlement area. In any event, the men do not perpetually farm in a single location, nor do they feel compelled to work within a set of borders which they consider to be the community. Perhaps most important, friends, kin and godparents are spread over the entire countryside. Such networks of persons are more dense within a settlement area, but they do not stop at arbitrary community boundaries.

Thus, the total *campesino* population is spread across the countryside. Some of the people, however, do live closer to one another and do have a higher intensity of interactions. Such population segments often are recognized by the people and by various outside agencies as constituting some type of grouping. These small-scale 'villages', however, are not corporate and as domiciles and relationships in the countryside shift so may their definition. Los Boquerones, then, is not a precisely defined social unit and for these reasons I view it as the field of inquiry but not the entity to be studied. Thus, when I refer to the community or village of Los Boquerones it should be understood that I mean an overlapping social, geographic and political entity. For statistical purposes, however, when I refer to Los Boquerones I mean the *regimiento* or political unit. The virtue of defining the village this way for a census is that at a particular time everyone must be a member of at least one but no more than one such community, and the identification is based on how the people themselves perceive their group. I have no reason to believe that a differently defined community would alter the conclusions or change the statistics I present in this book.

The community in relation to larger units

Even if the village were a separate entity in relation to other *campesino* communities, it certainly is not a closed unit with respect to the larger society. In this regard, I find it useful to approach the issue of the articulation between Los Boquerones and the broader society from two perspectives. First, there is the straightforward aspect of describing the empirical relationships which the countrymen maintain with others not of their stratum, such as representatives of governmental agencies, the church, or business organizations. Second, there is the more subtle task of delineating the relation between the culture of the *campesinos* and that of the larger Panamanian society. This issue in turn is connected to Redfield's distinction between the Great and the Little Tradition.[9] With respect to Panama the problem is that the countrymen have a culture similar to that of the larger Panamanian society and the broader Hispanic world; yet, they also have a distinctive configuration of customs. What is the relation between these levels? Is, for example, the difference between the countryman's religious views and 'official' dogma an historical precipitate, a result of the fact that the people have not been in continuous and close contact with the broader society? Will the newer teachings of the church be adopted in time by the *campesinos*? Conversely, will some of the countrymen's notions have an impact on the church's formulations? My approach to this problem is as follows. I recognize that something called 'Hispanic culture' pervades nearly every aspect of the people's life, and I am aware that there are historical reasons for this fact. I further recognize that institutions such as the state or commercial corporations have more power to implant their ideas upon the countrymen than the reverse. Nevertheless, I do not think it is useful to speak of a Great and a Little Tradition. The concepts held by the church and the state are not codified in a single book and themselves change over time: they do not provide a Great benchmark or a 'correct' version against which the Little cultural life of Los Boquerones may be measured. Instead, I understand the people's cultural notions to be one variant within a total system of temporal and spatial variants in the Hispanic world. Current church regulations, for example, exert a pull on the community, but they are themselves only one permutation of earlier laws and are interpreted in multifarious ways in the Roman Catholic world. Throughout this book, therefore, I place some of the *campesinos'* cultural notions within a comparative framework but I do not view their ideas as being less sophisticated, less integrated, or fragmentary versions of some larger correct form. For the people their own notions are alive and valid, and it is with this on-going 'practical' (Leach, 1968: 1) system that I am mostly concerned.

The problem

In general, *campesino* social life is fluid. Community boundaries are unstable; alternate forms of 'marriage' are practised; family units break up; household structures are moved; communal associations form and disperse; shifting agriculture is practised; land rights are impermanent; and there is little property to inherit. There are no corporate groups based either on collections of kin or rights to property. In what respects, then, is the social life patterned? Does the village have no social structure, as anthropologists sometimes use the term?

Loosely structured systems have, of course, been widely reported from Latin America and the Caribbean; and much of the ethnography I present here has its counterpart elsewhere. But few satisfactory analyses, explanations or models of these systems have emerged. Much of the reportage has remained at the ethnographic level. Whatever its faults, at least Foster's recent volume (1967) presents a framework for analysis, which is probably why it has drawn so much comment in the literature. The principal anthropological puzzle I have faced, then, is: what are the enduring constituents of social action in the community? I think I can claim to show that the village does indeed have a structure, which, given that Los Boquerones has its analogues in other parts of Latin America, raises the theoretical import of this study several fold; but the sort of structure I have found is not exhibited directly in concrete and persisting groups, offices or relationships.

Let me put it this way. This book is primarily a synchronic description and analysis of aspects of the villagers' lives. Such an account provides an all-at-once view and is out of time. The synchronic report is always an abstraction, either in the form of summary statements about observed behaviour, conscious or unconscious norms for behaviour, or the anthropologist's model. It never corresponds to the immediately perceptible. Yet, paradoxically, as a set of rules the synchronic is manifested through time, and indeed all would be chaos without some timeless structure underlying behaviour. To be valid, therefore, the anthropologist's synchronic account — which he hopes is related to that of the people — must itself persist. But this is quite a different kind of perpetuity from that of an actual corporate group. Therefore, my concern here is not only with observable ties and collectivities but also with the persisting factors producing these relationships. Such an inquiry leads one into the realm of ideals, concepts and their interrelations. Thus, my emphasis is upon the continuity provided by the category system, rather than that afforded by existing positions in the social structure. Viewed as a system of ideas, the rather loose social organization of the *campesinos* is neither disordered nor disorganized.

Given this perspective, the emphasis is upon repetitive (though not continuous) relationships and units. The people of Los Boquerones engage in diverse relationships both within and without the community, but the most repetitive unit in the countryside is the household group, and the principal relationship systems are the family and *compadrazgo* (godparenthood complex). My overall concern, then, is to delineate the pattern formed by the household, family and *compadrazgo*.

This focus, however, raises a new problem, which is the primary theme of the book. What sort of entity is a kinship system? In recent years a number of linked questions have emerged around this issue. First, there is the question, what is kinship? At the risk of simplifying I think we can identify three positions. Some have held that kinship is essentially biologically based. It is founded on fundamental facts of nature, such as sexual attraction, coition, conception, female childbirth, and so forth. Since these facts are invariant to the human species, kinship is universally found and the investigator can readily identify kinship in a foreign culture by searching for that relationship system which encodes these biological facts. Moreover, since kinship is defined by its direct relation to these facts, it comprises a discrete domain, both in the sense that kinship systems throughout the world all fall within a certain range of variation and that within a particular culture kinship can be isolated from other domains such as politics, religion or even metaphoric kinship. Thus, Gellner (1957) has attempted to establish an 'ideal language' for all kinship systems; the works of Scheffler and Lounsbury (1971) and to some degree Fortes (1969) are related to this view.

Others have held that kinship may have nothing to do with biological realities, being no more than a construct of the Western anthropologist derived from his own life experience and implanted wholesale on a foreign culture. Kinship here is treated as a cultural domain to be defined in terms of its differentiating symbols. Since kinship is not based on nature, the anthropologist cannot assume that it is a cross-cultural universal; conversely, within a culture kinship must be viewed in terms of the other domains to which it is related. Thus, Schneider (1969) finds that within America kinship does not comprise a discrete domain since its defining features — relations as natural substance and relations as code for conduct — also are features of nationality and religion. Of course, this position raises the practical problem of how the investigator is to define a domain or engage in cross-cultural comparison. Indeed, we reach the point where the anthropologist has no word to describe an unbounded domain which he does not know exists.

In fact, most anthropologists fit somewhere between these extremes, maintaining that kinship is neither a direct translation of nature nor pure symbol. Thus Barnes (1973) distinguishes between the mother-child link — a natural one explained in cultural terms — and the father-child bond — a cultural one framed in natural terms.[10]

Closely related to this problem about the nature of kinship is one concerning explanation. How is a kinship system to be explained or described? What are we really trying to do when we analyse a kinship system, however defined? Much of the discussion here has to do with whether kinship is 'idiom' or 'content'.

In general, the approach of Radcliffe-Brown and his successors was based on several assumptions. Kinship it was held is not a direct translation of biology, but it does bear a close relation to real-life experience. Since kinship has an ultimate biological grounding, or as Fortes expresses it, emanates from the familial domain, it constitutes a discrete sphere of social facts. As a social fact within a discrete domain, one item of kinship behaviour should be explained in terms of another. Therefore, although a kinship system is related to other domains of the social life, it may be abstracted as a distinctive set of ties and analysed as a largely independent system. Thus, the observed behaviour between two males may ultimately be explained as an expression of the 'unity of the lineage group' or the 'principle of alternate generations'. Moreover, these axioms hold because of the ultimate reality, the inescapable content, of kinship. For Fortes, kinship has a distinctive content — moral amity — and this content is related to its very nature: 'sucked in with the mother's milk' (1969: 251). The argument is internally logical: if kinship does derive from the familial domain, then it constitutes a discrete sphere and can be explained in terms of kinship principles alone.

A direct attack against treating kinship in this fashion was levelled by Worsley (1956) and Leach (1961b), who argued that some actions said to be determined by norms of kinship are in fact a response to ecological and economic conditions. Thus, Worsley has suggested that Tallensi males are influenced not so much by feelings of ancestral piety or patrifiliation but by such practical facts as where land can be obtained to support themselves. Kinship in this view is seen to be more of an ideology or 'idiom' (Worsley, 1956: 63) for other underlying realities. This alternative approach can lead to an under-playing of the ideological distinctiveness of kinship, as Fortes (1969: 220-31) has argued. And, as Schneider (1964, 1965a) has asked, if kinship is only an idiom for something else, of what does it consist itself?

Yet a third issue has to do with the level of analysis undertaken by the observer. Radcliffe-Brown and his followers placed primary emphasis upon the analysis of social structure, which meant abstracting from a broader context systems of social relationships, such as a kinship or political system. To perceive and isolate this dimension of social action was an immense breakthrough, but in the hands of a rigorous social structuralist culture sometimes is relegated to being simply the 'clothing' in which the underlying relationships are 'expressed'. For example, in this view it may be held that the social relationship between a subject and ruler is expressed culturally by bowing behaviour or verbal salutations. Clearly, a Tylorian definition of culture is too broad, but the structuralist can be just as one-sided. Thus, explanations of kinship behaviour have been offered in terms such as the 'unity of the sibling group' not only because kinship is viewed as a discrete sphere but also because for the structuralist explanations are phrased in social structural terms.

If, however, we define culture not as residuary to social structure, but as a pool of meanings, as the shared ideas and beliefs which confer meaning on experience, then a different dimension and a deeper under-standing become possible. By culture I mean the entire realm of belief systems, ideologies and values. Social structure I take to refer to the level of social relationships, organizations and institutions. But let me be clear, for I am using the word culture in two possible ways. At the broader level I understand culture to refer to the entire description which is phrased in terms of concepts and ideas. Within this I dis-tinguish the level of social structure, such as relationship systems, from the overarching and encompassing level of cultural meanings in which they are embedded. By contrast, in some renderings of this distinction culture refers to the symbolic order while society refers to *actual* relationships (Parsons, 1972: 254), a definition which, it seems to me, runs the risk of confounding the culture/social structure distinction with that of the ideal and actual.

This discussion brings me back to the Panamanian situation. I shall focus on the countrymen's relationship systems, but I do not think their kinship system is a fabrication of the observer. Kinship in Panama is an existent set of relationships. At the same time, I do not believe the people's kinship (or *compadrazgo*) system can be abstracted analytic-ally and presented as a discrete set of social relationships. To under-stand and explain such a system the outsider must view it within the ideological context which defines, informs and suffuses it with meaning. Analytical focusing may be the hallmark of social science, but it must be undertaken with caution; in the case of kinship the anthropologist must be careful not to 'bracket away' the cultural meanings, which energize the social relationships, and substitute his own explanations. My purpose, then, is to place the countrymen's ideas about kinship (and the *compadrazgo*) within the total framework of their notions about humans and their relations to others. The people's concept of kinship, I show, is inseparable from other ideas they hold concerning the *compadrazgo*, the household, the person and their own place in the world. I illustrate that for the *campesinos* kinship is comprised of both genetics and residence, that the shape of their kinship system is influenced by ideas they hold about locality, that the kinship and *compadrazgo* systems are interrelated, that both these systems are tied to and shaped by ideas about the individual, and that certain religious formulations provide a buttress for and pervade the entire system. Kinship in rural Panama is neither pure genealogy nor a construct of the anthropologist, but also it is not a complex of bonds to be abstracted from its cultural context.

The organization of the book follows the structure of my argument. I begin with a description of the formal political relationships the villagers have, the principal points of articulation between the *campesinos* and the larger society, and the voluntary associations within the community. All these relationships are important but relatively nonenduring. I then turn to a description of the environmental setting and economic life to show that the economy in itself does not require perpetual institutions nor does its study provide much understanding of the principal relationship systems. The following chapter, concerning religious beliefs and practices, marks a transition to a more conceptual approach and leads directly into my argument, for I show how the people's conceptions about man, his place in the world, and his relation to God provide one set of meanings for the kinship and *compadrazgo* systems. This chapter also concludes my more conventional treatment and arbitrary divisions of the ethnographic material. Following it I turn more completely to the people's ideas, and the reader will find that in later chapters 'things economic' or 'religious' reappear but under different guises. I show next how the individual, as a concept, is linked on the one hand to the religious conceptions and on the other to the household-family-*compadrazgo* complex. In the following chapter I consider the household as an idea about residence or locality, and I show that the household concept is used to express ideas about the individual. The next five chapters are about the family system, and my concern in all five is to describe the intricate relations between kinship and residence, and beyond this to delineate the connections between the kinship system on the one hand, and the concept of the individual and the religious beliefs, on the other. Throughout these five chapters I am wrestling with the ghost of those who would explain kinship by reference only to 'kinship principles'. In the next two chapters the same themes continue but in relation to the system of godparenthood. I show how the *compadrazgo* is linked to the family, to the household, to the individual, and how ultimately it can be apprehended only through an understanding of the religious conceptions.

In sum, my emphasis throughout is upon the people's concepts which define and make meaningful their principal systems of relationship, and upon the continuities among the *compadrazgo*, kinship, the household, and the individual. Although this is an analytical study, the argument is less elegant than I should desire; but perhaps to that degree it captures something of the *campesino* world.

2   Village life and ties to the larger society

By law the *campesinos* are full Panamanian citizens, but this is a legal entitlement only. In most of their relationships with the larger society power lies with the persons from the outside, and such relationships tend to be transitory. Within the village several voluntary associations bring diverse people together on different occasions, but these groupings, too, are relatively non-enduring and are not community inclusive. To show in what way the primary relationship systems are influenced by aspects of the broader social organization, I consider here the countrymen's formal political life, some of the ties they have to outsiders, and the formal community associations.

Governmental and political institutions

All Panamanians above the age of twenty-one have the right to vote; however, the political participation of the *campesinos* has been minimal. In effect, political power is held in Panama City flowing out from there to the province capital and countryside. No administrative officers of the national government reside in the village itself, and politics and government do not have a dominant impact upon everyday life in the community.

Formally, Panama is a republic. The nation has had a number of constitutions, though basically all have been similar. Divided into three branches, the government consists of a presidency, whose occupant serves a four-year term and is elected directly by popular vote, a unicameral assembly comprised of one deputy for each 25,000 residents, and a hierarchy of courts culminating in a Supreme Court of Justice, whose members are appointed by the President and approved by the National Assembly. The nation is divided into nine provinces each of which is administered by a governor appointed by the president. Provinces are divided into districts, of which Veraguas Province contains eleven. Districts are administered by a mayor *(el alcalde)*. In most areas he is an elected official but in certain cases is appointed directly by the president. The Santiago mayor is a presidential appointee, although often the president first solicits the recommendation of the local district deputies. Districts are composed of subdistricts called *corregimientos,* which normally have a minimum of 4,000 inhabitants. The district of Santiago contains five *corregimientos* plus a sixth area called the 'head of the district' which is governed directly by the district mayor. *Corregimientos* are administered by a paid *corregidor,* a local resident appointed by the mayor of the district. As noted, within the district a further subdivision, the *regimiento,* is sometimes recognized. *Regimientos,* are headed by an unpaid *regidor,* who also is appointed by the district mayor. The *regimiento* of Los Boquerones falls directly within the head of the district of Santiago, and therefore comes under the immediate jurisdiction of the Santiago mayor.

The *campesinos'* relationship to the government on the national level is tenuous, although the people are aware of the different political leaders and governmental crises. Many exercise their voting rights but the gap between the ideal of representative government and its actuality is large. With respect to the countrymen most of the politicians' efforts are focused upon garnering votes at election time. On election day a candidate normally provides the *campesinos* with free transportation to Santiago. His agents frequently give potential voters drinks, goods or cash, and more extreme measures to obtain votes also have been used. Occasionally, the people have tried to obtain community-wide benefits in return for promised political support, and this has met with varying success. In 1964 one candidate promised supplies for the community's chapel which was then under construction. Directly prior to the election he brought out some building materials, but when he subsequently lost he retrieved the goods. By contrast, in this same election a small group of neighbours promised to vote for a different candidate in return for a water pump to be located in their area of the village. The candidate arranged for a drilling rig to be brought out to the community prior to the election, and after he won the work was completed and a pump was installed. The most well-known form of political patronage is called the *botella* (bottle), a government job which has few or no duties attached.[1] None of the community members has obtained a pure *botella,* although one or two have been rewarded with personal favours.

Politically, then, a short-term contract, the exchange of goods for vote, takes the place of a long-term contract between voter and representative. The consequences are twofold. For their part, many of the national deputies do not feel obliged to maintain an interest in the people whom they represent; some at least consider it proper to recoup their election expenses once in power. From the *campesinos'* standpoint the voting practices undermine the conception of popular representation and effectively remove them from political participation.[2]

As citizens the people have few fully-formed ideas concerning what they desire from the government. Some express the wish for an orderly and disciplined polity. None is concerned about foreign affairs or, in particular, the relation of the Canal Zone to Panama. Most would like to see the government provide more work, even money, for the *campesino,* and some would like to see market goods subsidized for the countryman. The national government and certain other agencies, none the less, do provide several important, though not overly effective, services for the *campesinos.* Currently for the villagers one of the most important units is the agrarian reform agency, which is in the process of dividing up and selling to the people the land on which the community resides. This agency, along with the mayor, is also appealed to several times a year to settle disputes over rights to house or work land. In such cases an agent will visit the community and try to divide the land equitably between the parties concerned. But both formal and informal communications between the agrarian reform people and the *campesinos* are infrequent.

A team from the malarial control agency, which is supported by national and supra-national organizations, visits the community approximately once every six months to spray all the houses and other structures. In Santiago a private health organization, which focuses on preventive medicine, provides low-cost consultations and medicines. It also has a unit which travels to some of the larger district capitals, and a set of inspectors who visit the smaller communities giving general health advice and working in the schools. But the visits of the health inspector to the community are infrequent, and for most of their medical problems the *campesinos* consult one of the local curers or a private doctor since the situation normally is not one of prevention and since they receive more rapid service from a private practitioner.

Other agencies which in varying degrees affect rural life are CARE, CARITAS (Catholic relief organization), FAO, the civil-action arm of the national police force, and a semi-autonomous government department, the Instituto de Fomento Económico (IFE) which is responsible for economic development programmes lying outside the jurisdiction of other agencies. One of IFE's tasks is to offer agricultural loans; however, it requires of the debtor collateral or a trustee, a stipulation which effectively bars most *campesinos* from receiving loans.

The governmental organization most centrally concerned with countryman life is the Ministry of Agriculture, Commerce and Industry. One of its major offices is located in Santiago. The ministry provides a diversity of services from soil testing to fomenting agricultural and fishing co-operatives. Agricultural agents are assigned to work directly with the countrymen. This agency, however, is frustrated in its efforts by a number of problems, one of which is a shortage of staff, and thus far only a few community members have been affected by, or even been in contact with, the local agent.

For the people the most important ties to the government come through the school teachers, the Santiago mayor and the local *regidor*.[3] The three school teachers, who are paid by the government, do not live in the community. But during the school year they are in the village five days a week for the greater part of the day. The school, built within the last fifteen years, has only six grades; however the impact of the teachers upon the village extends beyond their purely teaching function. The school keeps a small garden, and through this medium the teachers attempt to introduce new agricultural techniques to the children. Often a governmental agency will contact the community through the school. The teachers also try to introduce and enact political ideas. The school children elect class officers as does the school association of parents. The teachers see that the national holidays are celebrated, at least by the school children, and on the community level they have been a driving force behind the acquisition of a community saint and the celebration of the saint's day within the community. At public meetings they tell the countrymen to have a greater sense of pride in themselves, the village and the nation. What impact they have is due partly to their role as outsiders but mostly because the adult generation, being largely illiterate, values education as one of the few means of advancement. A number of school teachers grew up in the countryside, and the job itself is respected and seen to be within the potential of some of the younger generation.

The *regidor* is appointed and dismissed by the mayor. In the past fifteen years six different persons have served as *regidor*, who is always a resident of the community. Before making a new appointment the mayor normally solicits names, particularly from the local association of school parents and the school teachers. From the mayor's standpoint the *regidor* is the first authority in the community, though what power the *regidor* actually has is unclear. Verbally, at least, the mayor says the *regidor* performs the same job within the *regimiento* that he, the *alcalde,* performs in the whole district, but he also views the *regidor* as his own representative within the community.

The *regidor* has no specified list of duties but the folllowing are some of the tasks he should perform. When it is announced once or twice a year that the grass along the highway and feeder roads must be cut to prevent fires, the *regidor* must organize a work group or see to it that each person cuts the area which pertains to his house. If the government is going to vaccinate animals or make a census, the *regidor* should announce this, and assist the visiting team. If the animal of one person damages the crops of another, the injured party may come to the *regidor* and ask that recompense be made. In the case of a suspected robbery the *regidor* may serve as a witness that a good was owned by one person and not another. When the Santiago mayor settles a case he may send an order to the *regidor* who, in turn, must transmit it to the parties concerned. In theory, then, the *regidor* is the local arm of the government and the first authority in the village.

The facts of the job are somewhat different. In the first place, the position is unpaid, and both the current and past *regidores* complain about the time it takes — visiting damaged fields in the community, talking to people, and travelling to and waiting in Santiago. Second, most *regidores* have found it difficult both to maintain their friendships in the community and to enforce the law, for in most situations the *regidor* must side with one of his neighbours against another. If he is assiduous in his tasks, he makes enemies; if he is lax, the people complain about the lack of order in the community. Third, though a *regidor* can suggest a settlement between two disputants, if one disagrees, the case must go to Santiago, for only the mayor can enforce a solution. Finally, the people feel that a case in which potential damages may amount to more than $10.00 should be taken directly to the mayor anyway.

Thus, the *regidor* is in an ambiguous position. As an appointee of the government he does have some authority, and the job does give him some prestige. But he has no direct revenue base nor even a salary, and he cannot actually impose a decision. Although the mayor solicits communal opinions, the *regidor* is not popularly elected, which means both that he may lack support in the community and that he serves at the convenience of the mayor. Given the structural position of the *regidor*, both the villagers and the *regidor* find it easier to allow the broader society in the form of the mayor to settle most disputes in the community, with the result that at this level, also, their own sense of political participation is minimal. The people invidiously contrast a *regidor* to a *corregidor*. A *corregidor* is paid and serves in his job full time. He can attend to difficulties immediately, and he has the authority to settle a case directly in the *corregimiento*.

The current mayor of the district is knowledgeable about Panamanian law and the situations in the countryside to which it applies, and most people seem satisfied with his decisions. A number of the villagers know him personally. The mayor also is aware of the difficulties which a *regidor* has and, therefore, he claims to support the *regidor* whenever possible. For example, in most cases he requires that an individual have a witness testifying on his behalf; he does not require one of the *regidor*. In addition to strengthening the position of the *regidor,* the mayor would like to see the *campesinos* develop a greater sense of duty to the state.

Political power, in sum, filters from Panama City into the countryside. No true political officials live in the village and the government has little impact on the daily affairs of the people. At the local level there is little political manoeuvring and few political leaders, if only because there are no political spoils. What few advantages there are must be obtained on an individual basis by means of a link to a more powerful person outside the village. Subject to the laws of Panama, the countrymen generally accept these norms; the values of the community are not opposed to the forces of the nation. But the political tie between nation and country village is tenuous. In national politics the *campesinos* are passive participants.

Santiago and the larger society

In addition to their formal ties to the government the countrymen have interchanges with other representatives of the larger society. Outside the community the town of principal interest to the people is Santiago, now easily accessible by passenger bus. Through the district and provincial capital are funnelled the villagers' primary relationships with the larger society. Located there are governmental agencies, commercial establishments, doctors, a hospital, a church, and bars. Santiago is the home of a secondary school and is the locale of the principal teacher

training school for Panama. None the less, Santiago itself is rather small
and decidedly rural in character. Its main street, of concrete, houses the
finer stores and leads directly up to the church. Leading off the central
avenue are dirt roads many of which become almost impassable by car
during the rainy season. Only portions of the town hold much interest
for the *campesinos*. Although *campesinos* can be found going into the
bank, the more expensive stores, the municipal offices, the hospital or
the church, countryman life generally is centred about the marketplace,
which is located one block from the main avenue. The link between
countryman and the larger society is funnelled not only through Santiago but through one part of the town. The *campesino* is a part of the
national society yet in many ways inhabits a world of his own, which is
reflected geographically. Compared to their behaviour when in the
community, the demeanour of the countrymen towards the town
dwellers is deferential.

The ties between *campesino* and town dweller are non-enduring. No
one, not even the village storekeepers, can obtain credit with commercial organizations in Santiago, even with some of the small food sellers
at the marketplace. Santiago also is not a major market for *campesino*
produce. From a commercial perspective Santiago serves primarily as an
outlet for national market goods to the *campesinos* rather than the
reverse.

Aside from Santiago the people have ties, though of lesser importance, to other towns in the area. Friends and kinsmen may be located
in neighbouring rural villages; añd some have relatives in other provinces. The two mills to which the *campesinos* sell their sugar cane are
located in the vicinity of Aguadulce, a town forty minutes away by
highway. The men now must travel through Aguadulce to collect their
cash earnings and loans, and to arrange various affairs with the mills.
Most, however, go directly to the mills without stopping in the town
itself. Most of the men have been to Panama City but only to find a
temporary job, to sell or buy an article, or to see a member of a
government agency about a problem which cannot be solved (or is
stalled) in Santiago. Many of the women have not even been to the
national capital.

The communications networks linking the *campesino* to the larger
society are various. The people make little use of the Panamanian mail
service. In a neighbouring community a telegraph is operated, but it is
not used by the people of Los Boquerones. Newspapers seldom reach
the village and few adults can read. The most popular form of one-way

communication with the larger society is the transistor radio, and nearly every household has one. Of special interest to the people is an evening programme devoted to reading out private announcements. Over this programme a community can advertise its forthcoming *fiesta* or an individual may send a personal message. The most important change in the communications system has come in the last fifteen years with the betterment of the roads. The Inter-American Highway now is plied by small passenger buses called *chivas* (female goat), which carry people, produce and even messages.

Social life in the community

Some of the organizations based outside the community have a direct impact upon specifically village groupings. Within the community personal interactions are organized along several lines. One level of exchanges consists of kinship, *compadrazgo* and household relationships. Economic interchanges, which themselves are not entirely independent of kinship bonds, constitute a second level. A third level is comprised of interactions among friends and acquaintances, while a fourth, of concern here, consists of voluntary associations in the community. Most of these village groupings bear some sort of link to entities from without, but none provides a cohesive framework for the community itself.

The most important and inclusive of the communal societies is the Padres de Familia (Family Parents), an association concerned with the village school. Technically, it is composed of parents who have children in one of the six school grades; in fact, it normally includes any adults in the community who are willing to attend the meetings. The association meets at infrequent intervals, averaging about once a month. Elected officers direct the group but the school teachers provide the dynamism for it. The functions of the Padres de Familia, though focused on school activities, may range beyond such affairs. Directly next to the school is a small sugar-cane field the profits from which help to defray school costs. Throughout the year the Padres de Familia is responsible for caring for this field and, at appropriate intervals, for levying a day's work on community members. The teachers use the meetings to stress the importance of education and of having the children attend school regularly, or to transmit information from a government agency. The group also sometimes makes small loans to community members. Neither community inclusive or exclusive, the Padres de Familia is a voluntary association with a flexible membership that has no formal means for forcing people to attend its meetings or to contribute labour to its projects.

A second organization is the chapel society, composed of all those who wish to help care for the village's chapel. The association has elected officers, both male and female, and new elections generally are held every year. The primary source of revenue for the society is the patron saint, *San Martín,* to whom monetary vows are paid. Once or twice a year the society asks for help in cutting the grass around the chapel, and occasionally someone will be requested to repair a door, fix a corner of the roof, or perform another odd job at the chapel. As the saint's day approaches, meetings become more frequent so that preparations for his *fiesta* may be made. Membership in the chapel society is open and every meeting sees different persons attending, although there are perhaps 15-20 people in the village who are most concerned with the chapel.

A small but vibrant group is the 'pre-cooperative' association. The group currently is composed of nine men, several of whom live outside the village. In 1964 a new bishop was installed in Santiago, and he expanded the social arm of the church by helping to develop an organization to work with the *campesinos.*[4] The principal activity of this secular organization has been to initiate and encourage the forma-tion of co-operatives in some 20-30 communities around Santiago. Each community co-operative (or 'pre-cooperative') is now a multi-functional venture, being at once a savings society, a source of loans, a dissemina-tion point for new agricultural techniques, a lesson on communal work, and an agricultural organization. Thus far, however, the society's activities have taken up only a small part of each man's productive efforts, and in terms of the rest of the village the co-operative society has had relatively little impact. All males are free to join, but the entrance fee is $15.00 and the group is composed of some close friends; others are suspicious of joining them and of committing their own resources to the venture. Indeed, it may be that the co-operative society has had some success precisely because it is composed of a small, closely knit group.

At times different individuals have formed a variety of *ad hoc* groups, most of which eventually have fallen apart. For example, one man began to talk about forming a funeral society which would collect money periodically from its members and then pay the funeral costs of the associates who died. His suggestion did not take hold, but then he and others formed a savings and loan society. This group in turn had a chequered existence. Eventually, several members resigned, and non-attending and non-saving associates were eliminated. When I left, the group was still functioning, had about $80.00 in savings, but had dwindled to ten members.

Of these several, specific-purpose voluntary organizations in the village, some have had a stable history and undoubtedly will continue. Others seem to take hold for a few years and then fade. The stronger ones have closer ties to and are influenced more powerfully by outside agencies. The school and chapel committees perform community-wide functions, but the village as an entity still has no enduring organization associated with it.

Within the past 10-15 years the larger society's political and social influence on the community has increased, and the *campesinos'* interactions with persons from without the village are growing. But the impact of these ties is not yet pronounced, and the countrymen are not tightly linked socially or politically to the nation. In most of the people's relationships with the broader society the outsiders make the decisions and the *campesinos* face outside organizations as individuals, not as members of a group. Within the village itself the communal associations are impermanent. Thus, the formal political and social frameworks presented by the larger society and institutionalized in the village do not yet present or require a highly organized, stable community. They permit a relatively free flowering of other relationship systems within the village.

3   Economic organization

The villagers have a 'household economy' in that the production, distribution and consumption functions primarily are focused upon and occur within the household group. In times past the economy was based almost entirely on subsistence, slash-and-burn, farming, but within the last ten years the people have moved toward a mixed system of subsistence and market production. I consider in this chapter the broad outlines of the economic system to show its relation to household organization and the rest of the social life, to show in what way the *campesinos* are tied economically to the larger society, and to indicate some of the transitions which currently are taking place.[1]

The setting

The geographic and climatic settings provide the stage for and dictate the timing of most of the people's productive activities. The year is divided into two seasons. The dry season or summer begins in December and terminates in March or April. The rainy spell or winter lasts roughly from the middle of April to early December. During the peak periods of rain sudden thunderstorms are a daily occurrence, often in the afternoon. The humidity in the winter ranges from 80 per cent to 90 per cent (Fuson, 1958: 28-30), and this, combined with a daily temperature which often exceeds 27°C, can make living uncomfortable if not, at times, arduous.

The community, as mentioned, covers less than 2,600 hectares of savanna and forest land. Much of the area is relatively flat, but portions of it are dotted by gently rolling fields and steep inclines. Much of the land is certainly below 60 metres and one lagoon area is not far above sea level. A number of dirt roads leading off the highway and innumerable footpaths criss-cross the land. In the rainy season the area is cut by many small rivers and most of the dirt roads become impassable by car, truck or oxcart. Some of the roads and paths become so waterlogged that even the pedestrian must make frequent detours. The land itself varies in fertility, but it is not a rich soil. Under conditions of too intensive use it becomes susceptible to erosion, evidence of which is provided by the shallow lifeless gullies which are found in a number of areas.

Land history and ecology

Two further elements conditioning the people's agricultural life are the land-holding system and the ecological situation, and both of these must be seen in the light of several historical changes. While the particular conditions I describe are unusual to Los Boquerones and nearby communities, the overall situation is quite typical of rural Panama. In general the countrymen are not land owners nor are they perpetually bound to a local village.

The land which the *campesinos* of Los Boquerones work has always been owned by outsiders. The community lies in the area first deeded to the heirs of Columbus. In 1821, when Panama declared its independence from Spain, a large part of Veraguas, including what is now community land, was taken by José de Fábrega (1774-1841), a local general who was born in Panama City. Rights to the property were passed down in his family for several generations, although pieces of it were sold to outsiders. The Fábregas used the land for grazing cattle. It was not until the early part of this century that the first *campesino* resident of the village moved into the area, but he was soon followed by others, all of whom were looking for cultivable land. The countrymen were permitted to move on to the land but were not allowed to build permanent houses. In return for $1.00 or a day's labour per year, they were granted the right to cut down the forest or bush (el monte) for use in slash-and-burn cultivation of dry land rice, maize and other crops.[2] They were not, however, permitted to seed perennial crops nor to plant any single large area of land, and it seems likely that many planted in more than one locale. These restrictions, none the less, were congruent with the traditional system of agriculture and with the prevailing mode of building houses. Folk tradition has it that in the earlier portion of this century, land and forest were plentiful, and harvests were ample. The Fábregas viewed their own action as a form of renting the land, and the *campesinos* recognized that they had rights only to the crops which they raised.

By the 1940s the yearly fee had been raised to $5.00 or several days of labour. In the very early 1950s the owner, Julio José Fábrega, died. At this point the history of the land became complicated. Five of Julio José Fábrega's six children survived him. They decided to dispose of the land, and in the early 1950s reached several agreements with some large cattle owners. Before the contracts were fully consummated, however, one owner erected a number of wire fences on the land and threatened to dispossess many of the *campesinos* of their somewhat nebulous squatter's rights. The people tore down the fences and appealed to the president of the country.

Finally, in 1961 the government agreed to buy the land from the Fábregas, and on 29 May 1963 five of the six Fábrega parcels were purchased by the nation through the agrarian reform agency. The government bought the most populated areas of land; the sixth area was purchased by an in-law of the Fábregas.

Within the past twenty-five years several ecological changes have complicated these legal developments. First, the population has increased, a consequence of improved health practices and a predominance of in-migration over out-migration. Second, prices have gone up while many of the natural resources such as game, firewood, and even the vines used in constructing houses have diminished. The price increase has meant that most *campesinos* are no longer able to buy and to feed hogs and cattle, animals which in the past nearly every household possessed. Third, some 20-30 years ago large cattle owners introduced to the central provinces a new type of forage grass called *faragua (Hyparrhenia rufa)*. This drought resistant grass survives burning, spreads quickly, and has made incursions into the community, for the people do not have enough cattle to keep it under control. Where the grass takes root, the necessary thick forest is not regenerated. A fourth development is that in the late 1950s the villagers began on a large scale to raise sugar cane as a cash crop. This sudden growth in the raising of sugar was due to a conflux of factors. Highway improvement and an increase in Panama's sugar quota to the USA made it economical for the mills to haul the cane from Los Boquerones. Further, the Fábregas had always prohibited the seeding of a perennial, but once they left the *campesinos* were free to plant sugar cane, and the lure of cash prompted them to do so. A field planted in sugar yields a profitable harvest for four or five years, never ceases to produce a little, and wears out the soil. Where it has been planted the forest cover has not returned.

These four historical developments are now having some important impacts upon the lives of the people. The population increase has led to less land being available for each household, while the introduction of the quick-spreading cattle grass and the sugar cane has had the effect of diminishing the forest area available for the swidden cycle. The total consequence is that less good forest land is available to each household. The rest cycle for the land and forest has been shortened, and harvest sizes have been dropping. At the time of fieldwork the people had not reached a crisis point, but they are caught in a rapidly worsening situation.

The historical and ecological changes have increased the value of the land to the people, and though it is owned by the government, a folk set of usufruct rights has arisen. These rights are not systematically organized nor agreed upon by everyone; however, the people now mention the following rights when discussing their tie to the land. First, a person has the right to harvest the crops he planted. If he seeded perennial fruit trees, he has the right to the trees, although not necessarily to the land on which they reside. A man also has the right to be recompensed for the work he has put into the land, such as cutting down and clearing the forest. He has the right to retain an investment of capital, such as wire fencing used to encircle a field, and an encircled parcel gives a person some right to the field itself. A man also has some right to an area he has worked and is currently resting. Occasionally, one person will sell to another his rights, though all know that these are not rights of ultimate disposal. Despite the pressures, not all the land is claimed and some resources are available to everyone. For example, reeds in the lagoon area, used to weave saddle blankets, may be secured by anyone.

This is the historical and ecological context in which the agrarian reform agency is beginning to put into effect its plans to sell the land to the *campesinos*. For the time being the agency does recognize certain of the people's rights to the land, such as land which is being worked, land which is being rested, and land which has been worked in the recent past. The agrarian reform agency also recognizes rights to house sites which have been improved. The agency, however, has a detailed plan for dividing up and selling the land, which was officially announced to the people at a meeting in July 1967, one of the last months of my fieldwork. According to the programme all houses are to be located on one or the other of two strips of land bordering the highway and extending 200 metres deep; the rest of the area will be divided into 10-hectare plots for farming.[3] The agency aims not to throw anyone

off the land, and will not let outsiders purchase community land until
the present inhabitants have had a chance to do so. By law also the
agency cannot sell the land for less than the original purchase price of
approximately $30.00 per hectare. The *campesinos* are not averse to
buying the land, but as I was leaving they were much concerned that
only a few, perhaps 6-8, would be able to pay immediately what will be
a minimum of $150.00 in cash, not to speak of making a yearly
monetary payment in the years to come.

At the time of fieldwork, then, the pattern of land-use and the
ecological situation were much as they had been in the past, but
changes are occurring and further changes are on the horizon. The
forest is a waning resource and the people now recognize informal rights
of land use. But because they have never had permanent rights to the
land, because some land is still available for farming, and because
out-migration is still to some degree possible, land rights have never and
do not now provide the basis for permanent estates. The *campesinos*
have never been perpetually bound to the land or community. This
particular constellation of ecological and historical factors obviously
pertains only to Los Boquerones and the villages in its immediate
vicinity, but the general situation is absolutely typical of rural Panama.
For example, by 1960 only 9 per cent of the 21,231 farms in Veraguas
Province were owned by the people who operated them, and only 1.5
per cent of the land had been affected by the land reform programme
(*Censos Nacionales de 1960,* vol. III, 1961).

Productive activities

The *campesinos* raise agricultural products for subsistence and for the
market. The most important crops grown are dry land rice, maize and
sugar cane. The countryman, however, is not solely an agriculturalist;
he raises animals, and is adept at countless tasks around the house and
fields.

By means of the basic productive activity, slash-and-burn agriculture,
the subsistence crops of rice and maize are raised.[4] The rice is harvested
from August through October, while the maize is harvested in August
and September; sometimes a second maize crop is planted and then
picked in December. The annual round is contained within a larger
cycle. A field seeded in rice will be replanted one or more times
depending on its fertility and on whether sugar cane has been added.
Ideally the people would like to farm a plot for 2 years and permit it to

regenerate for 8-10. Because of the recent historical and ecological developments, the rest cycle has been shortened to 5 or 6 years.

It is difficult to provide exact figures on current 'profits' and harvest sizes since they vary widely, depending on the fertility of the land used, the season, the size of the area planted, the exact amount seeded, the rice market, and so forth. Such calculations are made more complicated by the fact that the *campesinos* sometimes do not measure the size of their harvests, and in some cases the harvest — such as a second seeding of maize — is picked only as needed. None the less, to provide an idea of the quantities involved I have listed in Table 1 the steps involved in the raising of one hectare of rice, the requirements for such work and the equivalent monetary costs.[5] Normally the people are not far from a 'break-even' point and seldom have a rice harvest which exceeds their needs for a year.

TABLE 1   *Costs and harvests for one hectare in swidden agriculture*

Activity		Expenditures	Range of Monetary Costs ($)	
1	Cut down forest	10-15 man/days	10.00	15.00
2	Burn off wood	With friends at night	—	—
3	Clean off remaining rubble			
	Strong fire	3 man/days	3.00	—
	Poor fire	5 man/days	—	5.00
4	Seed	25 lbs from house supply	1.50	1.50
5	Seeding	8 man/days (done in 1/2 day units)	8.00	8.00
6	First weeding	10-20 man/days depending on weed growth	10.00	20.00
7	Second weeding	0-15 man/days	0.00	15.00
8	Harvesting	15 man/days	15.00	15.00
9	Transportation	Oxcart from field to house	5.00	5.00
		Total	52.50	84.50

Harvest: 20-5 *quintales* (1 *quintal* = 100 lbs) of unshelled rice.
Equivalent selling price = $5.00 per *quintal*

Therefore:			
	Harvest	$125.00	$100.00
	Costs	52.50	84.50
	'Profit range'	$72.50	$15.50

In 1966 on the best available land one man harvested about 33 *quintales* of rice plus two harvests of maize which had a total value of approximately $150.00.

The important characteristics of this slash-and-burn system are the following. First, the producer puts in much labour but invests little capital. His basic tool is the all-purpose machete, and the entire task of regenerating the land is left to nature. Second, the amount produced is limited by the forest available and by the labour the producer can mobilize. In particular, three bottle-neck operations must be completed quickly and on time: the seeding, the first weeding, and the harvesting. Since, for various reasons, individual schedules are staggered, a man normally can harness enough labour to farm one hectare of land, but few exceed this amount, since it is difficult to gather a large enough labour force, and since most do not wish to risk loss of even part of the crop. Third, the system does not require an elaborate social or political superstructure, and from an economic standpoint, the countryman need not be a member of a tightly integrated society or community. To practise agriculture a man need only secure forest, and labour for certain crucial points in the cycle.

The people have always raised sugar cane, but until the last ten years it was grown in small amounts for home consumption only. The increased production of sugar is having several impacts, one of which is its effect on the ecological balance; the cane is also a source of cash. The amount of money a grower receives varies according to a number of factors. Harvests are about 40 tons per hectare. Ordinarily individuals have between 3 and 5 hectares of cane, and many clear as much as $200.00 profit in the year.

The sugar cane is sold to one or the other of two refineries located 20-5 miles away. In addition to the impacts the mills are having upon the cash economy of the *campesinos,* they are effecting other, somewhat more subtle, changes. Both mills are trying to introduce more modern agricultural techniques, efforts which have met with varying success, and both are involved in complex relationships with their countrymen producers. The companies provide interest-free loans to finance the crop, settle some disputes between neighbouring cane owners, maintain the system of mud feeder roads, rent tractors, sell agricultural goods and regulate the transport system.[6] In short, the countrymen are now entangled in a series of relationships with the mills from which it will be difficult to extricate themselves. Yet, the mills do not make a large capital investment into the *campesino* sector, and it is the countrymen who bear most of the risks of production, their only insurance being a concurrent system of subsistence agriculture.

In addition to the principal crops others are raised in the fields or at house sites, such as yuca, yams, tomatoes, seasonings, fruits, coffee and tobacco. Not everyone seeds every crop, but in general the *campesinos* have never been dependent upon rice, maize and beans alone. Further, though the people are becoming more dependent upon purchased items, they have always used the environmental resources extensively: brooms are made from bushes; vines are utilized in basket and house construction; gourds are used for hauling water or are made into drinking vessels.

Most of the people keep animals. Nearly every house has at least half a dozen chickens which are fed scraps of food and maize. Chicken raising is not profitable; the animals are kept for home consumption and as a bank account. Some homes have cattle encircled in a pasture, but hog raising has nearly died out. The people also engage in a diversity of temporary and permanent occupations, such as hunting, fishing, making fishnets, making unrefined sugar using a home mill and cooker, securing reeds and weaving saddle mats, and running an oxcart. Several people own small stores. At times some of the countrymen also have been able to secure outside salaried jobs on a temporary or more permanent basis, such as working on the roads, driving trucks, or working in a restaurant. Some of the women have worked in Panama City as domestics, and a few men have found odd jobs there. But with respect to such salaried work, the *campesino* is a marginal member of the national economy, passing into and out of occasional jobs. Essentially, the people are agriculturalists.

The economy has a basic periodicity. Money is most plentiful from late December through April, while the sugar cane is being harvested, and in these months a man makes his major purchases, such as clothing for the family. The months of May through July are difficult ones. The crops require great care, but cash and food supplies are nearly if not completely exhausted. Fortunately, at this time the mills make loans for weeding the cane; instead of fully investing in this work, most of the people use a portion of the money received to purchase household necessities. From late August through October the major food crops are harvested, but there is little cash. In November and early December there is enough food, though money still is scarce. Since the work in these months is little, many go fishing if they do not spend the time catching up on other jobs.

Organization of labour

Agricultural work is done primarily by the men, while women work mostly in the home. Certain of the agricultural activities require or are facilitated by a group of men working together. Such jobs either are too big for one man to accomplish alone or must be finished within a relatively short time. The people mobilize and organize a labour force by several means, although some of these now are used less frequently. The principal patterns are the *junta,* the *peonada, peón* for *peón,* and hiring *peones.*[7] Conceptually the four are distinct, though in practice they shade into one another and may be intermixed. The *junta* is a large group of labourers which is organized by one man and lasts for one day only. The 'owner' provides his workers with food and drink; he also may incur an obligation to return the labour, a debt which may remain outstanding for years. The *peonada* consists of a group of men, usually from 8 to 12, who work the fields of one another in rotation throughout the agricultural year; they keep account of the work owed and paid, and make a general settlement at the end of the year. Both these forms of labour organization are seen far less frequently now than in the past, due primarily to the increased use of cash and the greater diversity of agricultural activities. On the individual level, a person may agree to trade his labour with another, but without cash payment; this is known as 'earning a *peón'.* By contrast, a paid worker is reimbursed immediately in cash or kind, such as with rice from the freshly cut rice harvest.

Labourers are chosen on the basis of friendship and kinship ties, on availability, and on personal ability. But kin and friends are not obliged to work together, and persons from distant communities often are found working with a collection of villagers.

In all four forms of labour organization debts of time, money or goods are contracted on an individual basis. Only in the case of the *junta* may such debts remain outstanding for more than a year. The *peonada* is the only form of organization which involves a group working together over time, but even this group disbands after the harvest.

Sources and disposal of goods

As an economic entity, the household has both sources for, and uses of, goods. On the disposal side most agricultural produce is destined for home consumption, although some of the items are exchanged for cash. The sugar cane is sold to the mills, and a small quantity of rice may, from time to time, be sold to another *campesino* in the village, to a rice buyer or store in the village, or to one of the rice mills in Santiago. Hogs and cattle are disposed of in several ways. In a few cases an individual slaughters his own or a purchased animal and sells the meat in the village and its environs. Such animals also may be sold live to buyers in Santiago or to other individuals. Occasionally, minor agricultural products such as yams, bananas or yuca are taken to the highway and sold to persons in passing cars; and an individual sometimes will sell fish, fruits, or homemade molasses from house to house. But most of the *campesinos'* products are used in the home. Aside from household need, the reasons for this minimal participation in the national market include: inadequate transportation and preservation facilities, small quantities of goods produced, and sporadic demand.

A household has several sources of goods. Most of the produce comes directly from the fields, but the people are beginning to purchase more on the national market. Market goods reach the countrymen in several ways, the two primary conduits being local stores *(la tienda)* and commercial establishments in Santiago. Of the four community stores, two sometimes shut down or carry few items; the other two are open through the year. All four are inside, or extensions to, private domiciles. Although owned by men, they are run by women who are at home during the day. The range of goods sold is limited; the essential stock includes staples, such as rice, beans, and sugar, kerosene, soap and tinned goods. The profits from a store are not great, and a 'large' well-run one probably clears less than $.50 a day while the earnings of a small one may be less than one dollar per week. The inventory of the store varies by the season; in the cane-harvesting months as the demand goes up and his own resources increase, the storekeeper augments his stock of goods. By November, a store's shelves may be nearly bare.

Most villagers prefer to make their purchases in Santiago, if possible, for there prices are lower and a greater range of goods is offered. At the marketplace and its immediate environs most of the goods and services the countrymen desire can be found. Lottery tickets are sold in the marketplace, and it is to this vicinity that a man will bring a chicken or hog in hopes of finding a buyer. The entire market is most active on Saturdays, and most of the people arrange to make their purchases on Saturday morning. In sum, as buyers and sellers the people are participating more and more on the national market, but their basic subsistence still comes from goods grown in the fields. In Figure 1 I have summarized according to their relative importance the major sources and uses of household goods.

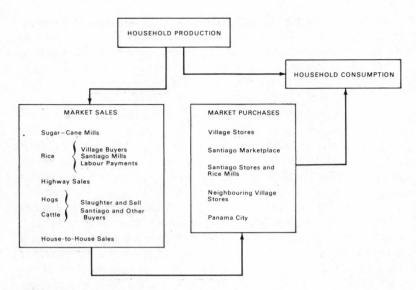

FIGURE 1   *Sources and uses of household goods*

Household units

In the home the crops destined for consumption are elaborated into a variety of dishes. The people take three meals a day, though if food is short they make do with two. Household diets vary according to the supply of food and money. Normal fare includes a breakfast of coffee and boiled plantains or yuca. If a household has maize then a type of tortilla may be made, or if cash is available, rolls or bread may be purchased. The midday meal and supper are focused about rice, though the comestible is rarely ingested by itself. Spices and flavourings are added, and the people try to have beans or a few slices of meat at least two or three times a week. Men speak of the sense of security they feel when they see rice stored in the loft above the kitchen and many are embarrassed not to have a supply. If a household has exhausted its rice, this is the first item purchased; and if goods must be sold to raise cash, the rice is saved to the last.

If all necessary food were to be purchased a small family of three (two adults and one young child) could subsist on about $.40 a day or $3.00 per week. The money would be used to buy rice, beans, cooking oil, onions and coffee. But such a family would have no matches, sugar, meat, or tobacco, and this level could not be maintained for long. On

$4.00 a week three persons could eat adequately, though not elaborately. These costs are large compared to the $1-1.25 per day that a man can earn when wage work is available, and the figures illustrate why a family head must be certain to seed rice every year and to maintain a diversity of crops beyond this.

Clothes, like food, are basically simple. Today most people purchase their vestments. Men wear khaki trousers and coloured shirts. Most women wear print dresses. Both sexes go barefoot or use sandals.

Given the lack of cash, the people sometimes must borrow. Credit at one or another of the local stores is available to some but rarely exceeds several dollars per person. Beyond this a man will turn to his kin and friends for aid. A person normally solicits money only to buy food or medicines. Usually, people borrow money and not goods; requesting a loan is embarrassing but asking for food is even more so. Interest is not charged on these minimal transactions among friends, which usually range from $0.50 to $1.00. A $5.00 loan is unusual; for a sum of $10.00 the lender might require a witness to the transaction or collateral to be held by himself. Elaborate networks of debtors and creditors, however, are not built up, and most loans are private affairs. The people point out that everyone has at least one other person to whom he can turn for help, and they sometimes repeat an old proverb: 'He who doesn't owe isn't a person' *(El que no debe no es gente).*[8] Since fortunes are variable, most are aware that a current debtor is a potential creditor. Aside from lending, there is not a large amount of reciprocity. If a household has a surfeit of ripe fruits, it may offer some to another; if a family is about to eat, a visitor may be offered food, though he will never ask for it. When men gather at a bar, drinks sometimes are bought on a reciprocal basis. Such gifts, however, are not of great economic importance, nor are they public matters. In general, households are not and cannot be financially dependent upon one another.

The rate of capital formation and level of capital itself are low. Very few think in terms of a profit, although everyone is aware of his monetary and labour costs, and most keep track of their harvest sizes. A person's primary concern is to raise enough crops to have sufficient food for the year, which in the first instance means having enough rice. As one person said, 'We want to live, nothing more'. Another expressed it as, 'We think of working in order to eat. We don't keep accounts of gains and losses. We think of getting enough food for next year'. Such an outlook should not be taken to mean that the *campesinos* do not want to accumulate wealth; to the contrary, everyone speaks of 'advancing' himself, but as the people see it the opportunities for doing so are few and the attendant risks are large.

Within the community one or another often will say, 'All of us are poor.' By the standards of the larger society, the *campesinos* are impoverished, but the utterance is also an assertion about the basic economic equality of all countrymen. Within the community there is no system of economic stratification nor are there marked status differences, although the countrymen do recognize that individual fortunes vary over time, and that some are better off or richer than others. The person who has a passable existence, it is said, does not have to sell his crops or borrow money; he has the necessities. The wealthier person, besides having sufficient food, may own cattle. None the less, there have been few traditional means for displaying wealth. A man is pleased to have a large rice field, a loft filled with rice, or cattle. In the past gathering a large *junta* to harvest rice may have been a kind of display, and everyone likes to have at least one white dress shirt, a pair of trousers and a pair of shoes for use on special occasions. A house made of cinder blocks also represents a large investment (more than $400). But display is muted and, it is said, and probably true, that economic differences rarely become permanent. This assertion of economic equality is both part fiction — for some are impoverished — and part truth. In either case, what wealth differences there are do not have a pronounced impact on the rest of the social organization. A man gains 'respect' in the community by other means.[9]

To illustrate the general level of wealth and the lack of marked economic differences, I list in Table 2 the major assets (i.e. lasting more than one year) of fifteen households in the community. The fifteen homes were chosen randomly from the total of ninety-one in the community, and a study of the economic transactions of each for the calendar year 1966 was made. For every asset, I have given an approximate monetary equivalent, assuming that each item could be disposed of on the market. My purpose here is to provide a general idea of household assets, and I have not taken account of certain facts, such as that some household groups seed more incidental crops than others or have a larger rice harvest. The monetary value of the oxen is low as they are usually purchased through a government loan.

TABLE 2 *Major assets of fifteen households*

House Number	Number in house	Number working males	House type	Present value agr. implements	Hectares in sugar cane	Oxen	Swine	Horses	Cattle	Fowl	Other	Total
1	4	1	Wood & Thatch / $30	$8.00	3½ / $210	0 / $0.00	0 / $0.00	1 / $25.00	0 / $0.00	18 / $21.50	None / $0.00	$294.50
2	6	1	Wood & Thatch / $30	$3.50	2½ / $150	0 / $0.00	0 / $0.00	0 / $0.00	0 / $0.00	16 / $19.50	None / $0.00	$203.00
3*	8	2	Wood & Thatch / $30	$4.75	0 / $0.00	0 / $0.00	1 / $20.00	0 / $0.00	0 / $0.00	10 / $12.00	Bldg. blk, h'se & sav / $100	$166.75
4†	6	1	Wood & Thatch / $30	$0.70	0 / $0.00	0 / $0.00	0 / $0.00	0 / $0.00	0 / $0.00	15 / $18.00	None / $0.00	$48.70
5	3	1	Mud / $60	$9.50	2 / $120	0 / $0.00	0 / $0.00	1 / $25.00	4 / $320	20 / $24.00	Titled land & cash / $1000	$1,558.50
6	3	1	Mud / $35	$3.90	3 / $180	0 / $0.00	0 / $0.00	0 / $0.00	0 / $0.00	15 / $18.00	None / $0.00	$236.90
7	2	1	Wood & Thatch / $30	$4.00	7 / $420	0 / $0.00	0 / $0.00	0 / $0.00	7 / $500	30 / $36.00	None / $0.00	$990.00
8	4	1	Wood & Thatch / $30	$2.00	0 / $0.00	0 / $0.00	0 / $0.00	0 / $0.00	0 / $0.00	30 / $36.00	None / $0.00	$68.00

House Number	Number in house	Number working males	House type	Present value agr. implements	Hectares in sugar cane	Oxen	Swine	Horses	Cattle	Fowl	Other	Total
9	5	3	Wood & Thatch / $30	$7.00	4 / $240	2 / $40.00	1 / $20.00	3 / $60.00	0 / $0.00	40 / $48.00	Oxcart & Sugar C. Press / $300.00	$745.00
10††	2	0	Mud / $45	$0.00	0 / $0.00	0 / $0.00	0 / $0.00	1 / $25.00	6 / $420.00	5 / $6.00	None	$496.00
11§	1	1	Wood & Thatch / $30	$4.50	5½ / $330	0 / $0.00	0 / $0.00	0 / $0.00	0 / $0.00	0 / $0.00	None	$364.50
12"	6	3	Cinder Block / $500	$13.00	5½ / $330	2 / $0.00	3 / $180	2 / $50.00	32 / $2200	15 / $18.00	Ox-cart / $250	$3,541.00
13	7	1	Mud / $40	$4.00	5 / $300	0 / $0.00	0 / $0.00	0 / $0.00	0 / $0.00	20 / $24.00	None	$368.00
14	7	1	Mud / $40	$3.00	7 / $420	0 / $0.00	0 / $0.00	2 / $50.00	0 / $0.00	9 / $10.80	Small store / $10	$533.80
15	3	1	Wood & Thatch / $30	$3.50	3 / $180	0 / $0.00	0 / $0.00	0 / $0.00	0 / $0.00	5 / $6.00	None / Owes $225	$(5.50)

*   Female-headed household: one grown son has steady job outside the community.

†   Head works as truck driver with earnings ranging from $10 to $40 a month.

††   Eldest person in community; unable to work now.

§   This bachelor has no one to watch over household animals.

"   This household has had three grown sons. One recently left, the other two will also in the near future; this will splinter some of the assets.

The economy and its social implications

The ecology and economy set parameters for the social organization. In the first place, the form of production and the geography permit and to some extent encourage a dispersed settlement pattern. The people are not required to live in compact communities. Second, the economic life does not necessitate a large or permanent investment of capital. The land still is not owned by the people; until now houses could not be permanent establishments; and in the agricultural system capital is neither invested nor amassed. The slash-and-burn system probably never was in true balance, and the countrymen, it appears, have been accustomed to moving across the countryside as the demographic and ecological conditions have required. In short, the economy has never tied the people to a locality on a continuous basis.

Economic life is organized around household units. Exploitation of the environment does not require the support structure of a complex social organization nor units larger than the household group. To be sure, some co-operation is a necessity in the bottle-neck operations of the agricultural system, but a simple method of recruiting labour satisfies this condition. Beyond transfers of labour, households depend upon one another for goods and loans; however, the needy usually have alternative sources of credit and there are no permanent networks of exchange between households or individuals. Within the system each household is basically equal, although wealth differences do appear. I am not claiming that the mode of production requires the people to have a household economy; this is a cultural fact, the reasons for which I examine in later chapters. I am arguing, however, that the productive life presents the opportunity for the independence of and non-continuity between households.

The people's primary economic tie to the larger society comes through the sugar-cane mills. The refineries now impose a further 'condition' on the economic system in that they afford permanent sources for disposing of cane as a cash crop and themselves require labour during four or five months of the year. The mills are national corporations, and the cash received from them enables the people to purchase goods manufactured by the larger society, although the countrymen buy only a selected range of items. Aside from the sugar cane the people's products reach the market sporadically and in small amounts. Their tie to the national market, then, is rather limited in that it flows through certain channels. The *campesinos* are members of the Panamanian economy but compose a well-defined stratum within it.

The village of Los Boquerones, like many other communities, is in the midst of several important changes. Many of the traditional resources are being depleted: the forest is diminishing and the land is becoming less fertile; firewood and vines are no longer found in abundance; hunting is now only a sport; thick wood for building houses is harder to find and no longer free. In the past the response presumably was to move to a new area. This is still possible, but the proposed system of land-ownership rights and the planting of sugar cane, a perennial with high initial costs, undoubtedly will increase the people's tie to the community in the future. Further, with the advent of the cash crop and its impact on the forest, the *campesinos* are beginning to move away from subsistence agriculture toward greater dependence on the mills, greater use of money, and more participation as consumers on the national market. Thus, several economic transitions are beginning to take place in the community, but so far they are only rumblings within the traditional social structure. The relationship systems and general social life do not yet evince signs of great change; they are still informed by traditional values. The economy itself has retained many of its old characteristics and the new modes of production have not yet burst in upon the social organization in a dramatic manner.

4   God, the devil and the saints

The *campesinos* formally are baptized and confirmed members of the Roman Catholic Church. Several permanent and visible markers in the community provide evidence of their faith: a cemetery, a chapel in which is kept an idol of the patron saint (San Martín de Porres), and religious images which are kept in private homes. Various rites are practised, and the people voice a set of beliefs concerning God, the saints, the devil and his helpers. Orthodox or not these ideas and practices form a systematic pattern, each element of which must be viewed in terms of the overall structure. The set of religious conceptions provides several designs for living in the sense of affording explanations or meanings for events which have occurred, and of providing orientations, or pathways, for behaviour that should occur. Ultimately, these beliefs justify and legitimate the central social relationships in the village.

God and man: destiny and faith

The personages of God, Christ and the Holy Ghost are not clearly distinguished. The expression 'the Father, the Son and the Holy Ghost' sometimes is said to be a benediction referring respectively to the priest administering the mass, the people at the mass, and God; other times all three are said to be God. The figure of Jesus Christ occupies a curious position. On the one hand, Christ is both God and a man who came to the earth before the world was totally formed. As no one believed in God, Christ appeared in order to convert the unbelieving through his presence and by his miracles. Christ, however, is not thought to be close to the people; he is God himself. On the other hand, one particularly important and effective saint is known as 'Padre Jesus de Nazareño', and Christ is often said to be the head of all the saints. Christ, then, does not serve as an intermediary between man and God; rather he has two separated capacities.

Mary is thought to be the wife and mother of God, and the wife of
St Joseph. Joseph never had sexual relations with Mary. Once he locked
her in a room alone but she became pregnant; it is said to be hard to
understand how she remained a virgin.

God created man. As a spiritual creature man has a soul, and this
soul leaves him only on the ninth night of the wake following his death.
There is a vague notion that every human also has a spirit which departs
from him at the moment of death. Each person, too, is born with a
guardian angel who follows him from behind but is rarely visible. The
angel helps care for the spirit, helps protect the individual against the
devil and committing errors, sometimes helps shield the person against
worldly dangers, and, like the spirit, leaves the individual at death.

God is both in the sky and on earth; his power is absolute and he
orders the entire world. The manifestations of his power are many. For
example, a delay in the onset of the rains, causing crop loss, may be
viewed as a punishment sent by God because of man's sins. True stories
(un cuento) illustrating God's power also are recited:

> One day a man came to a house and asked a young woman there for
> a drink of water. Her mother replied that she was the mistress of the
> home and that she was the one who would give the water. She gave
> the man a gourdful of water but placed a spider in the bottom of it.
> The man drank the water down and asked for more but added that
> this time he would like it without the ice cube. Only God could have
> changed the spider to an ice cube.[1]

The central concept concerning God's power is the notion of
destiny. A human's total life from moment of birth to instant of death
is governed by the destiny which God has placed upon him. Thus, men
are born to be agriculturalists, cattlemen, hunters, carpenters, hard
workers, slothful, rich or poor. Since God places a destiny on every
man, it is contradictory to say that there is life without destiny. As one
person put it, 'The person without destiny cannot live; life is destiny'.

The world, however, does not consist simply of a juxtaposition of
beings with different destinies; events happen through the meshing of
destinies — 'like the workings of a clock'. Thus, it was said to be not
only the destiny of one man in the community to be killed at a certain
moment by a bus on the highway, but that of the driver and passengers
to be there, too.

The concept of luck *(la suerte:* luck, fate) is complementary to that
of destiny and is distinguished from chance or accident *(la casualidad)*.

In contrast to destiny which refers to a total life, luck designates short-run changes. Through bad luck one may lose some seeded rice or sugar cane, a cow may die, or one's house may burn down. Through good luck one may win in the lottery or have an exceptionally good harvest. Luck refers to the short-term fluctuations which punctuate a destiny, and one proverb is: 'Luck can come overnight' (*La suerte peude venir de la noche a la mañana*). Nevertheless, since the world is totally ordered, luck is not understood to be a consequence of probability or randomness. Such an idea is more nearly expressed by the term *la casualidad:* however, the people relate even the idea of accident or chance to the divine will. In this connection, a further proverb is sometimes repeated: 'From luck and death no one escapes' (*De la suerte y la muerte nadie se escapa*).

From one perspective these concepts concerning destiny and luck furnish the people with an explanation for every event. The idea of destiny does provide a *post hoc* explanation absolving man from searching for the causes of his successes or failures. However, to view the notions in this manner is to reduce them to a different framework. The people do not simply invoke destiny, when necessary, to provide an explanation for past events; it is a more encompassing concept. Destiny is life itself.

God's worldly plan is never revealed to man, but man is actively engaged in life, for God requires that he have a belief and a faith in God himself. As a primary expression of this faith each must search out his destiny. A man's eventual destiny may be to grow wealthy in farming, but since he does not know it he must grasp at every opportunity which comes his way. Even if a man's destiny is destitution, he must continue to work, for if not, his life will be even poorer. Man can never lose the hope that his life will change, for though God places a destiny upon each man, he also has the power to change it, and God likes the man who continues to struggle. A frequently repeated proverb is, 'Help yourself so that God may help you' (*Ayudate que Dios te ayudaré*).[2] In this connection a story sometimes is told, concerning the time God and St Peter were walking upon the earth:

On their first day of travel God and St Peter came across a household. Being thirsty St Peter entered to request a drink of water. He found the man of the home lying in a hammock and a messy interior which was evidence of a poor housekeeper. The people were lazy and hungry. The following day God and St Peter walked in the same area. When they came to the house St Peter asked God to help the

poor inhabitants but God refused, pointing out that that was precisely what they wished. Then, as they travelled further, the pair
came across a man vainly trying to lasso a cow. Both realized that
the man was trying to steal the animal but that he was doing so in
order to feed his household. St Peter pointed out that the man was
sinning, but God said, 'He who helps himself, God helps'. Then God
aided the robber for he was doing all that was humanly possible to
provide for his family.

The story may be interpreted in several ways, and I shall elaborate
some of these in conjunction with a complementary tale below, but the
people tell it simply to illustrate that each man is expected to help and
to be responsible for himself. Life is often said to be a struggle, and
because man's destiny is unknown, he must have faith and express this
faith by struggling onwards.

The faithless person who thinks that he alone does his work is said
to be stupid, worthless, and little more than an animal. He is alive but
lacks 'interest' in his work, and like an unfettered animal, he is incapable of carrying out purposive activities. Except for the dog, animals
'know' their owners only in the sense of recognizing *(reconocer)* them.
They are incapable of knowing *(saber)* in the sense of understanding,
and are, therefore, powerless to sin. Man has the capability of knowing
right from wrong, and thus he can and must have faith in God.

Concretely, faith in God means having faith in the future – that
crops will grow when planted, that activities will lead to fruitful results.
Faith also means having respect for and fearing God and his power. The
people's own fear and distance from God is graphically demonstrated
by their reactions to some of the new teachings of the church.[3] Young
and energetic priests, recruited by the newly installed Bishop of Santiago, began in 1966 to hold masses and to give lessons in the community's chapel. In one lesson a lay teacher stressed that man should
love and not fear God. Afterwards several people expressed disbelief in
his teachings and said that without fear one could not believe in God;
they concluded that the new teacher was a Communist!

Faith in God also is expressed by various practices and actions. If a
person is speaking of something he intends to do, he adds 'if God wants
it'. When a man leaves his house in the morning to work or goes on a
trip he says a short prayer: 'In the name of God and the Virgin'. The
same words with the addition of 'may it grow up well' are spoken in the
fields when a man begins to seed. In addition to these regularized
expressions of faith, one should fight sinning and pray to God asking

for forgiveness and a good heart. Further expressions include crossing oneself in the morning, respecting other people and the saints, observing *fiesta* days, erecting a cross at the house or where one works, marrying in the church, lighting candles and attending or paying for a mass.

The devil and man

A second power also exists in the world, the devil: and in fact man may have faith either in God or the devil. The devil's home, hell, is a place on earth, and he is assisted by helpers, known as 'Jews'. The helpers also are on earth, and just as the devil offers a precise analogue to God, so his helpers are the counterparts of the saints. The devil's helpers, dead humans who live in hell, are non-Christians; God's helpers, dead humans who live in heaven, are paragons of the Christian life. Both are intermediaries between the mysterious power and man — one on the side of good, the other on the side of evil.

Logically, the idea of the devil is a necessary complement to the concept of God. In terms of category oppositions we could argue that without the idea of evil and the devil there could be no conception of good and God. None the less, the fact that the devil has power within the world poses a logical problem. If God is the original force, then how is it that the devil has power to influence men's destinies unless God himself created the devil? Conversely, if God is good then the existence of the devil is proof that he is not all-powerful. The countrymen explain that God does not compel anyone to have bad thoughts or to sin. All evil comes from the devil. God's power, however, is greater. He sets the destinies of men, while the devil can only try to enter men's souls and lead them to sin. Man himself, then, is basically good, being more a creature of God than the devil.

The relative power of the devil and God is illustrated by the following story:

One day both God and the devil were on earth. The devil locked a group of men in a room and asked God to guess who was inside since he was all powerful. God responded that the room was full of pigs. The devil laughed, opened the door, and pigs came out! For this reason Jews, the devil's helpers, do not eat pork. Everyone was a Jew in those times.[4]

Although the *campesinos* relate the story only to illustrate that the devil's power is opposed but subsidiary to God's, we may note other facets. As in the preceding tales the action occurs on earth where miraculous powers are exhibited. The story is also an analogue of the tale of the Virgin Mary who was locked alone in a room by Joseph but exited pregnant. In both stories God performs a mystical transformation inside a locked room. Mary, a normal human, gives birth to a supernatural being, as a result of whose work humans became spiritual beings. The devil's helpers, non-Christians, are changed in the other direction, from being humans to pigs. Animals in general are faithless, while the term 'pig' is applied specifically to 'uncivilized', sloppy humans who have little sense of shame and are incapable of respecting others.

Because God and the devil together rule the world, they constantly compete for men's souls, and the final reckoning between them is made each year on 2 November, All Souls' Day (Día del Juicio Final). At death each individual's spirit rises to the sky. Preceding the annual day of judgment the recently deceased is placed in a temporary spot where the soul cleanses itself. (This provisional location is likened to being sent to prison in Santiago before being transferred to the state penitentiary on the island of Coiba.) Then, on All Souls' Day, at the Gates of Heaven a tribunal consisting of God, St Peter and the devil sits with a Roman scale, an apt symbol. The recently deceased are called forward and the sins and acts of good of each are recounted. A person's soul is aided by 'lawyers', who are saints and dead *compadres* of the deceased; and remembrance prayers from earth asking God to save the soul may help ease its passage. God overlooks small sins and only makes an accounting of the major ones. If an individual knew what he was doing and committed three or more mortal sins then he is condemned to hell; however, God is more lenient if the person did not know he was sinning. It is also said that an individual's good and bad acts are balanced on the scale. Too many sins tip the scale in favour of the devil and the soul proceeds to hell. If tilted in the other direction, the soul is admitted to heaven. What happens once the soul enters heaven is unknown.

The comparison of the after-life with the legal system of Panama is made consciously by the countrymen. Sometimes God is said to be like a 'governor' (of a province). But it would be incorrect to deduce the religious from the legal; rather, it is through such terrestrial comparisons that the religious conception is thought out and made concrete. Indeed, it provides one model for conceiving the political system.

Judgment occurs only after death; the fight for men's souls takes place every day. The devil and his disciples sometimes trick people and lead them to have faith in the devil himself. The devil particularly pursues those who are 'more sacred'. He goes after local 'prayers' *(rezandores)* and specially likes it if church-married couples or *compadres,* both of whom are joined by sacred bonds, begin to fight.[5]

Evidence of the devil's power is seen in the fact that man sins and commits vices. The earth, it is said, once was white like sugar; because of the devil's influence man has sinned and these sins being heavy have dropped to the ground and turned it dark. Vices and sins are not clearly distinguished, and sins are not always hierarchically ordered, but fragments of more 'orthodox' Catholic theology are evident in the beliefs. Mortal sins are considered worse than venial sins, though which errors are which is not always clear. Some of the worst sins are to hit one's mother or father (or other kinsman), to renounce God, or to fight with a godparent or *compadre.* To a lesser degree, to speak badly to any of the above is also a sin. And just as killing is a sin, so having an abortion is a mortal sin. To insult, lie, and gossip about others is sinful, as is stealing another's wife. But having sexual relations is an ambiguous act. According to some the sexual urge is unnecessary and sinful. God showed that he could make the world with virgins only; the devil introduced sex. According to others, coitus is not a sin, for without it there would be no world. In any case, a distinction between public and private sexual relations is always made; again, a common folk story is told in illustration of the point.

One day God and St Peter were walking on earth. A church-married couple, walking along the street to mass, had the urge to fornicate. The woman said 'Where? Here?' and the man replied. 'Since we are married it doesn't make any difference. It isn't a sin to do it here in the street. Come on'. Many people passed by since it was the day of the mass and saw them there. Then, God and St Peter came upon them in the act and asked them what they were doing. They laughed and told him. God, then, turned them into a mare and stallion, for as he explained to St Peter the couple were acting like animals. The next day God and St Peter were again out walking. This time an unmarried couple had the urge to fornicate. The man wanted to do it right in the street, but the woman said, 'No, here in the street all the people come and will see us. It is better if we go off here to do it and hide'. The man agreed. They went off the road and hid among some leaves where they began to fornicate. As St Peter came along the road he had the desire to defecate and went into the same bushes where the couple were. He asked them whether they were married, and they replied they were not. St Peter pointed the couple out to God, but to his surprise God left them alone. St Peter then asked God why he cursed the married couple but not the unmarried ones. God replied: 'Because they "eat" in confidence; the married couple did it in public and that is not right. Those who are married must keep the set order. The "friends" were the ones who kept order; they respect more the public and the presence of God than the married ones.'

In form, this story bears a similarity to the one concerning God, St Peter and the robber. In both, God and St Peter are walking on earth and the action takes place on two successive days, which permits different human actions to be contrasted. St Peter, who was a human, is implanted in the story and voices the questions of the audience; God's supreme power also is made evident. Focusing on this story alone, the central point concerns public versus private sexual relationships. The married/unmarried opposition heightens the contrast. The message concerning the public and private nature of the act appears to be that both man and animals practise sexual relations, and in this respect they are similar.[6] None the less, man is different from other animals in that he can control his urges; to do so is to be human and to live in God's grace. Thus, even those countrymen who claim that sexual relations are natural do say that public coitus is sinful. The handling of sexual relations signifies one difference between man and animals, and it is the religious man who is able to direct, guide and combat his natural impulses.

Depending on the necessity which impels them, certain actions may be good or bad, an idea well illustrated by the earlier story about God, St Peter and the robber. To stress the point of need, the story specifically contrasts a sin and a vice. In the tale the first man God and St Peter encountered, lay about his home, and was dominated by the vice of laziness; the second was stealing a cow and committing a sin. Yet God refused to help the slothful and assisted the robber. Even a lesser sin committed from necessity may be condoned by God. He does not condemn the lazy, but he does not help them either.

It would be reductive to ascribe the countrymen's beliefs about the devil to their position within the larger society, but it is important to note the correlation of the two. Although it is a person's destiny which makes him poor or wealthy, it is also said that God only helps man to have a passable existence. The rich are thought not to believe in him, and he does not favour them. Of wealthier people within or without the community, the people say either that they are particularly pursued by the devil or that their good fortune is the result of his work. Some, it is suggested, have made pacts with the devil by exchanging their souls for worldly riches. Such a belief linking the wealthy and the devil does provide an explanation for the people's impoverished position within the broader society. None the less, there is no evidence to suggest that the one is prior to the other, and there are no grounds for supposing that the belief in itself inhibits the *campesinos* from striving for material success; on the contrary, most everyone does desire to emulate the townsfolk and have a more affluent life.

The belief in and practices of faith, then, are important not only with respect to God but in relation to the devil, for it is man's faith in God which is attacked by the devil. The concept of the devil not only 'explains' evil in a world dominated by God's power but gives to each individual the responsibility for his own actions. To combat the devil man must express his faith. As one person said, 'It is not much but you have to do it'. And man should fear both God and the devil — God out of respect, the devil for his evil power. With these precautions the devil will be unable to find a reason for 'checking you off on his list'.

Women, snakes and fruit trees

In addition to these general orientations concerning man, and his relations to God and the devil, the religion presents several, more specific conceptions which afford models for behaviour. The two most important ones are the Virgin Mary and Eve. The former provides, in many respects, the prototypic image of the mother, the latter that of the sexual partner and of fallen man in general. A discussion of these figures, however, raises a number of difficult preliminary issues, and while I do not wish to consider these in detail they must be mentioned. In the first place, the people themselves do not verbalize a direct connection between their daily life and either of these religious personages as models of or for behaviour. This, of course, does not vitiate an effort to draw such links, but it does make it more difficult. In the second place, the Biblical stories which concern Mary and Eve are believed or at least told in a vast number of societies, some of which bear little resemblance to rural Panama. These multi-faceted images clearly allow for a diversity of folk interpretations. None the less, some understanding of the female role in rural Panama is gained by viewing it in terms of the complementary images of Eve and Mary.[7]

Mary is said to be the mother of God, and she was the wife of St Joseph, although a virgin. In the feast cycle Mary, or rather different refractions of her image, are given special attention. She is one among other saints but perhaps the most important. One day in particular, 'Painful Friday', identifies her with women as mothers, just as all men are linked on a different day with St Joseph. The mother-child bond is the steadfast tie in the family and the mother, like Mary, must be prepared to accept countless sorrows and trials.

Mary, the virginal mother, is also important for the contrast she presents to Eve, the sexual temptress who led man to sin. Indeed, the concept of virgin birth makes little sense unless taken in conjunction with some other non-virgin birth. Given Eve's sin the only way Christ, the son of God, could be born was from a virgin. The concept of Mary presupposes that of Eve.

Eve, by contrast to Mary, provides a model for adult female-male relationships, or, to put it differently, provides the pattern by which the people comprehend the female person as a sexual being. For example, it is women who are thought to have a higher sexual passion, who must exhibit shame for this passion, who are responsible for accepting or rejecting the advances of a man, and who can sexually burn their husbands. Men are consciously seen as the active sexual aggressors, yet they also are the passive agents since it is women who attract them. This basic division between males and females, has ramifications throughout all domains of the culture.

Having provided these brief suggestions concerning Eve as a model for women let me elaborate by analysing structurally five beliefs and practices of the people which have a bearing on the concept of Eve. The customs themselves are not consciously interconnected by the people, nor even said to be 'religious', yet I shall treat them as linked statements which are connected to the Genesis story. In essence, the beliefs are a retelling of certain of the Genesis themes, a recoding from the written bible to unwritten beliefs and practices, which masks their import but assures that the meanings are carried over time. With respect to the story of Genesis, Edmund Leach has already furnished one, structural interpretation and I begin, therefore, by reviewing a few of his points.[8]

Leach divides Genesis into three creation stories: the seven-day creation, the Garden of Eden, and Cain and Abel. In his treatment fruit trees, creeping things, and women all occupy structurally anomalous but similar positions. 'Eve in the second story replaces the "Creeping Things" of the first story' (1962: 32). He does not explicitly link these two categories to fruit trees, but the comparison is implicit in his diagrams.

It is relevant also to recall certain portions of the Genesis tale. In 'story 1' on the third day God created vegetation, plants yielding seed, and fruit trees (grass, cereals, fruit trees) (I: 11-12). On the sixth day cattle, beasts, and creeping things were created (I: 24-5), followed by the creation of male and female. In 'story 2' the Garden of Eden was created with the tree of life and the tree of knowledge of good and evil (II: 8-9). Man was permitted to eat from every tree in the garden except the tree of knowledge (II: 16-17). God created helpers fit for Adam — cattle, birds and beasts — but no helper like man was encountered. Woman was created (II: 18-23). The serpent tempted woman; the woman ate fruit from the tree of knowledge, offered some to her husband, and their eyes were opened (III: 1-7). God then cursed the serpent to crawl on his breast and to eat earth. He put enmity between the snake and his seed, and the woman and her seed. Woman was cursed to experience the pain of childbirth and to be under the power of her husband. For Adam the ground was cursed so he had to toil to eat and had to return to it in death (III: 14-19). After the pair were expelled reference is immediately made to the fact that Adam 'knew' Eve, linking the tree of knowledge to sexual desire (IV: 1).

The five beliefs and practices of the people which I wish to consider are the following:

(1) If a snake bites a person, that individual may never touch or pick fruit from a fruit tree. If he or she does, the tree will slowly dry up and die. The bitten person remains contaminated for the rest of his or her life.

(2) If a man has had sexual relations with a woman and in the next twenty-four hours picks fruit from a fruit tree, the tree will die. After twenty-four hours he may harvest fruit without damage to the tree.

(3) If a pregnant woman or her spouse picks fruit from a fruit tree, the tree will die.

(4) If a pregnant woman looks at a snake, the snake will stop moving until she takes her eyes away. The snake is only stopped, it is not killed. This faculty is called *la fuerza de la*

vista (the power or force of sight).[9]

(5) If the spouse of a pregnant woman kills a snake and then looks at its twisting dying body, his mate will have a difficult childbirth; the child will twist and turn as it comes to leave its mother.

These propositions are at once beliefs, prohibitions and sanctions. Custom two undoubtedly was transgressed, but for the most part the people appear to follow the prohibitions.

Certain folk explanations and other ethnographic facts are relevant for an understanding of the customs. The prohibitions regarding fruit trees apply only to picking fruit. A person bitten by a snake can seed fruit trees. Most fruit trees are planted in the 'garden' which is at the side of each house; the prohibition does not apply to harvesting crops such as rice or maize which are planted in the fields. The fruit tree dies only if picked, but it is the sight or vision of the contaminated person that actually kills the plant. The bitten individual is said to be unclean or poisoned. Similarly, the poison of the snake and the power of a pregnant woman are in their eyes, 'like the evil eye'. The first belief holds true for all classes of snake. All snakes are said to be poisonous to some degree, and a snake bite always poisons the individual. When he is in a strong state the bitten person can 'cut' the poison quicker, but he remains poisoned forever. In fact, although the people know that some snakes are deadly poisonous and some not, they fear all snakes.

Pregnant women are considered to be in a special state. Ordinarily they try to hide and seldom outrightly admit to their condition. The spouse of a pregnant woman is said to be poisoned because his mate is. Similarly, in regard to custom 2, a man who has had sexual relations is poisoned because he has had contact with a woman, just as one may contract a sickness from another by sleeping in the same room. If a man is going to pick fruit in someone else's garden the owner often will say, 'Pick it with care', meaning have you had sexual relations with a woman recently? Lastly, these are the only prohibitions which result from being bitten by a snake or having sexual relations with a woman. For example, a man may cohabit with a woman after being bitten by a snake.

Given these folk explanations, I shall treat the five customs as a whole in comparison to Genesis. (This does not exclude the possibility that other variants may exist in Panama or in other Hispanic cultures.[10]) Relying solely upon the ethnography it is possible without distorting them to rewrite the five propositions as comparable statements, divided into phrases (see Table 3). The folk explanations justify my elaboration of the propositions.

In this form phrase A refers to an action, phrase B to its consequence. Phrase C refers to a further action and phrase D to a further consequence. The phrases under B were either explicitly expressed by the people or filled out from the ethnography provided. Phrase A of 3, 4 and 5 is the passive transform of phrase A in 1 and 2. Phrase C refers to the prohibitions which are observed. In this comparable form the statements and phrases may be read simultaneously across and downwards.

A comparison of statements 1 and 2 shows that snakes and women are metaphorically linked. Both poison man through 'biting'.[11] The snake's power, however, is greater for it can affect both men and women, and the poisoning incurred is permanent. From a snake there is no cleansing, from a woman there is. Thus far, this interpretation is perfectly consistent with a Catholic reading of the Old Testament in which original (statement 1) and actual (statement 2) sin are distinguished; the latter is remissible, the former is not. And in Genesis itself the woman's evil is differentiated from and considered to be lesser than the snake's. The snake led both Adam and Eve to evil, Eve only led Adam.

In statement 3 both man and woman are affected as in 1, but as in 2 the venom goes away in time. The male in 3 is associated with his pregnant spouse by contact or contiguity. Comparison with the Genesis story and statements 1 and 2 provides, I think, an understanding of this belief. In statements 1, 2 and 3 phrase A implies that mankind has eaten (or will eat) fruit from the tree of knowledge and has gained sight. Therefore, man has the ability to procreate and have descendants. In Genesis the result of this action is the expulsion and man's curse:

And he said: Behold Adam is become as one of us, knowing good and evil: now, therefore, lest perhaps he put forth his hand, and take also of the tree of life, and eat, and live for ever. And the Lord God sent him out of the paradise of pleasure, to till the earth from which he was taken (III: 23-4).

The *campesinos* have simply recast this belief in statement 3. Having eaten from the tree of sexual relations, as implied in phrases A and B, man and woman are prohibited from re-entering the garden and eating from the tree of life, as implied in phrases C and D. Statements 1 and 2, then, are variants of this.

TABLE 3　*Five customs in rewritten form*

Phrases	A	B	C	D
Statements 1	Snake bites/ man/ poisons woman	man/ poisoned for ever woman	poisoned man/ picks (touches) & fruit woman sees	fruit tree dies
2	Woman sexual relation man	man poisoned twenty-four hours	poisoned man picks (touches) & fruit sees	fruit tree dies
3	Pregnant woman/ 'Pregnant' man	poisoned nine months	poisoned woman/ picks (touches) & fruit man sees	fruit tree dies
4	Pregnant woman	poisoned nine months	poisoned woman sees snake	snake stops
5	'Pregnant' man	poisoned nine months	poisoned man kills (touches) & snake sees	'kills' wife & child

Considering the three statements together, in 3, pregnancy and having descendants poisons both man and woman, but in 2, sexual relations alone affect only a man, not a woman. The juxtaposition of 2 and 3 leads to the conclusion that woman is not the exact equivalent of man. Further, as I have implied, in 1 and 2 a similarity but not equivalence of woman and snake is established. Finally, the statements clearly single out fruit trees, linking them to the woman-snake complex. All three are anomalous and have ambiguous powers: snakes bite but lead man to the tree of knowledge; women poison but provide descendants; the tree of knowledge provides sexuality but excludes the tree of eternal life.

Statement 3 links 4 and 5 with 1 and 2. In 4, a pregnant woman stops but does not kill the poisoning snake. Poisoned woman is in no immediate danger, but the snake can return later to bite her; original sin recurs again and again. In Genesis, of course, the snake is cursed to have the enmity of mankind, specifically Eve and her descendants. By contrast to 4, in statement 5 the spouse of a pregnant woman cannot stop a snake, but must flee it. There is an association of a twisting dying snake and a twisting birthing child; killing the snake can lead to the death of the child. This image in 5, C and D is simply the inverse of that in A and B of 1 and 2 where a potent biting snake equals having sexual relations (and the possibility of descendants). Statement 5, phrase D, is also a re-statement of the woman's curse: she must submit to the power of her spouse and suffer the pain of childbirth.

Several messages, then, are encoded in these customs. One concerns the paradox posed by sight and man's mortality. If man and woman had not listened to the snake, i.e. the devil, and eaten from the tree of knowledge and seen sexual difference, they could not have had descendants. By listening to the snake, however, they gave up eternal life. Since mankind has chosen to have descendants it is forever tainted by original sin and condemned to be mortal. Second, the customs reiterate the other curses of Genesis, particularly with regard to women suffering the pains of childbirth and being under the domination of men. Third, as in the biblical story male and female are clearly differentiated, and women, like snakes, are poisonous. They bear the primary guilt for the Fall.

Beyond their manifestation in the five customs, these issues are important ones in the people's lives. I point out again the ambiguous status of sexual relations. According to some people, sex was introduced by the devil; others maintain that coition is necessary if there is to be life. The crucially important relationship system — the *compadrazgo* — is founded on the notion of original sin from which all men must be cleansed. Furthermore, men do toil in the fields; fruit trees are raised in gardens kept at houses; and young children who have not yet learned how to sin are kept at home — the Garden — until they reach sexual maturity. Childless couples, in fact, often foster small children because it is said they help to keep the devil away. The people are fastidious about separating themselves from the earth around the house, which is said to be dirty because man's accumulated sins have dropped on to it, but which is also where the snake is condemned to crawl. More important, women, like Eve, should be and are under the domination of their spouses, and it is the female who must have a heightened sense of shame for her sexual passion. In a fundamental respect women are thought to be tainted in a way that men are not, and it is they, not unexpectedly, who are principally involved in the religious celebrations within the community.

I am arguing, then, that the religious conception offers two important and interrelated models in the figures of Mary and Eve. Certain facets of these figures have received emphasis in rural Panama. The two images are not everyday models in the sense that females consciously pattern their lives after or think of themselves in terms of either figure. Rather, Eve, the impure woman who created descendants, and Mary, the ideal, virginal mother, stand as prototypes about females, and these assumptions about women as spouses and mothers are deeply embedded in the secular social structure. The five beliefs and practices I have briefly analysed are but one manifestation of these presuppositions about females and their relation to males.[1][2]

The saints and man

The people's most elaborate beliefs and rites centre about the saints; indeed, for the *campesinos* they have assumed an importance far beyond that specified by the church.

Saints stand between man and God in a manner analogous to 'Jews' who stand between man and the devil. Just as the 'Jews' assist the devil in his work, so the saints help to focus and guide men's actions in the truly religious life. Saints are identified as all those listed in the almanac. They were humans who performed extraordinary sacrifices and did not sin. But more important, 'they made miracles', and folk accounts of the saints always take note of the fact that they were touched by the supernatural.

Saints, like people's souls, are in heaven; God gives them a lesson each day, but they have no other heavenly duties except in relation to persons on earth. There is no conceptual hierarchy of saints although some are said to be closer to God, just as on earth some are better friends than others; however, it is unknown which saints are nearer to Him.

The interest in and importance of the saints is congruent with the people's conception of God as an all-powerful but distant entity. Since Christ is not a mediating figure between man and God, this separation of the natural and spiritual presents a problem in that man seemingly has no direct link with God. It is, I suggest, the saints, the miraculous humans, who occupy the mediating position between man and God and who provide one means by which man can reach God.

The distinct role of the saints may be seen in the differing acts of worship made toward God and the saints. Man must have faith in both, but since God is all powerful, man can only pray to or beseech him, asking for forgiveness and salvation. Man cannot offer God anything. By contrast, through the institution of the vow an individual may offer a saint an act of devotion and request immediate help in his material life.

A variety of saints are recognized, and the people's connections to them are formed in different ways. Some links are personal, based for example on the connection between personal (saint) name and the saint in heaven. One saint is known as the Virgin of Fatima or the Virgin of the Miraculous Medal. Her image circulates through the community itself, passing from house to house each day and thereby giving each home an extra measure of good fortune. The patron saint of the village is San Martín de Porres. The idol of San Martín was acquired in the early 1960s. According to the villagers San Martín was a *mestizo* who lived in Panama.[13] His life was virtuous and touched by the miraculous.

The people say that it is better to have a patron saint, for he serves as a guide for the entire populace. Invoking the political-legal metaphor, they suggest that being without a saint is like lacking a *regidor*. Having a patron saint and a chapel re-enforces all men's belief and faith in God and it particularly leads the younger people to have a deeper understanding of him. A patron saint gives a community greater respect in the eyes of others, and in concrete terms through the institution of the vow or prayers the saint may help protect the community against misfortunes. But people must have faith in San Martín. If San Martín fails, it is only because the community lacks faith in him.

Since the acquisition of San Martín's idol a small *fiesta* has been held each 17 November, the date when the idol was first brought to the community. (Officially, the feast day is 3 November.) On the saint's day a small procession is held and the idol is paraded about portions of the village. The cavalcade includes the school children and women; only a few men participate. Some from outside the community attend the *fiesta*, usually coming to complete vows made previously to San Martín. Many of these vows are monetary or have monetary value, such as the presentation of a calf. The people note that although San Martín is the patron of Los Boquerones he does not ordinarily take money from people of the village. He earns it from outsiders, and this money can and should be used to finish construction of the chapel which honours him. In addition to being a religious celebration the *fiesta* is a mark of community pride.

At least twenty-five further saints are celebrated during the course of the liturgical year, many of whom are patrons of neighbouring villages. Some of these saints are celebrated by performing no work, others are venerated by attending lively *fiestas*. Some saints mark good days for planting, others propitious times for fishing. On the day of some it is said to thunder, while others may be prayed to if the season is dry. On Our Lady of Sorrows or 'Painful Friday' (the Friday before Palm Sunday) women should do no work out of respect for Mary who raised Christ. The pains refer to all the pains a female has — menstruation, pregnancy and birth, and housework. Conversely, St Joseph's Day (19 March) should be kept by men.

The most important time in the liturgical year, however, is Holy Week. The designated and important days are Holy Wednesday, Holy Thursday, Holy Friday, Saturday of Glory and Easter Sunday. According to the countrymen Christ died either on Wednesday or Thursday, was buried on Friday and arose on Saturday. This emphasis on the early part of the week is probably connected to the fact that until the recent changes in the official ritual, masses were said on Thursday, a procession was held on Friday, and the Easter vigil rites were performed on Saturday morning.

Friday is the day when Christ gathered together his disciples; hence, one should visit his family and mother on this day. One may have a cross blessed in the church on Friday and then place it on the house for protection against the devil and strong winds. In a number of the larger towns processions are held in the evening.

Nevertheless, this is a very sacred time and the people's activities are marked by a number of prohibitions. First, beginning at noon Wednesday through Sunday no one should work. Men should not work in the fields or around the house. Women should not wash clothes or dishes, or shell rice. At most they should cook once a day. It is even bad to light a fire. Second, from Monday onwards no one should eat meat; fish are permitted. Third, sexual relations from Wednesday onwards are prohibited. Fourth, one should not drink alcoholic beverages, though a few do. Holy Week is the only time when sexual relations are prohibited.

With respect to these prohibitions it is particularly instructive to look comparatively at all the interdictions which are imposed on the celebrated days. Roughly, the interdictions fall along a continuum stretching from heavy work in the fields to light work in the house. As I shall show in a later chapter, male/female work categories are thought out through this same opposition of the fields and household. In general the interdictions always start at the field end, and then are imposed successively towards the house end. Since the division of male and female work parallels this continuum, the circumscriptions fall first on men and then on women. Additionally, there is a correspondence between the number of prohibitions and the sanctity of the day celebrated, which brings us to the interdictions of Holy Week. During this time all classes of men's as well as most women's work are prohibited. But the interdictions apply not only to field and house work, they extend into the most private area of the home, the bedroom — sexual relations are prohibited. In some respects, then, the prohibitions serve to purify the actors, by removing them from nature and animals, and placing them within the domestic unit. The degree of needed purification varies according to the significance and sanctity of the holiday.

In addition to their role in the religious cycle it is through the saints that man can most effectively reach God by means of the *manda*. The term *manda* comes from the verb *mandar* (to command, order, will, rule). In some other parts of Latin America this same transaction between man and saint is known as a promise. Theologically it is an elaboration of ideas concerning vows and votive offerings.

The *manda* is formed between one individual and one saint. It consists of a request to the saint for divine help on earth and a promise to perform or dedicate an earthly duty to him. The saint repeats the appeal to God who in turn does or does not grant it. *Mandas* are always made through the saints as intercessors, they are never made directly to God. If aid is given, the promise must be fulfilled by the earthly petitioner; failure to do so may bring further misfortune.

Usually, requests are focused on the restoration of the normal order. Most requests centre about the three valued items of humans, animals and crops. The offerings vary in expense and hardship from offering candles to making a pilgrimage. If one saint fails, another may be tried; when a saint proves effective for an individual he may be returned to again and again.

The offering of the *manda* in some sense stands in place of the offerer. It is part gift, part payment, and partly a sign of submission. But the *manda* is viewed mostly as a penalty or hardship — a punishment the individual must bear for a prior, though perhaps unknown, wrong. Through the promise of this symbolic expiation the petitioner hopes to gain divine aid.

Because God is distant and man is on earth, intermediaries to reach the divinity must be used, and it is the saints who provide this transition. The unitary force of God is refracted, divided and classified in the celebration of each saint; and through the saints, God and God's ordering of the world are made manifest throughout the year. Through the *manda* the gap between godhead and human is temporarily narrowed. And in this respect it is worth noting again that the Christ image, the central sacrificial and intermediary figure in the orthodox religion, is suppressed in the folk version, hence the importance of *mandas* and the saints.

In this chapter I have examined the beliefs and rites which define and express the man-God, man-devil and man-saints relationships. This total system has a profound impact upon the idea of man, his place in the world, and his relation to other beings. In terms of relationship systems the religious conceptions lay the groundwork for the *compadrazgo* in that every person is thought to be born with original sin from which he must be cleansed through baptism. Images of woman as suffering mother and sexual temptress are both presented, and these have an impact not only upon the idea of woman but also upon male-female relationships. Children, by contrast, are born innocent of sexual desire.

In the creed itself the key elements are an unshakable faith in the existence of God and the belief that he sets and controls the destiny of every man. Through careful observation of rites man will remain in

God's grace and away from sin, but his religion provides him with little sense of spiritual uplift. God, in the form of Jesus Christ, is not on earth, and there is little feeling of personal redemption, participation or -communion with him: Christ's death, not his resurrection, is stressed; man must endure his destiny and fulfil his religious obligations; 'happy' songs are not sung at *fiestas*; everyone, and particularly woman, is tainted with original sin; man expiates his sins through the *manda* and seeks divine help only to restore the normal order on earth. In practical terms, as exhibited in the proliferation of *fiestas* and the role of the *mandas,* it is the saints who are the most prominent figures in the religion, and their salient position undoubtedly is related to the clear separation of the divine and natural spheres.

If these beliefs do not promote a sense of oneness with God, they also do not further social groupings on earth. Each person has a separate destiny, and the strength of his own faith is never the same as that of another. Every individual, too, seeks out his own saint, appeals to him in times of personal misfortune and offers an oblation of his own choice. The people as a congregation are united only during certain *fiestas.*[14] In everyday terms the only religious group in the community is the chapel society, a loosely-structured organization predominantly concerned with the practical problems of keeping the chapel in repair and preparing for the yearly *fiesta* of San Martín.

5   The individual

In Los Boquerones the term *la persona* refers to the concept of the person. All individuals are considered to be equal in that they are composed of identical qualities, although these common elements are distributed uniquely. Each person is a total being and a particular refraction of humanity.[1]

It is important to distinguish between the individual as cultural conception and as empirical object. Societies obviously consist of human beings, but the way in which these entities are conceptualized differs markedly. The person is categorized as a totality and dissected analytically in culturally specific ways. Among the *campesinos* the individual is not only conceptually defined, the concept itself is a significant and ordering idea in the culture. The concept of the person is a central one, providing the link between, on the one hand, ultimate beliefs about the world and, on the other, the social relationship systems. At the juncture between culture and social structure, the concept of the individual is the point of articulation for translating values into relationships.

Classes of persons: the individual within the larger society

The countrymen as Panamanians use a number of concepts to locate themselves within the larger society. Some of these are related to personal characteristics, some are descriptive, others are evaluative.

A *capitolino* is one who lives in a capital or *pueblo* (town, village). A *campesino* is one who resides in the *campo* (country, field) or not in the town. Since a variety of persons actually live outside the major towns additional characteristics sometimes are added to distinguish the *campesino* from others. A *campesino* is not a cattleman *(el ganadero)* but an agriculturalist or farmer *(agricultor)*, although this term is not applied to females or children. The countrymen also distinguish themselves from large-scale farmers; an agriculturalist 'throws' the machete for a living. He works in the fields raising rice, maize, and other crops.

These terms are not only descriptive but evaluative.[2] The people consider that it would be easier and better to be a cattleman, a teacher or to have a business in a capital. The evaluation placed upon the category *campesino* receives clear expression in a set of terms which the countrymen, and to some extent, the town dwellers employ. These words define a graduated scale of 'civilization', a concept which has social, spatial and temporal meanings. At the top of the social scale are the *capitolinos;* at the bottom are the Indians *(los indios)*. Indians are seen as a separate group with their own language and customs. They are said to lack civilization and to be backward (*atrasado*). The concept of the backward Indian provides the reference point for the word *cholo*. Literally, *cholo* is a racial term referring to a dark-skinned person who has a mixture of 'white' and Indian blood. Used in this sense only the term could be applied to a very large proportion of Panamanians in both countryside and city. But the word also has social connotations. *Cholo* refers not to a discrete group of people but is applied down the social scale. To the city dweller everyone in the countryside, regardless of racial origin, is a *cholo*. For the countrymen a *cholo* is someone who is behind others in the graces of civilization. Sometimes the villagers speak of themselves as *cholos* in relation to town dwellers. Individuals would confide to me: 'Here we are all *cholos*'. But most times no one admits to being a *cholo*. 'They' are said to be the ones who live in the most distant areas and who come to work for the people as *peones*.[3] To these more distant *campesinos*, in turn, a *cholo* is beneath them. Finally, at the bottom of the social scale *cholos* are Indians. In addition to its racial meaning, then, *cholo* refers to crudeness or backwardness and to those people who live farther away or toward the mountains.[4] Employed in this manner it refers not to a group but to a relationship between the speaker and the observed.

Other labelled categories convey similar ideas. The term *montuno* (derived from *monte*) refers to the old style of *campesino* clothing which is no longer used; it also means backwardness of a certain type. A *montuno* is unaccustomed to speaking with people, is timid and shy, and lacks social graces. For example, if a meeting is held in the community school, the ones who stand outside and look in through the windows are the *montunos*. The term, like *cholo,* is used comparatively, is applied down the social scale, and has spatial connotations. In Los Boquerones the *montunos* are the people who live farthest from the highway. But the *cholo* and *montuno* are not equivalent. Both are backward and lack social manners; however, *cholos*, it is said, cannot even read or write whereas *montunos* may have these skills. Normally, then, the people say that in Los Boquerones there are *montunos* but not *cholos*.

A partial synonym of *montuno* is *cimarrón*, a word meaning wild or untamed.[5] The term is applied also to the corn liquor *(la chicha fuerte)* which is made illegally in the countryside, and this brings out yet further reverberations of the idea of civilization. For the people civilization has a temporal dimension. The *campesinos* note that over time they have become more civilized. They used to make *chicha fuerte,* the *cimarrón* or untamed liquor. Now, a law prohibits its production. Over time civilization has come to the countryside in the form of new styles of clothing, metal pots and plates, drinking glasses, fencing wire, and radios. Now, it is considered embarrassing to be found using a wooden spoon or plate, or a gourd for drinking or hauling water.

Further, the *cimarrón* is wild or untamed: lack of civilization also implies animality. For example, the word *cochino* refers to both a swine and a dirty person. In the past, swine were permitted to roam in the bush where they scavenged for food; unlike horses, dogs and chickens they were not fed by humans. A *cochino* person is one who takes no care of his body or speech, and it is said that an individual is a *cochino* or not in accord with the civilization he has. The people also state that compared to townspeople they are *brutos* (coarse, brutish) and *crudos* (crude, harsh).

Thus, civilization is understood to run in descending degrees from the *capitolinos* to the animal-like and backward ones, it penetrates over time from the city into the countryside, and spatial proximity to a population centre partially determines the degree of civilization that a person has.

A different set of social terms concern categories of colour, the principal ones being:[6]

Negro (black): considered to be a very ugly word.[7] It should not be used in address. However, a man may affectionately call his spouse *'negro'*, though if he uses the feminine form *negra* she will be insulted.

Moreno (dark, brown, coloured): refers to a slightly lighter colour than *negro*. It is an acceptable and frequently used word, and should be used in place of *negro*. A number of popular songs refer to *'mi morena'*. It is sometimes said that there are no *negros* only *morenos* in the community.

Trigueño (swarthy, dark): infrequently used. It refers to a somewhat lighter colour than *moreno* but is said to be its synonym.

Amarillo (yellow): employed for a number of persons within the village who have an exceptionally light but not white skin colour.

Blanco (white): used for a few persons within the community.

Other more strictly 'racial' terms such as *cholo* also are utilized. *Cholo* is said to have been first used by Columbus, who came from Africa, discovered Panama, made it into a country and was the first Panamanian. Columbus married an Indian woman who had beautiful hair; when calling her he would say, 'come here my *chola*'. The *campesinos,* it is occasionally said, are descended from this pair. Sometimes the term *chombo,* also considered to be ugly, is equated with *cholo.* More properly it is used to refer to certain 'Jamaican characteristics': dark skin and tight, coarse hair. *Prieto* (dark, black, compact) is a synonym of *chombo* and also refers to Jamaicans. (The people themselves have no adverse feelings toward Jamaicans, and one well-regarded man in Los Boquerones is said to be descended directly from Jamaicans. West Indians have not always been welcome in Panama, however, and in the early 1940s their citizenship rights were withdrawn, although later they were restored.)

These terms, then, refer primarily to overt physical characteristics. But they have social overtones, for in so far as a person's colour is related to that of his parents, skin tint can have implications about ancestry. Within the community, however, there are no social classes; and colour and ancestry have only a minimal bearing upon a person's social standing within it. Still, lightness of skin is valued and darkness is not. *Negro* and *chombo* have pejorative connotations, and there is a tendency to say that darker colours actually are lighter. *Moreno* (brown) is substituted for *negro* (black); *trigueño* is sometimes used in place of *moreno.* Although I found no evidence that persons seek light-skinned conjugal partners, a few young women do use umbrellas when running an errand in the sun, and several older ones who had worked in Panama City reported with pleasure how much lighter their complexions had become when their work kept them indoors.[8] Thus within the village, skin colour is evaluated but is not linked to discrete social positions. The evaluation emanates from the larger society where colour is connected to class of work, ancestry and socioeconomic standing. In that 'civilization' is valued by the *campesinos,* skin colour also helps define the identity of the person. Unlike the strictly social categories, however, colour differences penetrate into the community itself and differentiate one person from another.

One portion of the person's identity is defined by his relation to the larger society. In this context he is an individual, or one in a class composed of other individuals. Compared to town dwellers the *campesino* lacks civilization with all its implications. Theoretically the individual has the potential to rise in the social scale since the characteristics which define him are not inherited or permanent, and since he is not defined by or bound to a discrete group in the countryside. Hence, at times, but not always, the countrymen accept the town dwellers' low estimation of themselves while entertaining the hope of advancement for their children.

Classes of persons: the individual within the community

The social and colour categories connect the individual to, and separate him from, the larger society. Within the community further categories define the place of the person. Each individual recognizes about him categories of persons based on social proximity. Although the particular humans occupying the categories change, the categories themselves remain constant. It is to these categories that I first turn.

Every person distinguishes between friends, enemies, and *particulares*. Friends are of two types: *de confianza* (of confidence, trust, familiarity) and *de la calle* (of the street). A friend of trust is also called a friend of the house *(un amigo de la casa);* a street friend is sometimes labelled a work friend (*un amigo de trabajo*). Conceptually, then, the two types of friends are distinguished on the basis of the household versus the street or work. Needs and problems may be confided to a friend of confidence, and it is to such friends that one turns for help. A house friend may be relied upon to respect one's spouse as if she were a mother or *comadre;* and with such a friend a spouse may be sent on a trip to Santiago or Panama City, situations in which even close kin might not be trusted. A street friend is one with whom amicable contact is maintained, although only conversation and drinks may be exchanged. More generally, a friend of the street is said to be one who is not an enemy, and an enemy reciprocally is one who is not a friend. Enemies are said to be angry *(bravo)* with one another. They do not greet and usually have fought in the past. The term *bravo* connotes not only anger but also ill-temper and wildness; when men drink to excess they often become *bravo* and fight. Like things in the wild outside the community, an enemy's social presence is ignored.

Nevertheless both friends and enemies are individually distinguished, and against these two categories is ranged a further one: *particulares* (private individuals, citizens). A *particular* may or may not be personally known; relations with him are infrequent or non-existent. However, such a distant person is identified as a *particular*, a unique being, and not as a member of a social group. *Particular* designates a category consisting of individuals.[9] Of course, the manner in which these categories are 'filled out' varies by the individual, and a friend in one year may become an enemy in the following. Even the category friend has its ambiguities; a friend in front but not behind *(por adelante de atrás no),* because speaking behind the back violates the essential norm of trust, is no friend at all.

The sense of responsibility towards others is congruent with this set of categories. Aside from aiding kin and *compadres* it is said that one should help close friends and then neighbours in times of sickness, shortage of money and death. Neighbours, who also are friends, loan salt, kerosene, and other basic necessities. They offer help when an emergency arises at night. But a person is not obliged to help a friend or neighbour who is persistently in need. Beyond this friend-and-neighbour level there is a lessened sense of obligation toward others. All, it is said, have an equal, though minimal, responsibility to 'advance' the community. In practice this means giving labour time or a small sum of money to the school or chapel. One should attend the funeral of a community member and may offer help to a household struck by sickness. But if an individual is carrying out activities which harm a number of people within the village, no one is obliged to join with others to impede his actions, and there are no formal mechanisms which may be deployed in order to coerce a person to offer communal aid. Should the need arise, aid ought to be offered to the province; but helping the nation of Panama is not considered to be a duty.

In contrast to the previous categories, these concepts and obligations concerning the person designate him as a unique being at the centre of a series of concentric circles: friends of the house, friends of the street, enemies, other individuals. Each category includes unique beings, and each category is defined in relation to its opposite in a series of binary discriminations. The notion of duty towards others weakens as the more distant categories are reached. At the level of the community (which includes house friends, street friends, enemies and a few *particulares*) a sharp break is encountered; there is a sense of duty to the community but not beyond where the world is populated only by other private individuals.[10]

The terminology for referring to and addressing others also provides a set of categories for discriminating individuals. A complete analysis of the nomenclature system lies beyond the scope of this book, and I only note here some of the links between the different terminology systems and the systems of relationships. Although the terms designate classes of individuals, they never refer to relationships between individuals as members of groups. They designate the person himself as a category.

Terms of address and reference in the *compadrazgo,* which are described more appropriately in chapters 12 and 13, with only a few exceptions, override or replace other forms. For example, a brother who becomes a *compadre* is called *compadre* and not brother, although the relationship itself retains aspects of the sibling bond. Second, kinship terms, also described later, normally take precedence over other forms of reference.

A third system of naming is based upon age. For example, as she grows older a female passes through the categories of *niña, muchacha, señorita,* and *mujer.* These terms are descriptive but may be used in direct or indirect address. A young female may be addressed as *niña* or referred to as *la niña Francisca.* Even the dead are specially marked. In reference, the name of a recently deceased is prefixed by *'El difunto'* (the deceased, dead). The term is used, it is said, because the named is dead and must be distinguished from the living. Widows are distinguished by terms of reference, but widowers and orphans are not. Correct form is to label the widow by reference to the first name of her husband, for example, 'the widow of Juan'. A widow also may be referred to by her own name, such as 'the widow Paula' or merely 'the widow' when the context makes the reference unambiguous.[11] Thus, with respect to the life cycle, certain linguistic labels mark important changes in the individual. Such modifiers are optionally used for the living and invariably employed for the recently deceased; no ambiguity is permitted as to who is alive and who is not. The use of widow (but not widower for a single man) seems to indicate that a female's self is partially defined in relation to and enveloped by a male's.

A fourth set of terms is used in the context of respect, power and prestige differentials. The honorific *Don (Doña),* used with a first name, is employed for extremely wealthy or prestigeful outsiders. Only a few in Santiago are addressed by the people as *Don. Señor (señora),* also prefixed to a first name, is primarily a term of respect which may be used in both direct and indirect address. It is employed for such outsiders as wealthy landowners, school teachers, and government officials. Within the community, among adults, the title is deployed for older persons (primarily males), for most males by females, and for an individual who merits respect. However, an elder person need not address a contemporary as *señor,* and not all older individuals are addressed by the term. The formal and informal you *(usted/tú)* also are used to denote positions of respect. *Usted* is employed for all older persons, by females for males, for *compadres,* godparents and godchildren, for acquaintances who are not close friends, for God, and for outsiders. *Tú,* which connotes a lack of respect, is used for children, for animals, for close friends, and for age contemporaries. It is used among children and may be employed by an older adult for a younger adult. In Santiago and Panama City the term is commonly used for any acquaintance, a practice which often impedes communication between the *campesino* and town dweller.[1][2]

The formal and informal 'you' differ in use from the honorific *señor. Señor* always connotes respect, but its lack of use does not necessarily connote a lack of respect. By contrast, the opposition *usted/tú* obligates the speaker to choose between respect and familiarity. *Usted* is employed in all situations where *señor* is used, but the reverse does not always hold. Thus, an older person may respect a contemporary and employ *usted* for him but not call him *señor. Señor* connotes respect in an asymmetric relationship. *Usted* may connote respect in asymmetry or in distance.

Finally, surnames, first names, and nicknames are classification devices and terms which denote the unique position of the individual. Currently most of the people have two surnames, a patronym and a matronym, placed in that order. The matronym is rarely used. A child's patronym is the patronym of his father, his matronym is the patronym of his mother. A surname therefore is composed of the patronyms of the paternal and maternal grandfathers, and in a strict sense there are only patronyms. If a man has daughters only, his patronym continues in the first generation as a patronym, becomes a secondary form as a matronym in the following generation and then is extinguished. In a consensual union a woman does not assume the surname of her spouse. If legally married, she keeps her patronym and adds that of her husband preceded by '*de*'. Like a widow her identity is partially defined in relation to her mate. In general, then, surnames of all but married women classify individuals by reference to their grandfathers.

First names are allocated on quite a different basis. A child's first name should be the same as that of a saint who is celebrated on the day of his birth, although parents sometimes do not follow this rule. On All Souls' Day of each year God and St Peter come out to the gates of Heaven and call out the names of those who have died in the preceding year. The name used to call a recently deceased is that of a saint from his day of birth. Therefore, to avoid confusion at the gate of Heaven and risking God's displeasure, it is said to be better to name a child according to the rules. From a different perspective, however, we may say that what God calls forth on All Souls' Day are not individually named persons but classes of people grouped by saints' names. At birth a human is not named; he is allocated a pre-existing named position according to the date when he entered human society.

Proper names, then, are classification devices, but they also have the function of individuating the human. The stock of names is finite. Theoretically, new names are created only when new saints are recognized, but since new saints were humans, their names too must have been drawn from the pre-existing stock. The names used in Los Boquerones are comparable to those found in many Latin American communities.[13] The bank of names is large but closed. Within this stock of names parents try to choose one which is not occupied by others. Persons bearing the same first name address and refer to one another as namesake *(tocayo)*. A sense of similarity unites them, and a namesake is said to be like a relative. Parents particularly avoid giving their child a name which has been associated with a disreputable person or which has bad connotations. For example, one young man in the community, who shares the first name with another, has a history of epileptic fits. His illness is not fully comprehended by others and he is generally shunned. His namesake, in particular, studiously avoids meeting him and resorts to circumlocutions when referring to him. Thus, namesakes are persons who belong to the same class of individuals, and they are therefore metaphorically linked. In order to individuate their children in relation to the community parents try to draw on unutilized names from the pre-existing stock.

But this logical tie between namesakes has a spiritual basis. Through his first name an individual is linked to a saint whereas through his second he is linked to a family. In theory the first name is assumed when a child is baptized, that is, admitted to the spiritual world, although in fact parents address him by his first name before baptism.[14] The family name is assumed at birth, or more precisely when the child is officially recognized as an offspring of a man and a woman. The two names reflect a contrast of nature and spirit in the individual. One classifies the child as a natural member of society and a family which continue through time. The other classifies him synchronically and allies him with the spiritual world. First and last names alone designate parts of the person; together they denote the total individual, and cross-cutting one another they provide the person with a unique position in the society. Names, then, are natural and spiritual classifications at the level of the individual.

Within the community, persons may be referred to in several ways. Unless a kinship or *compadrazgo* label is used, first names are normally employed, since their uniqueness and the context make the reference unambiguous. But two types of nicknames also are used. Certain first names have standard nicknames, i.e. Vicente = Chente, Marcellino = Chelo, Antonio = Nino, Victor = Vito, Francisca = Chica, etc.[15] Other nicknames derive from different sources. One well-mannered, light-skinned young man is called *Cholo.* An older man who has produced ten children is sometimes called 'the rabbit'. Such nicknames are largely confined to males. Unlike those found in many comparable areas they are not pejorative nor are they inherited (Foster, 1964: 119-21; Kenny, 1966: 86-9). *Cholo* in this context is said to be a term of affection, and 'the rabbit' enjoys the occasional use of his nickname as much as the rest of the community.

The terms, 'that man' (*ese hombre*) and 'so-and-so' (*fulano*) are used interchangeably in several contexts. If a person wishes to refer to another but does not know his name, he employs one of the expressions. But the terms also may be used in a derogatory manner to refer to someone who is known by name to the speaker and his listeners. By employing the circumlocution the speaker protects himself from passers-by who might overhear and from the disrespect of directly labelling the person. In both usages the speaker identifies the other not as a particular person but as a human in a broad class of others that he does not individually recognize.

Some broad principles may be extracted from these systems of nomenclature. Kinship terms, *compadrazgo* terms, and first and last names are permanent labels. The contrast of *compadrazgo* and kin terms parallels the spiritual/natural dichotomy of first and last names. However, kin and *compadrazgo* terms are relational whereas within the community a human has a personal name with respect to everyone else. By contrast, the age labels are impermanent and classify all individuals within the village. Terms of respect, though frequently based on age, are relational but not permanent. Thus, an individual occupies a permanent position with respect to kinship, *compadrazgo,* and personal labels, and he has an impermanent one in relation to age and respect terms. His relationships are defined dyadically by kinship, *compadrazgo* and respect terms. Personal names and age labels classify him; the latter group him with a number of others, the former individualize and dissect him. No terms identify the person as a member of an existing social group.

Classes within the person: the individual divided

Having described some of the principal concepts which place the individual within the community and larger society, I turn to those categories which pertain directly to the person. Above all the individual is thought to be divided into natural and spiritual parts. The natural portion in turn defines his essence as a sexual being.

As a natural being the person is thought to be included within a larger system of classification which includes all natural objects: the opposition of hot and cold.[16] Throughout Latin American this binary scheme of classification is largely associated with medical practices, but the contemporary system is only a remnant of a broader and older conceptual scheme. At the time of the Conquest the essential concepts were part of Spanish scientific medicine; later the system or parts of it filtered into the folk areas of Latin America. In the historical system there were thought to be four primary physical components in the world which were combined into two pairs of opposites; hot/cold and dry/moist. All humans were thought to have four humours which were said to represent combinations of the four elemental qualities: blood (warm and moist), yellow bile (warm and dry), black bile (cold and dry), and phlegm (cold and moist). In addition, there were thought to be three vital forces in the human body: the brain (wet and cold), the heart (dry and hot), and the liver (wet and hot). Each individual was said to have a different proportion of the humours, and a person's health was thought to depend upon their proper blending. Food, also classified according to whether it was hot or cold, wet or dry, was said to furnish the material with which the humours renewed themselves. Medical practices consisted primarily in diagnosing the cause of a diseased body's imbalance and prescribing an appropriate category of food or drug to restore its characteristic prior equilibrium.

Such a scheme is potentially a system of total classification. Theoretically all phenomena in the natural world may be reduced to a combination of the four elemental qualities. Man himself is conceived as a natural being within the scheme; yet each human is unique in having a special configuration of humours.

In Veraguas the present system is but a shadow of its former self. The wet/dry dimension as well as the degrees of the qualities are not recognized.[17] Hot and cold as temperatures, however, are distinguished from hot and cold as classes of objects. In the latter sense the terms refer to the quality (*la calidad*) of an item which derives from its nature (*la naturaleza*), although the class of an object is sometimes based upon its actual temperature. No individual can produce the entire classification, and in some cases there is disagreement about the category of certain objects. The items that may be classified as hot or cold include humans, bodily changes such as pregnancy, birth and post-birth, sicknesses, medicines, animals, plants, topography, and meteorological objects. A number of everyday practices are still based on the system; for example, a person who has been working in the hot sun should not eat physically cold food or take a cold bath.

Concepts about man as a natural being are unelaborated, and only fragments of the classical scheme can be discerned. Life is made up of blood, food, water, and a spirit (*el espiritu*) or air (*el aire*) which comes from God. Blood is the life and essence of the human; when it ends life also finishes, and many physical ailments are ascribed to 'low' or weak blood. All humans are warm, and have a distinctive humour (*el humor*) and nature (*la naturaleza*). These three concepts – humour, warmth, nature – are the central ones and are themselves interconnected. The location of the humour in the body is unspecified, but it is said to emerge as one breathes and is reflected in human perspiration and bodily odour. Warmth is associated with humans in a number of ways. For example, a common expression is that a garden of fruit trees needs the heat of people (*el calor de la gente*) in order to grow. Nature refers not only to the class of an item in the hot and cold system but also to the sexual urge.[18] Of the three concepts, nature is ultimately the determining force in an individual's physical makeup.

These three notions of heat, humour and nature are used to classify humans according to sex. Men generally are thought to be cold, women hot. For example, it is sometimes observed that men begin to shiver on a cool day while women stay warm. Further, women are said to have stronger humours than men and a higher *naturaleza*.[19] And nature, as specified, refers not only to an object's quality but to sexual passion.

Thus, these three characteristics of the human — warmth, humour, and nature — are thought to be in heightened form in women. At this basic physical level differences between males and females are recognized.

These attributed physical differences between males and females have ramifications for the man-woman relationship. To begin with, a stronger humour is thought to endanger a weaker one. Since the body remains in one place at night, the humour gathers in concentrated form; therefore, a male and female should not sleep together in the same bed, although either may sleep with a small child. Conjugal partners should have humours which join well together; otherwise the one with the stronger humour, almost always the woman, will 'consume' the one with the weaker, particularly through sexual intercourse.[20] For males, the stronger sexuality of females is an ambiguous power. Men say they desire to have a 'hot' woman. Some even give potions to their wives to raise their *naturaleza*. (Others take pills and potions to raise their own.) Yet a hot woman is dangerous to man. Physically she can enfeeble him;[21] socially she is more liable to cuckold him. These conceptions about humans as physical creatures are congruent with the religious view of woman as the temptress, Eve.

Hot and cold refer not only to the sexes but also to comestibles, and through the hot/cold system a connection is established between sexual relations and eating. Just as the human must seek a hot or cold partner who will be in accord with and not damage his nature, so also he must ingest hot or cold foods in accord with his internal state. Thus, it is said that a hot woman will 'consume' a cooler man; he will grow pallid, weak and lose weight. Unmarried men sometimes say they have had their 'fill' of a young girl. The man who is sexually potent may be said to have a 'hot hand'. Of the girl who is pregnant it may be asked, 'What did she eat? ' The categorical opposition of male and female, however, is not limited to sexual relations and eating, for it is also expressed in other domains. I only wish to establish here that the sexual division is thought to have a physical basis in the individual.

In addition to his natural aspect man has a spiritual character. The religious conception emphasizes the singular role of the individual. Salvation is not attained through co-operation with others.

Man carries a heavy load of sin from which he must be released through baptism and against which he must struggle through his life. Like Adam and Eve, the woman brings sex to the man, and it is she who must bear the primary sense of shame for this act. Woman, too, like Eve, is under the domination of man. At the same time, Mary, the sinless mother, presents the ideal contrast to Eve.

The concepts of man as a natural and spiritual being separate him from all other animals. Each portion of the individual leads him to be enmeshed in a system of natural and spiritual relationships, but neither of the two conceptions justifies the exercise of authority within the community. On the one hand, God exercises supreme control over the world; on the other, natural law derives from the larger society. There is no conception of a corporate social body, only individual responsibility, and this sense of personal accountability, which differs by the individual, is connected to and summarized in the concepts of respect and shame.

The total person: respect and shame

Respect *(el respeto)* is an evaluative concept about the person and his behaviour. As an action it is manifested toward certain categories of people and specific qualities in persons, and it is deployed across several relationship systems. Since respect is an evaluative attribute of all persons and their behaviour, it is the one concept which sums up the individual's total social standing. With its allied notion of shame *(la vergüenza)*, respect is the central category in defining the place of the person in the community.

Respect and shame in Panama are linked to the values of honour and shame reported from the Mediterranean,[22] though at least two significant differences may be noted between the areas. Respect refers primarily to the individual; it is not linked to the honour of a family group or name. Second, respect, unlike honour, is non-competitive and non-antagonistic. Since respect is not tied to wealth, prestige or political advantages, it is not a scarce good to be gained at another's expense; the emphasis is upon avoiding its loss.

It is easy to equate mistakenly the Panamanian words with ours and lose the shades of meaning which they have in Veraguas. In the first place, respect encompasses a wider range of behaviour for the *campesinos.* Second, respect is an aspect of behaviour, which is expressive of the statuses of the persons concerned. Finally, the concept of respect has what may appear to be several paradoxical qualities: (1) Respect refers both to inner qualities of the person and to aspects of his overt behaviour. To show respect the inner state must be exhibited. (2) To say that an individual has respect *(tener respeto)* means that he respects others and that others respect him. To be respected he must himself exhibit respect, while a person cannot have the quality without the social validation of receiving respect.[23] (3) Respect is paid to categories of persons and to individual qualities. This distinction, which is not made consciously by the people, is similar to, though not identical with, the logical shift made between honour as precedence and honour as virtue.[24] Respect, in sum, is a quality of the person deriving from his position in society and his sense of worth. To be recognized by others it must be exhibited in behaviour; to be validated it must be returned with the respect of others. It is a part of the individual which is exhibited only in social relationships.

Respect is linked to certain other concepts in the culture. To keep or observe consideration *(guardar consideración)* or to consider another is synonymous with keeping respect. The term honour *(la honra)* is used in a slightly more restricted sense. A person who is honourable *(honrado)* is financially honest. He repays his debts to the last penny and does not steal from others. Honour presumes financial independence, and as such is a prerequisite for having respect, although the person with honour is not necessarily respected. Shame *(la vergüenza)*, unlike our notion, is a valued quality of the person, though to be put to shame is not. Shame refers to the individual's awareness of and regard for the rules of social intercourse. It is an inner quality which makes the person sensitive to his own position of respect and to others' opinions about himself.[25] To have shame is said to be equal to having respect; the former is manifest in the latter. Conversely, to respect another as an individual aside from his social position is to respect him for his sense of shame. Like respect, shame is not a quantity that can be accumulated, though it can be lost. The term embarrassment *(la pena)* is sometimes used synonymously with shame. The individual who is embarrassed by his actions or feels shame says '*me da pena*' (it embarrasses me). In other contexts *pena* refers to hardship or penalty; for man's sins God may place a *pena* upon all men. 'To be worthwhile' is *valer la pena*. These latter senses of the term help provide a better understanding of the former. *Pena* is embarrassment in the sense that it imposes a kind of hardship, penalty, or even grief on the individual. Finally, in many contexts the opposite of respecting and considering others is to sin.

Heredity, raising and the social order

In the individual, respect has a dual origin. On the one hand, each person is born with his manner of respecting others; it is a function of his heredity and destiny. On the other hand, there is no continuity over generations in the respect positions of family members. Each individual must be taught the qualities of respectful behaviour by his parents. The unseemly behaviour of a child, therefore, reflects upon his parents as genitors but mostly as teachers.

The term *criar* (to breed, bring up, rear, educate) is used to describe the process of educating and teaching a child to respect others. The word is employed in a number of contexts, but its central meaning always refers to domestication. Thus, kin are distinguished in importance according to whether they were or were not 'raised' together, meaning brought up in the same household. Children and household animals are 'raised' while animals in the field are not. Proper training (*criar*) leads a child to have shame and to have respect. The young person who does not have respect for others is said to be *mal criado* (ill-bred, badly raised).

Respect and shame are the characteristics which define the individual as a proper social being. A person without shame is said to be 'for nothing' or 'worthless'. He is like an animal and has no faith in his fellow men or God. By contrast, with a sense of shame and respect, the individual can defend himself *(defenderse)* and not be dependent on others. A common expression is 'No one rules me' *(nadie me manda)*, for if one is ordered by others then one can have little honour. A sense of shame should and to some extent does inhere in all individuals, and in this sense all are equal within the community as human beings. But 'the quantum' of shame differs by the person and the very notion requires a certain exhibition of self-independence; hence it also differentiates one human from another.

Shame links each person to the social order. If the social structure were to be viewed as a network of positions, shame would fall in the interstices, for it attaches to individuals, not offices. It is a special quality inhering in the human apart from the formal structure of society. In this sense shame might be seen as a 'charisma' of the individual in that it is the quality which makes each person unique and of special value. This unique quality leads the individual to observe and to respect the proper order of society. Shame legitimates the order and impels the individual to do so; respect rewards the order and the person who does so. Respect behaviour, then, is a way of expressing that the individual recognizes the social categories about himself and accepts his own position in relation to them.

The modes of respect

As a form of behaviour respect is variously expressed: words, lack of words, actions and bodily movements. For example, proper use of honorific titles is a sign of respect. To insult or embarrass another is a sign of disrespect. Sexual joking with anyone but a friend is disrespectful. To walk in front of another who is talking or to interrupt him is disrespectful. Taking water from a person's house or picking a mango from his overladen tree without first asking is disrespectful.

In these forms of behaviour it is possible to distinguish two modes of respect. Respect implies distance as opposed to closeness and/or deference as opposed to condescension (Brown, 1965). On the one hand, respect is opposed to intimacy, closeness and friendship. It implies constraint and formality.[26] The self is kept distant and honour is preserved. Respect as distance also entails the notion of fear. The respectful person does not fear the other but offending his dignity and in turn exposing himself to criticism. Respect, then, is a type of avoidance behaviour. One recognizes the quality of shame in another; to notice his lesser attributes is to treat him as a shameless one.

Respect as deference is exhibited only in the context of status difference. A male in the community will respect all other men in the sense of maintaining proper distance, but he will never respect them in the sense of allowing himself to be ruled by them. By contrast, women respect men, and children respect adults both by maintaining distance and by deferring to them. If called by an elder, a child should answer, 'command me' *(mande me)*.

Respect and social categories

The countrymen do not consciously separate respect paid to social categories from that paid to personal qualities, but I shall do so for descriptive purposes. In terms of positions six axes define each individual as a unique being and allocate to him a special position of respect: man-God, villager-outsider, man-man, male-female, age, and kin and spiritual kin. The social life is organized primarily about these axes.

Greatest respect is due God. In this refraction of respect the notion of fear is predominant, and the relationship involves both distance and deference.

Powerful outsiders such as the managers and owners of the sugar cane and rice mills, store owners, or government officials are all treated with respect and deference. A stranger also is treated with respect until his social position has been established. And in a related way the people speak of fearing and respecting anyone who is known to be a fighter. The countrymen, however, see themselves within the context of a social scale. Downwards they do not respect less civilized persons; *cholos* should respect them. The social scale is characterized by a flow of respect upwards.

All persons, nevertheless, because they are humans and not animals, deserve some respect, if not as deference at least as distance. Thus, even a superior in the social scale should pay his inferior some respect. Animals, by contrast, need not be and are not respected.

Within the relationship systems of kinship and the *compadrazgo* respect should be exhibited. The *compadre-compadre* and godparent-godchild bonds must be and usually are respectful. Within the family greatest respect is due the mother, then the father and then siblings. After them more distant family are paid respect in lesser amounts.

Respect is given also on the basis of relative age. In general, respect must always be paid to an elder. Children are taught not to interrupt a conversation nor to walk between two elders conversing. The honorific *'señor'* is applied to older males.

Between the sexes respect is paid asymmetrically. Men owe respect to females for their shame, but women owe greater respect to males for their power. On one level shame and honour are attributes of all human beings; with respect to the sexes, however, the two concepts are divided (Pitt-Rivers, 1961, 1965). Shame as humility, reserve, modesty and chastity is the female ideal. A male should be manly and independent; men have the faculty, ability and power *(facultado)* to do as they wish. As seen, this sexual division is thought to have both a religious and a physical basis.

For the male a prerequisite for having respect and honour is physical ability. This capacity enables him to provide for himself and his family, and allows him to be independent. Yet this sense of self-independence cannot be unregulated. To have honour and respect a male must have discipline. Unregulated masculinity emerges as fighting when men get drunk, become filled with courage, hot, mad *(bravo)*, and forget themselves.

For their higher nature or sexual passion women must exhibit shame. A female has to look after or keep her powers under control *(cuidarse)*. A woman's place is in the home where she should carry out her required duties. Significantly, prostitutes in the community are known as 'women of the street', and are said to be out of control like drunken males. In fact, prostitutes are outside their homes no more than other women; the expression is indicative of the fact that they are inverting the basic expectations of womanhood.

These value conceptions differ with age. Young children are scarcely differentiated by sex. Older boys are permitted to wander in the street, while young women must remain at home, help their mothers and remain innocent of sexual matters. For adults the differing expectations become complementary in a conjugal union. The man is expected to work in the fields and provide while the woman should confine herself to domestic duties.

Respectful and shameless behaviour

Respect is paid also to qualities of the individual. These qualities are themselves representative of the person's sense of shame or embarrass-ment, and his sense of self-regard or honour. Thus, the people say they respect a person for his consideration, his seriousness or formality, his financial honesty, his sense of embarrassment, his sense of responsi-bility, or for his not embarrassing others. At times they speak of specific forms of behaviour which draw their respect, such as the quality of talking well, in the sense of not swearing or criticizing others.

By implication certain qualities may be neutral in relation to a person's imputed shame. The man who is skilled in telling stories, in holding vast quantities of alcohol or in having many women may gain renown but not respect. Prestige also is not a component of respect. The prestigious person, it is thought, has more social contacts within and without the village. He is not embarrassed to speak and is listened to in group meetings. Of the people considered prestigious within the village, some are respected and others are not. Wealth does not give a person greater respect in the community. The accumulation of riches, like the above qualities, is attributed to an individual's good fortune and is a part of his destiny. Being poor, however, may have implications for the respect a man receives. If, in spite of hard work, a man is poor, that is not his fault but God's. But if a man is poor because he is lazy or dominated by his vice of spending money or drinking, then he is not respected. He is not a provider and, therefore, is not independent.

With regard to qualities of the individual, however, the primary emphasis is upon avoiding the loss of respect or not exhibiting shame-less behaviour. The accent is upon criticism and in a sense respect is gained mostly by default. The quality of having shame, therefore, is contrasted with shameless behaviour *(sin vergüenza)* and lack of respect *(la falta de respeto)*.

The cover expression for one who lacks respect is 'badly raised' *(mal criado)*. But other terms also are used to describe varieties of shameless behaviour, and a person's behaviour may be minutely categorized in terms of the respect he fails to exhibit. Some of these words connote behaviour which is animal-like and lacks civilization and discipline *(bravo, macho, cochino, bruto)*. Others connote fear of the other or even arrogance *(orgullo)*.

Finally, a general term for shameless is *la cara pelada* (peeled, hairless, bare or penniless face or countenance).[27] The term refers to being put to shame or humiliated by another; correlatively it refers to being shameless and exposing one's own inability to defend the self. A man who asks another for a loan says he has *la cara pelada*. But if he is refused the loan he also says that he was left with *la cara pelada*, for the other has refused to trust his financial worthiness or honour. His sense of shamelessness has been confirmed, and he feels even greater embarrassment.[28] Hence, the people prefer not to ask others for loans or for credit at a store, and the man who does want a loan or repayment of a debt often sends his wife or child as an intermediary to shield him from face-to-face contact. The *campesinos* will complain about their sicknesses but never about being hungry which might be construed as a request for aid. One woman, by continually begging in the community, sacrificed all her honour and was known as having *la cara pelada*. By contrast, another would beg, but in distant villages. Since her activities were covert she did not have *la cara pelada* within the community.

Respect and individualism

From every perspective — social, political and religious — the person is seen as a unique being living in a collectivity of other such beings. This view is epitomized in the notion that each individual must have his own manner of honour and self-worth. He must 'defend himself' as a person. Such a notion of the individual implies that a sharp distinction be made between the self and the other. And if the former is to be trusted, the latter is not. Thus, the people assert and reassert their desire to live without contracts or binding agreements *(vivir sin compromisos)*; simultaneously they speak and despair of the distrust *(la desconfianza)* they bear for one another.

Communal associations. generally are ineffective, since the countrymen do not want to assume permanent responsibilities towards others. When a new problem confronts the entire community, it is often greeted with, 'It has nothing to do with me.' Individuals will aver in private that they disagreed with the action of another person or a group but add, 'I did not say anything.' In group meetings public votes almost always turn out to be unanimous; those who disagree with the majority leave before the balloting or vote along with the majority.

The other side of the coin to this rigorous independence is distrust of the other, which also is exhibited in a diversity of ways. Nearly every home has a dog to guard it and to warn the inhabitants of the approach of strangers. Preferably, houses are set at some distance from one another. The people explain that they separate their houses as protection against the spread of fires and to avoid fights between children and animals of different homes. Some men are said to want to seclude their spouses. But the separation of houses also preserves family privacy and security in a situation where there is great curiosity about the other. Constant complaints are made about stealing. Men say it is impossible to leave ripe crops in the fields. Further, it is common practice not to reveal one's destination when leaving the house. If a man is not at home and an inquiry is made of his spouse as to his whereabouts she replies, 'I don't know' or 'He is walking in the *monte*', an answer which can mean anything. Likewise, if asked where he is going, a man responds, 'to the *monte*'.[29] Men explain that others may wish to assault or ensorcell them, and then to steal their spouses. In fact, only once did I hear of an alleged attack in the fields and that occurred some time ago in a distant village. Finally, meetings of the various communal associations often are marked by indirect accusations among the members. In such meetings there is often a great reluctance to talk, and many place themselves as far as possible from the centre of the room, as if spatial distance could protect them from others.

If it is perceived that attacks and accusations are made upon the self, it is also true that everyone knows how to extract the maximum from his neighbours. For example, if crushed ice covered with sweet syrup is to be sold at a *fiesta,* the people know how to cut costs by adding food colouring and water to the syrup and by filling the cup half-full with water before adding the expensive ice. And numerous occasions occurred in which others indeed did not uphold their end of an agreement.[30]

Respect is based on a concept of the individual as a distinct entity. Yet, defending the person and preserving self-dignity produce a hiatus between individuals; and when carried to extremes, assertions of self-independence lead to distrust and the breakdown of personal relationships. Paradoxically, then, to have respect, the individual must also participate in a community where the value is recognized and the behaviour is rewarded.

The individual within the society and community

In relation to the larger society each person is defined as a unique entity within the category of the *campesino*. Within the community the individual defines others as being in the category of friend, enemy or other. The human himself has both a body and a soul. As a natural being, the person is akin to all other animals and plants, though characterized by a distinct combination of natural elements. Within the class human, females and males are distinguished, and each person is further perceived to be a unique configuration of elements. As a spiritual being each person has a special destiny and is responsible for his own salvation. The overall order of these destinies emanates from a power outside human society. Nevertheless, in that respecting the proper order of society is tantamount to accepting the order ordained by God, and in that having shame is being aware of this order and one's own fallen state, the social order itself receives religious validation.

Each individual occupies a unique set of statuses by reference to his age, sex, kinship, *compadrazgo* and friendship positions. Respect and shame, as integral parts of the individual, provide a means for ordering, expressing and validating these positions, and for uniting in a single statement the total social standing of the person. At the most abstract level, then, respect is a communication and a social currency. Furthermore, by respecting another, a person is respecting not only the other himself but the entire system upon which the social relationships are based. From this perspective the social and demographic fluidity which characterize the community and the individualism which the people themselves think is indicative of their life are not symptoms of normlessness but reflections of the fact that the structure inheres in the individual. The order of society is not externally codified and recognized in persisting offices and groups; the material components of society, human beings, are themselves the principal social units.

6 The household

The term *'la casa'* means literally house, household, or home. As employed in Los Boquerones the word has several referents. Depending on the context it can mean: (a) the physical structure where humans live, sleep and eat; (b) the physical structure plus the goods contained within it; (c) the physical structure, goods within, and the immediately surrounding area; or (d) the physical structure, goods, surrounding area, and the persons domiciled within. In this final sense *la casa* is best translated as 'household group'. In short *la casa* can refer to an edifice or to the structure plus its human inhabitants. In either case the term must be distinguished from *la familia* (family). Families may live in houses and therefore be household groups, but at least consciously the people separate the two, as when a man says, 'I work in order to earn for the house' or a woman states, 'My duties are in the home'. In this context both are referring to obligations of residence not the family. The family belongs to the realm of kinship, while the household is a concept about locality.

Household groups are the principal units of organization in the community. Within them the primary domestic, economic and social activities are carried out. They have rules of admission, 'heads', and a unity in contrast to other such groups. But households are not corporate units, for they have no perpetuity nor are enduring estates attached to them. Households as physical structures do not serve as fixed points through which generations pass.

As a concept, however, the household endures and is a focal point in the category system, for the household idea is linked to concepts emanating from other domains. For example, the common Hispanic opposition of male and female, the relation of the *compadrazgo* to kinship, which is rooted in Roman Catholic theology, and the bilateral kinship system of the countrymen which is an historical precipitate of the Spanish conquerors are all cross-cultural themes that are independent of residence. But in Los Boquerones their shape, the way in which these and other ideas are worked out and thought out, is influenced by the concept of the household. In this chapter I shall describe the household as an idea, delineate some of the ramifications of this concept, and show the importance of the household as an institution within the community.

Houses

Of the concepts concerning geography within the community only those pertaining to the household refer to areas which have discrete boundaries. Every home is located on a separate house site *(la vivienda* or *el hogar)*. Normally trees or fields separate one site from another. The house site itself consists of the house, a patio and a garden *(la huerta)*. The patio is a cleared area surrounding the home, consisting of grass or dirt. It affords protection from snakes and provides room for activities outside the house. Swept and cleaned every day, in a sense it is an extension of the interior domestic area. Adjacent to the patio is the garden. Used by itself the term *'la huerta'* refers only to a garden at a home.[1] Fruits, such as bananas, plantains, mangoes and avocadoes, and other crops such as coffee and spices, are grown here. Such seedings it is said need the 'heat of people', while crops in the field do not. In these respects the garden too is part of the domestic area. If a house garden is totally planted and has at least half a dozen large trees which provide considerable shade and cool, then it and the entire living area are known as a 'site' *(el sitio)*. By contrast, a similar growth of trees in the fields is termed a *finca* (ranch, farm). The entire area of house, patio and garden is frequently surrounded by a wire fence, which has little direct utility since no large animals are kept within it. Thus, houses and house sites are conceptually and physically demarcated one from the other, and as domestic areas they are distinguished from the fields.

By definition a house has a bedroom and a kitchen, and together a kitchen and bedroom always comprise a house, in one of its meanings. The kitchen is public; friends are entertained there. The bedroom is private; a person never enters the sleeping room of another without an invitation, which itself is rare. If a friend comes to a house and sees no one around, he stands outside and calls until the inhabitants in the bedroom have arisen and come out to greet him. I have already noted that a metaphorical relation exists between cooking (kitchen) and sexual relations (bedroom).

Empirically these concepts about a house are worked out in three different ways.[2] The most common type of home is the thatch-and-stick variety. All such houses have different layouts — individual styles — but each always includes a kitchen and bedroom. The bedroom is totally enclosed and has one entrance from the adjoining cooking room. The bedroom walls are constructed of long sugar-cane leaves hung upon a frame of wooden poles; the leaves are placed together so tightly that the inhabitants have complete seclusion within. The walls of the cooking/living room are made of thin poles lashed or nailed on to a wooden frame, making it possible to peer into and out from the kitchen. Visitors are entertained either in the kitchen or patio. Bedroom and kitchen normally are covered by a four-sided, sloping, thatched roof.

A second type of house (wattle and daub) has walls made of mud mixed with straw *(quincha)*, a few open windows with wooden shutters, and a tile roof. This variety too has a separated kitchen and bedroom. The advantage of mud domiciles is that they last longer and require fewer repairs than the wood-and-thatch type. But while a man at little monetary cost can build by himself a thatch-roofed house in twenty-five working days (monetary equivalent, $31.25), the construction of a mud home necessitates gathering a group of men and supplying them with food and drink for one or two days while the mud is prepared and plastered on to a previously constructed frame. The total cost of one such house including materials, hired workers, and the owner's labour time was approximately $110.00 (of which about 60 per cent was in cash outlay and 40 per cent in personal labour). In addition there are a few cinder-block houses with corrugated metal roofs. Located along the highway, most were built recently by wealthier members of the community. The cost of one equivalent in size to the mud dwelling described above would be more than $400.00. Because such homes are expensive, the people often build them in stages, accumulating first the needed materials and then constructing the home over the course of several years. Normally, adjacent to such homes is found a thatch cooking house.

Cinder-block houses are permanent dwellings. Mud-walled homes last at least ten years and well-constructed ones may endure twice as long. The wooden house has a more transitory life. Every few years walls and thatching must be restored and occasionally some of the major supporting beams must be replaced. Abandoned wooden houses fall to ruin within a year or two.

Thatch homes, in contrast to the others, are flexible dwellings and may be reshaped to meet the needs of the household group. The form or size of the house may be changed by shifting a doorway or moving a wall, which is done relatively frequently.[3] Also, thatch houses may be moved by demolishing the walls, lifting the roof structure off its base and placing it upon new supporting beams in another location. New walls must then be constructed.

In spite of their differences, the pattern of life and goods within each house type are much the same. The bedroom is usually crowded with beds made of bamboo laid across a wooden frame. Clothes and personal items are stored in cardboard boxes. The centre-point of the house is the kitchen, and here most of the activity is focused about the fireplace. The hearth consists of a waist-high platform of hardened mud, supported by poles sunk into the earth. Nearby, two large earthenware jugs sit on a wooden stand. The water in one is changed each morning and is used only for drinking. This water is said to be 'cold' and is called 'water asleep'. The water in the other, said to be 'warm', is not changed each day but is supplemented as necessary, and is used for all purposes other than drinking — such as cooking and washing dishes. If water from the drinking jug is used for cooking, it is thought that the portion remaining will become warm. The drinking water is changed each morning because during the night an enemy might secretly place a harmful potion (*el hechizo:* charm) in it.[4] The cooking water need not be thrown away each day since it is ingested with food only after being boiled, and this process destroys any potion added to the liquid.[5]

Kitchens normally contain an assortment of plates, trays, cooking utensils and so forth. Most households also have a transistor radio, and a few have store-bought chairs and tables in addition to their handmade wooden ones. Above the kitchen, wooden planks are placed across the roof beams to make a small loft *(el jorón).* Here, above the warmth of the fire where they stay dry, are stored the harvested rice, maize, and other agricultural products. A notched wooden pole is used to reach the loft.

In addition to the physical house and its contents, a household group has associated with it other forms of property. Most homes have a few fowl running free in the house and patio, some have cattle in pastures, and a few keep swine in pens near the domicile. Several people store and hide money by burying it in the ground at the house site or by embedding it in the wall of a mud home. The other forms of wealth associated with a household group are the crops growing in the fields and the land rights. The *campesinos* have developed a folk system of usufruct rights, and these temporary rights are critical to the functioning of the household, but their monetary value is equivocal.

Goods, animals, crops and land rights are the principal forms of wealth associated with household groups. This property is minimal and non-enduring, and the countrymen have no significant valuables to transmit from generation to generation. As a concept, however, the perpetuity of the household is not dependent upon the continuity of property ownership. The definition of what is a household and the set of ideas associated with it persist, although houses as physical entities and property-owning units do not provide a diachronic frame through which successive generations pass.

The household in relation to the person

Since the concept of the household is defined by reference to spatial arrangements, it is independent of ideas concerning the distribution of power or the organization of kinship relationships. The converse is not true, for these other domains must be expressed spatially. In particular, ideas about the person — his relation to nature, his sex, his kinship and *compadrazgo* positions, and his life cycle — are informed by the idea of the household.

The household provides a reference point for distinguishing domestic beings from field animals, for separating humans from domestic animals, and for differentiating women from men. To begin with, residentially occupied land areas are verbally distinguished from unoccupied areas. The domestic area, consisting of a house, patio and garden, also is clearly separated from the *monte*, a distinction implied in certain vocabulary. Cutting wood in the fields is *cortar;* at the house the same activity is *picar.* Lighting a fire in the kitchen is *encender,* while setting fire to the fields is *quemar.*[6]

This distinction between household and fields is used to separate domestic beings from natural animals. Again, the crucial term is *criar* (to raise, breed, educate). All animals kept at the house are said to be 'raised' by humans. Animals which do not live at the house are 'kept' or 'tended' *(guardar)* or permitted to run free *(en suelto).* Domestic animals are treated like children in that they too are addressed by the familiar 'you'. But more than the physical act of care is implied by *criar,* for the term refers to domestication and socialization. A worse insult than calling another badly raised is to suggest that he has no home at all. The implication of both statements is that the accused must be like an animal in the fields.

The household concept also serves to separate domestic animals from human beings. In this connection the people's concerns about dirt in the domestic area are important. The ground is said to be black because man is unclean in his heart, and his sins have been so great that they have dropped to the earth and changed its colour. Absence of dirt, then, is good and the people are fastidious about washing themselves, their clothes, and their eating utensils. But dirt also is associated with domestic animals, and in their care about not being dirty the country-men disassociate themselves from these creatures. Every morning the woman of the house carefully sweeps the ground in the house and patio, re-establishing the living area. As she sweeps she cleans up the excrement of the domestic animals. Even after it is swept, however, babies are not permitted to crawl on the earth precisely because it is dirty.[7] No adult ever sits on the ground, even inside the house; he squats or sits on a log, stone, or bench. Further, although thought to be incorrect, an eating utensil will be passed from person to person, but if dropped to the ground it is washed before being reused. Food accidentally dropped is left for the animals. Finally, most of the domestic animals are kept out of the house at night while the inhabitants sleep, and chickens and dogs are never permitted into the bedroom. Thus, domestic animals, by their association with humans in the household, are distinguished from other animals in the fields. Yet in other contexts they too are separated from the human occupants of the home. In both cases the concept of the household and spatial rights in the domestic unit provide the point of differentiation.

The household idea also is used to express the distinction between women and men. As explained this opposition is thought to have a physical and spiritual basis. The male/female opposition, however, is most fully worked out in relation to locality, for the division of the sexes is homologous with the opposition of the household versus the fields. From one perspective all humans must have shame and must be domesticated in a household. From another, females must exhibit shame and work in the household, while males must have honour and labour in the fields. A total set of expectations is encapsulated in the people's saying referring to work: The man is in the fields, the woman is at home. To illustrate, I examine in some detail the division of labour. The people divide material tasks into five fairly discrete categories ranging from field work to housework; work assignments run parallel from males' tasks to females' tasks, as shown in Table 4.

Most of the work in the fields and with the animals falls to the men (category 1). As a general rule, it is men who provision the household. They raise, harvest and transport all the crops to the house or market; likewise cows and horses are cared for and raised by men. In contrast, women distribute and prepare material goods for consumption (category 5). For example, once rice is brought to the house it is the woman's job to hull, shell and cook it. A woman does the housekeeping, laundry, mending, and hauling of water from a spring or pump.

Some jobs which are neither fully of the field nor of the house fall to both sexes or can be allocated between them (category 3). For example, wood for the cooking fire is secured in the forest and brought to the house by men. At the house it is cut into small pieces for storing and using. This housework of chopping may be done by either sex. Keeping the patio of the house clean is similarly the work of both sexes. The woman sweeps inside the house and directly outside where there is grass or dirt, but when the grass grows high or the bush surrounding the house needs to be trimmed, the man must cut it with a machete.

The care of household animals also falls into the middle category in that animals are non-domestic but living in the household. Twenty years ago, when pigs were allowed to run free in the forest, their care fell exclusively to the men. Now they are kept in large pens at the home with the result that both males and females feed them. The classification system remained constant; pigs shifted categories by virtue of a spatial change.

The work in categories 2 and 4 falls principally to one sex but on occasion may be undertaken by the other. Women sometimes seed agricultural crops and harvest rice, the bottle-neck operations in the agricultural cycle. But these are the only legitimate field occupations of women. In the contrasting case men sometimes help out in the house by hulling rice or 'thumbing' through it to clean it of stones. They may haul water, but they never wash clothes or cook, for these activities involve a deeper penetration into the woman's domain. And in this context it is worth recalling the story concerning God, St Peter and the robber. God refused to help the male who remained in the house; but he did assist the robber who, being in the fields, was closer to meeting the cultural prescriptions.

TABLE 4 *Work tasks and the household*

	1	2	3	4	5	
MALE WORK	Male only	Male but female may help	Both Sexes	Female but male may help	Female only	FEMALE WORK
FIELD (Examples)	Chopping down forest	Seeding, harvesting rice	Cutting up firewood, purchasing rice	Cleaning rice	Cooking rice, caring for babies	HOUSE

These categories of work based on a continuum of field to house are themselves coordinated with the prohibitions of the religious days, described earlier. In general the interdictions move inwards from field to house, falling first on field work and then housework. The more important and sacred the day, the more prohibitions are imposed and the greater the penetration into the household. During Easter week all classes of men's work in the fields, all types of women's work in the kitchen, and even sexual relations in the bedroom are forbidden. From this perspective the prohibitions serve to purify man by separating him from undomesticated things.

In sum, the household/field opposition is used to separate field and domestic animals, domestic animals and humans, and men and women. At the same time, a loose similarity between the three orders is established. Men, to some degree, are to field animals as women are to domesticated things.

The life cycle of the individual and the developmental cycle of the family also are expressed in relation to the household. At birth, children are thought to be like animals. To become human they must be raised in a home, and their growth is reflected in their changing relation to the physical structure of the house. Young babies are kept primarily in the sleeping room; older babies are kept in the house but off the ground; young children are permitted to play in the house and patio but are seldom allowed to visit neighbours; male and, to some extent, female adolescents begin to meet friends in the street; at a conjugal union the young couple leave their natal homes and occupy a new household; at death the household is reshaped to exclude the deceased's bed. Finally, the family and the *compadrazgo,* as extensions of the natural and spiritual portions of the individual, also are arranged with respect to — indeed they are partially defined by — their relation to the household; but these are the subjects of the following chapters.

The household in relation to other domains

The importance of the household also may be observed on the institutional level. Economically, households are independent units. Each is a replica of others and internally is characterized by a division of labour. Aside from the sugar-cane and rice mills, there are no intermediary organizations standing between households as units of production, on the one hand, and consumption on the other. Economic co-operation does occur between households, but it is sporadic and for the most part not required. The ecology and economy facilitate but do not determine this independence of household groups.

Socially, households are important units. Household heads exercise some control over the productive and reproductive powers of their members. People visit others at a house; no community centres exist where men or women congregate to talk. People do gather at some of the community stores, but these are simply part of an already existing house. The suspiciousness found between individuals also is acted out on the household level. A woman never tells outsiders where her spouse has gone to work. All the major goods of a household are stored within the home, for only there are they safe. Women rarely wash clothes together. And houses also have a symbolic unity, as expressed in the inviolability of the bedroom.

In certain respects households are political and religious institutions. The principal community organizations, although not functionally important, are made up of representatives from the different households. If a household group which is composed of a nuclear family splits up, then each of the remnants constituting a new household group has the right to be represented on the committees. If the committees levy work, then each household group, regardless of its size or composition, should contribute a unit of labour.

Religious customs bring out the importance of the household as an entity. The prohibitions on *fiesta* days are based on the household/field distinction. The 'travelling saint' passes from household to household each day. Some of the *fiestas* 'mark' the home, such as St John's day when dancers used to pass from house to house or New Year's Eve when a life size dummy is taken from domicile to domicile. Finally, every house has at least one, if not more, wooden crosses hung on a kitchen wall, and branches blessed on Palm Sunday may be hung up. The countrymen say the crosses and branches keep bad winds and heavy storms from damaging the house and, more generally, keep away the devil. In the sanctity of the properly protected home, persons are safe from the devil and his helpers.

Thus viewed as an actual institution the household group is the primary, albeit non-enduring, unit of organization within the community. Each household is multi-functional, distinct and nearly independent economically.

Let me summarize the argument thus far. In the last chapter I described the concept of the individual and suggested that the person as an entity is a principal unit within the social structure. In this chapter I have argued that the concept of the household is defined by reference to space and that the idea of the unit endures even though the physical entities do not. Additionally I have shown that other domains are worked out, at least partially, in relation to the home; in particular, aspects of the person, such as his sex role, are conceptualized in terms of the household. However, I have not argued that all aspects of the individual are expressed through the medium of the household nor held that those portions which are could not also be made manifest in some other way. The concept of the household does not determine that of the individual; it is only used to articulate aspects of it. Next, we turn to see how other characteristics of the individual, his kinship and *compadrazgo* positions, are filtered through or transformed by the concept of the household.

7   The household and the elementary family

Between the household and the family a complex relation obtains, and this connection, with which I am concerned in this and the following chapters, can best be approached by examining how the people define kinship.[1] For them the irreducible kinship link, the tie from which all others are derived, is the mother-child relationship. 'A mother is always a mother', the countrymen say. 'The link can never be denied for it has been seen by others.' Thus, for the people, the elemental mother-child bond is based on the fact of birth, but the tie is a biological given only because it can be and is socially recognized. The position of the patrifilial bond is slightly different. On the one hand, the father-child relationship is thought to be based on the fact that the father engendered the child. Most mothers are able to name the father if he does not wish to identify himself, and in doubtful cases the people will even deduce genetic links from phenotypic characteristics. The father-child bond, then, appears to be like the mother-child link with the single difference that it is not so easily identifiable. But there is a complication. Genitors do not always live with their children, even beginning at birth. A child, therefore, may be brought up by a different male from his recognized or even unrecognized genetic father. In many cases this second man may be said to be the father, by virtue of having lived with and having brought up the child, both of which are implied by the term 'to raise' *(criar)*. In such a situation, locality gives rise to a kinship bond.

We are, therefore, confronted with an intricate relation between kinship and residence. Can we say which is 'prior'? Certainly matrifilial and patrifilial bonds exist on their own and are not reducible to locality. Yet kinship is based on the recognition of birth in a household and is soon forgotten if not reinforced by locality. Conversely, ties of co-residence do become bonds of kinship, but such relationships must be patterned after something, and the model on which they are based is that of the elementary family.

My approach to this issue is to view kinship as partially including residence. Kinship for the countryman is based on genetic ties, but these relationships must be socially recognized in the sense of being seen. What, then, about a genetic bond which is not seen? Would this constitute kinship? For the countrymen it would not, since a putative father can deny his bond to a child. Regardless of the 'facts' of which he may be well aware, he can claim socially that no link exists. So long as he or others think no genetic tie exists, there is no kinship bond. Is the case of the mother-child bond similar? Does it, too, depend upon social observation? Here, the physical facts of pregnancy and birth make the genetic link obvious, and even in the limiting case of a female living alone she herself would always know that she had given birth. Thus, although the matrifilial bond also depends upon human observation, in practical terms it is a recognition which is nearly impossible to deny.

Most anthropologists, of course, have long maintained that kinship is something more than mere biology. My point is that among the *campesinos* the elemental kinship relations are recognized when made manifest in a household. The household, in turn, is defined without reference to kinship. Therefore, conceptions about kinship at least assume conceptions about residence, although they cannot be derived solely from them.

Given this point of view, the immediate problem which concerns me in this and the following chapter is why elementary families, and not larger or smaller units, are identified with household groups. The pre-eminence of the conjugal family is not directly dictated by economic or political factors although ecology does set broad constraints on the possible kinship and household forms. Similarly, household organization is not a direct outcome of kinship norms. Rather, domestic arrangements are a consequence of cultural ideals about the individual as these are specified in relation to the household and economic life. As a result of these ideals, of all possible kin arrangements, the nuclear family is selected as the most appropriate unit to occupy a household, and it therefore provides the model for the household group, although not all households consist of conjugal families. This argument is consistent with the preceding concerning the definition of kinship. In both cases I am maintaining that 'kinship' — albeit in different ways — is defined, shaped or operated upon by 'non-kinship' factors, specifically concepts about residence and the individual. Therefore, although this chapter is about the elementary family it includes elements which are not normally considered to be kinship.

Males, females and the conjugal relationship

Conjugal mates bear not only the statuses of spouse and spouse towards one another, but also those of man and woman, fellow community members, individuals deserving of respect, and so forth.[2] Persons as actors within the kinship domain bring statuses to it from other spheres. The conjugal relationship itself is influenced primarily by the larger domain of cultural ideas concerning male-male, female-female, and male-female relationships. In this first section I look at these broader concepts which underlie conjugal unions. The ideals about what a male person is and what a female person is, and their concomitant separation of functions, draw men and women together into conjugal units. These ideas about persons are themselves expressed through the concept of the household.[3]

To show the importance of the male-female role contrast, I begin with those factors which do not necessarily buttress unions: love, wealth, and prestige. As evidenced in songs, gossip, and recourse to potions, the concept of love *(el amor)* plays a role in male-female ties, and ideally one should choose a mate with whom one is in love. But as often as not two lovers consummate their relation outside a connubial bond, and if love is the motivating factor, it is rarely the sustaining one in a conjugal union.

Money and prestige rarely impel people to form conjugal unions, since nearly all the countrymen have an equivalent living standard, and none has appreciable capital. It is true, though, that young women do aspire to marry townsmen from Santiago or Panama City. This recurrent dream, as we shall see, is related to the structural position of females in the village. A few instances of such outside marriages have occurred and the girls concerned are considered to have been very lucky. But the opportunities for women to marry up are few. Men never consider it a possibility to marry a wealthy female from outside the community.

The people themselves voice various reasons for entering connubial bonds. Both sexes state they wish to have a companion *(el compañero:* companion, partner, mate) with whom to talk and laugh. Children also are mentioned as a reason for having unions, although it is up to God — a 'mysterious thing' — whether offspring issue from a relationship. When men and women are old and can no longer work, it is to their offspring that they must first turn for aid, and only rarely does a child renounce his parents.

The folk reasons may be convincing, but the key elements underlying the conjugal relationship are the cultural conceptions about the male and female person, a contrast expressed on several levels and projected on to the concept of the household. In terms of the conjugal relationship the most important aspects of this division are the separation of economic duties and the sex-linked concepts of manliness and shame. Material tasks, as explained, are divided into five categories consisting of the parallel levels: males' tasks/females' tasks, and field work/housework. This division of labour and the sanctions of respect which buttress it provide a foundation for, indeed impel people to enter, conjugal unions.

Single adults, as a consequence of the well-defined work categories, experience difficulty subsisting. Because the female's job does not fall in the productive domain, women have few opportunities for undertaking productive activities or earning money. Single women can earn money by planting, harvesting, washing clothes and hulling rice for others, but such jobs are not regular income-producing forms of work. If women are to live outside a conjugal union, to survive they must sell their sexual services or leave the community. Most enter a connubial union.

A man can more easily live alone because his jobs lie in the productive sphere, and he can skimp on his household needs or hire someone to fulfil his important ones. Nevertheless the single man also finds it difficult to live. He is unable to keep household animals and has to pay for certain of his domestic needs. Even then, his rice is seldom freshly cooked and hot, and he does not eat soup or beans (both of which require several hours of cooking). As one individual remarked, he 'spends more and lives less well'.

In addition to experiencing economic difficulties, the single man or woman loses respect in the eyes of others. Work of the opposite sex is not prohibited to an adult, but when a man consistently undertakes housework (or a woman field work) his actions reflect on what he is as a person. More broadly, this value judgment is based on ideas about the individual. A single man, it is thought, is uncontrolled. Whether true or not, it is perceived that he spends money excessively by getting drunk, going to *fiestas* or chasing after women. He stays out late at night and cannot work well on the following day. He does not think about his future nor is he serious or responsible. The bachelor, it is said, has few obligations *(el compromiso)* and makes little attempt to honour those he does incur. As a result he is 'nothing'. He does not show that he has a fundamental sense of honour and ability to defend himself. Since he has nothing to lose he cannot be trusted. A conjugal union can control the wildness in a man, and as it does so, he acquires and exhibits a greater sense of respect.

In a complementary fashion women are expected to 'guard' themselves. A single woman is always suspected of being indiscriminate, and a connubial relationship legitimizes her sexuality, just as it tames a man. In fact, even if a single female is circumspect, she too is not exhibiting her fundamental sense of shame. For example, of one woman who lives alone and works in the fields, it was said, 'She works like a man'. For this she is admired, but the very phrase implies that she is not totally a female, and she is respected less than one who stays in the house.

Both men and women also express the desire to have their own home *(la casa* or *el hogar:* home, hearth). The house and family provide a base about which a sense of stability, security and authority may form. With a home and family, a man has a place to rest or someone to look after him when he is sick. But more importantly, in his own home, a male is 'head'. In his natal house, a man is under the authority of his father. In his own home no one rules him, and this of course is a prerequisite for having respect. In her own home a woman also, although under the domination of her spouse, has more liberty and authority in that she is master of the domestic arrangements and can exhibit her womanhood by becoming a mother. Without a home in this full sense, an individual has nothing.

The consequence of this total division of labour is to draw men and women together into co-residential units of at least one male and one female. However, the fact that males and females are forced together into conjugal units does not mean that the unions themselves need be enduring. So long as a male and female live in a properly formed house they fulfil their expected roles.

The conjugal relationship

Given that the connubial bond is founded upon these larger, non-kinship ideas about the person, we can now examine the more specific tasks of the spouses. In addition to an exchange of sexual services, a conjugal union is based upon the performance of precisely enumerated material obligations. These duties also are expressed in terms of household tasks and follow from the broader male and female ideals.

The man's obligation is to provision and maintain the household. He acts principally within the external domain, linking the house to and supplying it from the economic or agricultural sphere. The male is expected to provide the house and keep it in repair. He must see to it that there is wood for the cooking fire, and he must furnish all the necessary food and clothing. If a household member falls ill, the man should purchase medicine or pay for medical advice. If his spouse becomes pregnant, the man should care for her.

The male officially rules the house and is responsible for all the household members. For example, if one of the household animals bites a stranger or damages the crops of another, the man must make amends. If his children are in school, the male is responsible for having someone from the household attend official school meetings and provide needed labour. Internally, the man governs his spouse and resident children. He has the right to send his mate on an errand to another community. She may refuse to go if she has cogent reasons, but if she refuses capriciously this is interpreted as a lack of respect for her spouse's authority and will often result in a fight. A man's rights over his mate, however, pertain only to her legitimate duties. He has no right to order her to earn money for the household. Only if she wishes to, need a woman make dresses, wash clothes or hull rice for others.

The female's duties are more specific than those of her mate. The woman's place is to do the work of the home. She is expected to keep the house and patio clean, straighten the beds, do the washing and ironing, provide the cooking and drinking water, feed the chickens, and keep her spouse informed about the food supply. Above all, a woman should promptly provide food for her mate. She must rise early enough so that he can have hot coffee before leaving for the fields. If her mate demands it, she should take hot food to the fields at midday. And when he returns from the day's work, she should see to it that a warm meal awaits him. Whether or not a woman promptly prepares food for her spouse is an indication of the state of domestic relations. Rice is a particularly apt medium for expressing the condition of a conjugal union. Women pride themselves on being able to cook rice well, and everyone expects to eat rice two or three times a day: 'He who has not eaten rice has not eaten'. The woman who does not have a hot meal, including rice, waiting for her mate has done so for a reason and opens the way for a fight.

So fixed is this division of labour that men will rest in a hammock for hours watching their spouses do countless household chores. In the contrasting case a woman disclaims any knowledge of her mate's work. Thus, a female's refusal to tell strangers where her spouse is working is not only an expression of mistrust but also a denial of her own knowledge and interest in masculine occupations. Some men claim that their mates do not even know how much money they earn.

In addition to her obligations the female is the *de facto* head of the house. Only she, it is thought, knows the state of the clothing or food supply. The woman makes the major decisions concerning purchases and generally handles the money. This aspect of the woman's role is not solely a function of convenience; it is thought that females are more responsible with money. The man with a large sum of cash — paydays during the sugar-cane harvesting season are apposite examples — is likely to spend it on drink, women or a *fiesta*. A woman, being ideally a creature of shame and hence more discipline, focuses her life more upon her family and household. For smooth domestic functioning, then, it is important that the female be in fact the head of the internal domain, for she has better knowledge about household necessities and usually allocates money more wisely than her mate.

Since their duties are clearly detailed, the default of one spouse in carrying out his or her obligations has an immediate and disruptive effect internally upon the household. Externally, the concepts of respect and shame also impel each partner to carry out his appropriate duty. If a man is found washing clothes or cooking he is embarrassed, for it is clear that he is unable to control his mate. His spouse too may lose respect for being lazy or unable to fulfil her womanly duties. A man performing opposite sex work will avoid losing respect only if the reasons, such as his spouse's sickness or pregnancy, are valid and publicly known. Similarly, should a woman attempt to supplement household income by undertaking a male's job in the fields, her mate would be embarrassed. But a woman does not even have to work in the fields for her spouse to lose respect. For example, Vicente for several years has not had his own rice field. He earns cash from his sugar-cane harvest and by working for others. Because he spends some of this cash on liquor and because his income is not steady, his children are less well-clothed than others. To help buy food his spouse takes in washing and earns about $1.00 per week. Although Vicente does work and drinks moderately, he is never mentioned as a respected member of the community.

Sexual relations and conjugal unions

The basis of a conjugal union is economic co-operation, but sexual
relations are an important facet of the bond. Coition, however, is not
the defining characteristic of a union, for it can play a part in other
relationships as well. Indeed it is precisely because men are permitted to
have sexual relations with women who are not their spouses that the
exchange of sexual services cannot be regarded as the defining characteristic of a conjugal bond. Nevertheless like the division of work the
sex roles of the spouses derive from the broader non-kinship concept of
the difference between male and female.

Various terms are used to talk about sexual relations. *Molestar* (to
molest, disturb) refers to when a man first begins to play with or make
advances towards a female. For coition the polite word is *actuar* (to
act). A common expression, however, is simply 'to have contact'. As
noted, in various forms eating or food are metaphors for sex. Less
frequently 'to live' may be employed, while in reference to a past
action 'to sleep' may be used.

Sexual relations between a conjugal couple are kept private; man
conceals his sexual acts in the bedroom. Two mates themselves do not
discuss sex, and it is considered improper to inquire about prior sexual
experiences.

The sexual roles of the partners are made clear by certain statements
and proverbs of the people. It is often asserted that a man has the right
– he can do it anywhere – but a woman should defend herself. And in
a statement which parallels that of the work categories the people often
say, 'The man is for the street, the woman has to keep herself.' An
oft-repeated proverb is: 'God has left man in the world to make love
even with his mother if he meets her in the street' *(El hombre lo ha
dejado Dios en el mundo paraque enamore hasta su madre si la topa en
la calle).* It is a man's right to 'bother' any woman; it is the female's
responsibility to refuse or permit him to do so.

Few men focus their attentions solely upon their mates for long
periods of time. And at least the men are certain that 'walking the
street' is as much a male's right after he enters a conjugal union as
before.

The women a man seeks generally are single girls, prostitutes, or
widows. The extra-conjugal relationship a man forms may be impermanent or have a more lasting character. Casual affairs usually involve a
direct cash payment from man to woman for the services received. In a
more durable relationship the services are repaid diffusely. None the

less there is no concept of keeping a mistress, and the woman involved usually gains her livelihood from more than one lover. An example of a durable extra-conjugal affair is provided by the case of Carlos and Luisa, a single woman. Carlos lived with Gloria by whom he had a son. Together they maintained an orderly, well-run household. However several years after the birth of their child, Carlos began to have an extra-conjugal affair with Luisa. For this he needed money and since he ordinarily gave Gloria all the cash he received or accounted for the rest, he had to begin to conceal small amounts. Carlos had few places to hide the money, for Gloria checked even his wallet. Finally he found that he could hide cash in his bed, and for over a year he was able to carry on the affair. Eventually he arranged for her to receive food on credit at a local store. Carmen, who ran the store, is Gloria's sister, yet she said nothing to Carlos's spouse. Carmen's behaviour provided a clear example of how the community condones extra-conjugal affairs, and how individuals ordinarily do not interfere in the lives of others. But Carlos points out that such behaviour could not be expected of everyone, and in return he has gone out of his way to assist Carmen when she has needed something.

From this example it may appear that men are free to pursue their extra-conjugal wanderings, but such is not the case. In spite of what a man's sexual adventures represent — potency, money and freedom — the woman-chaser does not gain respect or prestige. On the contrary an excessive woman-chaser may lose respect because people see that he has no secure 'stopping place'.

A further look at the case reveals other constraints which act on men. Carlos found it difficult to hide substantial amounts of money from Gloria, for she knew approximately what his earnings were. Luisa's house also was not well hidden, and Carlos could be seen entering her door. In time Gloria learned of Carlos's actions and pestered him to stay home and spend less money. Indeed after a year Carlos found it expensive to maintain his own household and pay Luisa. The real freedom of the single male did not exist for him, and he felt his household obligations. These sanctions plus Carlos's own flagging interest brought the affair to a halt. As he said wistfully, 'Now I don't do such foolishness, I use what I have for food.'

The sexual role of the woman is radically different from that of her spouse. If a female in a union takes liberties her behaviour reflects upon herself and her mate, and if he learns about her activities, he will almost invariably beat her and then leave. The basic concept behind the female role is that women must protect or defend themselves. Women who do not 'guard' themselves are said to have no shame and lose respect. Yet, according to the men, because women have a stronger nature, they cannot be trusted to defend themselves at all times. A woman can enfeeble a man by making too many demands on him or burn him by despoiling his bedroom. A rhythmical proverb captures the attitude: *'Mujer segura, no hay ninguna'* (Trustworthy woman, there isn't any). Men think the love of a woman is subject to rapid changes. The consequence for women of this two-sided view is that they have no right to undertake an extra-conjugal affair but they are never trusted not to.

Women engage in extra-conjugal affairs in two ways. Some leave their mates temporarily or permanently. I consider these patterns to be conjugal separations and describe them in chapter 10. Others carry on secret affairs while remaining with their spouses. Only a thin line divides a temporary affair in which a woman leaves and later returns from an affair carried on while remaining in the house, but the latter is considered more scandalous. It is more damaging to a man's reputation for his spouse to cuckold him while receiving his material support than for her to leave temporarily. Someone else is 'eating his food'.[4] An example of an extra-conjugal affair carried on while the woman remained in the house is provided by the case of Edilsa, who had an affair with a man from outside the community while remaining with her spouse, Clemente. She became pregnant by the man, and since he was dark-skinned while Clemente and she are not, Edilsa knew she could not claim the child was Clemente's. Consequently she had an abortion, although some of her other children are 'smuggled goods'. Clemente did not learn about Edilsa's indiscretions until several years had passed.

Supporting this conceptual difference are certain linguistic usages. The woman whose mate is unfaithful is not referred to in a special way, but the man whose spouse has other lovers uses and is called by a variety of terms. The general, though infrequently used, term for a man whose mate has a lover is *el cabrón* (he-goat, cuckold).[5] The term also can be used in several expressions: two men who share a woman are said to be 'her *cabróns*'. A more exquisite refinement is the following: a '*cabrón* of a poor whore' is a man whose spouse goes and returns with no money; a '*cabrón* of a rich whore' is a man whose mate goes out and returns with money. The latter expression is considered particularly degrading. A *chulo* is a male who is maintained by the sexual earnings of his mate. In current Spanish usage this term has several meanings (e.g. dandy, effeminate man), but in sixteenth-century Spain a *chulo* was precisely a person who lived on what women would give him (Caro Baroja, 1965: 122). All these words are infrequently used. Heard somewhat more often are the following. The word *'quemar'* (to burn, scorch) is used both by the man who has been cuckolded and by others in referring to him, as in 'She burned me.' *Ahuevado* (*ahuevarse:* to be dull, stupid, fooled; *el huevo:* egg, testicle) refers to a man who has been cuckolded and is the term which was used for Clemente.[6] The word *pendejo* (*pender:* to hang, dangle, depend, 'pubic hair'; *pendejada:* stupid, foolish action) is frequently employed but in different contexts. In the broadest sense a *pendejo* is cowardly or timid; for instance he is afraid to ride a horse. A man who does his spouse's work or is afraid to rule her is also *pendejo,* as is the one whose spouse desires him but he is afraid to or does not come to her. Finally, the man who waits for his mate to return after she has left to have an affair or a trip is *pendejo.* Men often assert that they are not *pendejo.* This word too was applied to Clemente and several other men whose spouses had left them and then returned. All the terms imply that a man has been degraded sexually and that he does not care. But several refer to the entire role constellation of the male person; when the terms are applied to an individual they imply that the normal expectations concerning the total male role have been undermined and endorse the fact that the subject has lost respect.[7]

In sum, the positions of the conjugal partners are related to the broader set of concepts concerning all males and females and to the idea of the household. The roles are complementary. In the area of material obligations the differing jobs are expressed in terms of household tasks and draw the spouses together. Reciprocity plus the external sanctions of respect and shame provide the sanctions on the relationship. By contrast, sexual practices do not provide so firm a foundation for the connubial link. The man has the right to do precisely what his mate cannot. He is constrained partly by practical considerations and partially by the possibility of showing himself to be a man without foundation. But a woman also can apply sanctions, for provided it is not too flagrant, an extra-conjugal affair will not shame her but will strip her mate of respect.

Parents and children

The second major role contrast in the co-residential family is that between parents and children. Children are born into the position of uncivilized, a-social animals. Through the process of being raised in the household they become social beings. As they attain equivalent status with their parents, two changes occur. First, the factors which previously bound them into the household impel them to leave and to form new domestic units. Second, as the age-status distinctions are obliterated those based on sex take their place. The parent-child relationship is not purely one of kinship but also residence. As with the spouse-spouse bond the role contrast of parents and children is expressed through the medium of the household concept.

Raising children

The people express the desire to have children, but offspring are viewed more as recruits to a domestic than a kinship unit. They are not coveted to carry on a name or perpetuate a kin group. Rather, children are desired because no household is considered complete without offspring. Childless couples often attempt to foster a child. A woman especially wants offspring because they are more likely to stay with her in the home than her mate who may always leave. As one person said, 'Without children a house is not well. It lacks emotion.'

Within the domestic family the mother-child tie is the basic bond. Only in an extreme case would it be denied, and the initiator of the renunciation would suffer a severe loss of respect, for 'a mother is a mother'. On the other hand, the father-child tie can be, and occasionally is, renounced by father or offspring. A man says he never really knows who the genitor of his child was since a woman can never be trusted.

The people believe that conception occurs with one insertion; however, they are unclear about a woman's fertile period. It is known that methods of birth control do exist, but they are too expensive to obtain. Abortions are sometimes induced by the use of herbs.

By some it is said that a child resembles the parent who had more desire or energy in the sexual act; however most aver that a child may resemble one, the other or both of his parents. Resemblance between parent and child can be in any form: bodily feature, bodily movement, or the mind. And even if a child does not directly resemble his parents he may bear a similarity to another close family member.

Males and females are equally desired. A boy will be able to help his father in the fields, but a girl may find paying work in a town and remit the cash to her parents.

A child at birth is thought to be like an animal, and parents must raise their child from this state by instilling human customs. Since children have the capability of knowing in the sense of learning and understanding, they can and must be taught to respect others. A child, for example, is taught not to spit in the house, not to talk while eating, not to intrude upon a conversation, not to speak in front of visitors and not to cross between two conversing adults. More importantly, a child must learn to respect his parents, to use proper modes of address, not to use crude words, and to respect the property of others. And children are educated in their appropriate sex-role activities, such as seeding and weeding for boys and cooking and housework for girls. When castigating children, parents often use the term *necio,* meaning stupid, ignorant, or stubborn. As one person summarized the beliefs, 'In raising a child you must teach him that he is not a hen or dog. If you don't teach this, he doesn't know anything. A child without training is like a hen. He thinks nothing, he doesn't know how to do anything.' This same comparison with domestic animals was drawn by others, and one man added that he wanted his child to be 'a person'.

The entire process of teaching a child is known as *criar* (to educate, bring up), and a further examination of this term brings out the connection between socialization and the household. A baby is called *la criatura* (creature, baby, child). A child raised by an adult, regardless of their kin relation, is a *criado* or *hijo de crianza* (raised child). Two siblings raised together are *'hermanos de crianza'*. As mentioned, *criar* is used in the context of raising house animals but not field animals. In the first place, then, *criar* refers to raising within the household. But the education of children is also referred to by the word *criar,* and the well-raised and respectful child is *bien criado.*

One aspect of education which is not undertaken in the home is the teaching of sexual practices; children must learn about the opposite sex outside the household. Parents also are circumspect in their own relations and when dressing and undressing in front of their offspring. Young children disrobe in front of others, but when they reach puberty they cease doing so. This prohibition upon sexual talk and provocative behaviour between parents and children fits with the respect that must obtain between them.

In their early years children are kept at home to play in the house patio. They are not permitted to leave the house alone on an errand, and only rarely do young neighbouring children visit each other. On the one hand, this custom of keeping children at home is a reflection of the mistrust that exists between households. On the other, parents prohibit their children from leaving the house because their offspring do not yet 'know' good from bad. Since they have not yet integrated the customs of proper social behaviour, they are thought likely to acquire bad habits or to get into fights in other homes.

Until they are five or six, children are raised primarily by their mothers. The mother is the principal disciplinarian and enforces her will verbally or by hitting the child lightly with a green stick. A mother also will threaten a young, misbehaving child by saying that the *tulivieja* or goblins will carry it away to the forest. As a second resort a mother may call upon the father to discipline the children more harshly; she, it is said, is less willing to hit the children. The dominant role of the mother in the early years is consistent with her central position in the internal domain of the household and the stronger and more affectionate bond she maintains with the children throughout her life.

Beginning at an early age both sexes are taught to undertake chores because it is felt that if they do not learn how to work when young, they will grow up to be lazy. Separation of the sexes by activity also begins at a young age, but it is not absolute at first. Five- and six-year-old boys and girls may be sent on errands, set to cutting firewood at the house, told to fetch water, or asked to find the right type of bush for making the household broom. However, even when a boy is only five or six it is thought time to begin teaching him specifically male activities. A father intermittently takes his son of this age to the fields and shows him how to do some of the easier forms of work, such as seeding or harvesting. Boys of ten or eleven are thought to be capable of handling a machete and earning token amounts of money. Indeed a generation ago, before there was a school in the community, boys of this age worked all day, as well as they could, and earned a portion of an adult's wages. Daughters stay at home and, as they grow older, are taught to participate more and more in the household duties. At first they may be set to sweeping the house and patio. If they are old enough they may have to care for a younger sibling. They may be sent on errands or to a store. But only very slowly are daughters allowed to undertake any of the cooking activities. Thus, as they grow older, the activities of boys take them increasingly out of the household, whereas girls remain in the home itself. But as long as a child lives in his natal home, despite his age, the authority for directing him is not relinquished by his parents.

The household and the elementary family 111

Property, getting an interest, and inheritance

Household property is minimal and non-enduring. Yet the rules concerning the ownership and partition of household goods are explicit and well-known. This seems paradoxical. A close examination of the rules, however, reveals that they are intimately linked to the dynamics of parent-child relationships and household fission, and it is as clear statements about the ideal inter-relations of household members that they are important. Most of the rules pertain to males and this is consistent with the fact that it is the men who are vested with authority.

While a boy is in his parents' household his father rules him. When he begins in earnest to work in the fields for money, at the age of thirteen or fourteen, his father decides for whom and where he shall work. As a young man grows older he gains greater but not complete authority over the allocation of his labour. A generation ago the goods or money a son earned were paid by his employer directly to his father, who then gave a portion of the money to his son. Now, with an increase in wage labour, this pattern has been modified so that the son himself collects his earnings. In some cases he turns this over intact to his father who returns a part of it to him. In other cases the son keeps the money and decides himself what portion he wishes to give to his father. The father uses his portion for the household, while the son can use his as desired.

The control which a father exercises over his son's labour and earnings is a function of his general position of authority in the household. Only when he establishes his own household does a son achieve complete power to allocate his own efforts and distribute his own rewards. (Daughters are similarly under the guidance of their mothers, but since they do not earn money, the issue of control is not so sharply defined.) Specifically, the pattern of the father's control over the allocation of his son's labour and earnings is part of a larger formula concerning property rights called 'getting an interest' (*coger un interés:* to catch, seize, or gather an interest). This important formula specifies how young men should be tied economically to the household and is linked to inheritance and fission in the group.

Officially the father, as head of the household, along with his spouse is owner of all the household goods. (If a younger member has purchased something with his own money, then it is his.) Some of these ownership rights, however, are relinquished through time to a growing child. When a male child is still young, most parents place certain goods in his name. This practice is called 'getting an interest'. For example, Marcelino who is five years old had several chicks in his name. The animals were kept in the household brood, but Marcelino gave them special attention. When the chickens ended their lives in the family pot, it was recognized verbally that the family was consuming Marcelino's goods. By the time he is seventeen or eighteen a young man usually has portions of both a sugar-cane and a rice field named for him. The son keeps this property when he leaves the household, and he possesses the ultimate right of disposal; however, while the son remains at home, the household head has the right to use the resource and to distribute the produce or income from it. Depending on the wealth of the particular house the son will receive a larger or smaller portion of the profits from this property.

The term 'interest' in 'getting an interest' is used, then, in a double sense. The custom, it is said, is practised to get a child interested in learning how to care for valuable property, by giving him a share in the household profits. A son gains an interest or desire in working as he gains an interest or share in the rewards. From the father's standpoint the custom also is useful, for by giving his son a share in the household assets and profits, he motivates him to remain at home and to maximize his labour contribution to the group.

The formula of getting an interest is itself part of the rules of inheritance. The inheritance system is composed of gifts *inter vivos* followed by equal part inheritance with a bias toward ultimogeniture. When a son leaves his natal home to form his own household, the goods which are in his name become his and a productive resource for the new household which he heads. (Daughters have fewer or no goods placed in their names and occasionally this is a cause for dissension.) Thus, the custom of catching an interest, which culminates in property fission when an offspring leaves the household, is a method of giving gifts *inter vivos*. It divides the inheritance prematurely. Later, at the death of the father any remaining property should be divided into two equal parts. One of the halves should be further divided into equal shares numbering one less than the total number of offspring. One of these shares should be given to each of the children except the youngest. The remaining half should stay with the mother. When she dies it should pass to the youngest child, who is known as the *bordón* (fig. a person who guides or sustains another). The *bordón* should remain in the house with his mother. However, if he leaves or has left the house when the father dies, he should divide the remaining half equally with his mother.

Whether he remains in the house or not, it is said to be the *bordón's* responsibility to look after the surviving parent. Theoretically, then, this method of dividing the household property is a means of assuring that at least one child assumes responsibility for a surviving parent. The *regidor* or mayor, it is said, even has the right to require the *bordón* to assume responsibility for his parents.[8]

In fact, parents may or may not live with or rely upon the *bordón;* sometimes several of the children aid in their support, and in only one instance had a household head inherited land and money. Indeed, because there is so little to inherit and the rules were so seldom put into effect, there was some disagreement as to whether it is the youngest or the last remaining male in the household who should receive the extra large share.

If normally there is little household and inheritable property, why should such an elaborate system of inheritance rights be maintained? The answer, I think, is that the system pertains not just to property but specifies proper household relationships. In the first place, the rules are skewed toward males in that catching an interest refers primarily to the father-son relationship. Partly, this is a reflection of the fact that it is a man who is always the authority figure and household head. The formula of catching an interest supports the authority of the household head while specifying how this authority should be relinquished over time. The rules also reflect the value placed on manly independence. Each male to be a respected individual must have his own foundation, which ultimately rests on financial independence. The goal of catching an interest is to emancipate each growing male. In short, the rules are consistent with the total ideology concerning men. In addition, the inheritance rules illustrate that a household is never conceived of as an enduring estate. Property is parted and held individually not corporately. Yet, the code does reiterate that each household is an independent economic unit; on the one hand, a resident son's share is used for his natal group, while on the other the inheritance is given *inter vivos* when the same son leaves to form his own household. Paradoxically, this independence of households is facilitated by the very lack of non-partible goods. The rules, then, are not really about kinship and property but concern kin in relation to household groups.

Parent-child tensions

It is considered far worse for a mother and child to fight than a father and child, for a father can always disown his offspring whereas a mother cannot. Ultimately it is she who must see to it that her children are raised, fed and clothed. Nevertheless, strains do occur between co-resident parents and children, and these arise principally from issues concerning the disposition of authority, property and money. Such tensions become strongest when a child has reached the age at which he could form his own household but has not yet left his natal home. Since father and son are more intimately connected in these respects, theirs are the strongest of the parent-child tensions. Daughters have less to dispute about with their parents, and are sometimes able to circumvent parental authority when problems do arise.

Between father and son a delicate balance of positive and negative factors obtains. A son who stays in his father's house is not responsible for maintaining a household of his own, but he is under his father's authority and controls little property. If he separates and maintains his own house, he is under no one's rule, but his duties never cease if he wants to eat. A father, on his side, gains more from having a son in his house than not, for the costs of maintaining his offspring are less than the value received. But the father must treat his son with consideration and give him money and freedom when he may not wish to do so.

The father-son relationship does not always give rise to serious problems, but in nearly all households the two do have a dispute at some time over the division of the son's earnings. The most extreme case concerned a young man, Calixto, who while living in his father's house, had a fight with his father and suddenly committed suicide. The motivations for his act were complex, and at least a contributing factor was his unrequited love for a girl who spurned him, but the immediate cause of his death was a quarrel with his father. Calixto's father owns a truck for hauling sugar cane and is slightly wealthier than most of the other community members. Calixto had an elder brother, also living in the house, who apparently had been favoured throughout their lives. Both Calixto and his brother worked for their father – in the fields, driving the cane truck and handling an oxcart he also owned. The earnings from these enterprises went directly to the father. Needless to say, the activities of the boys were of immense value to the household. One Saturday night Calixto wished to go to a *fiesta* and asked for some money from his father, who refused. Calixto stormed from the house and sat by himself outside. Later he returned alone to the separate sleeping quarters and shot himself through the jaw. This was a most unusual case, but the factor of strain between father and son underlying it is common.

PLATE 1 *House site*

PLATE 2 *Mud-and-tile home*

PLATE 3   *Harvesting sugar cane*

PLATE 4   *Relaxing after bringing lunch to the fields*

Since there is always some tension between co-resident father and grown son, it is considered best if a young man eventually leaves and forms his own household. In fact, most young men do separate by the time they are twenty or so. Thus, what originally binds a son to the house — the rule of getting an interest — later gives rise to disputes, which impel him to leave, and provides him with the resources to found a new household.

Siblings

Co-resident siblings are expected to, and usually do, have a close relationship. As long as they remain in their natal home they interact frequently. Siblings should treat each other well and respect one another. Parents emphasize that their children should not fight among themselves, and an older child especially should not hit a younger one. In fact, though there may be disagreements between them, open or physical fights between young (or even grown) siblings are rare and quickly punished. It is said that if a man wants to fight with kin, it is better that he do so with more distant ones.[9]

Children of most equal age in the house usually become closest, and some adults think that siblings learn more from and better understand one another than they do their parents. All the children of a house use the informal 'you' among themselves when young, as they do with their age-mates. If a family is large, older daughters from the age of seven or eight may assist their mothers in raising younger siblings. Siblings of the same sex share a bed and perhaps a cardboard storage box for their clothing. Parents usually try to purchase equal items for their children. If one child does have a store-bought toy or even candy, he is expected to share it with his brothers and sisters, and a child of six or so who is old enough to understand must always relinquish a toy or food to a younger sibling, waiting until his sibling is through before resuming his own activities. While still living in the same house it is impossible for one sibling to rob another, since what each has also belongs to the others.

Within a sibling group two special categories are recognized: the *cabecera* and the *bordón*. Leadership of the household is vested first in the father, then the mother. Following them the head is the leader of the sibling group. Known as the *cabecera* (head) he is usually the oldest but may instead be the most experienced. The functions of the head are minimal, and he usually becomes important only when the natal household has broken up and at least one of the parents has died. He concerns himself then with whatever family affairs the sibling group still has in common. The head has no legal or strong moral hold over his siblings and if there is a disagreement within the group he has difficulty enforcing his will. The job is not a prestigious one, people do not seek it, and it is not a defined role that suddenly can be assumed. Undoubtedly, the unimportance of the position is related to the fact that siblings, once they have formed their own households, have few material interests or duties in common.

The youngest sibling is known as the *bordón* or the *cacique* (lit. political boss, one who has an easy life). The term *'cacique'* – used also for the smallest issue of a litter – by extension may be applied to any child who is born small.[10] Aside from having an ideologically special position with regard to the inheritance and having a little more attention lavished on him at an early age because he is the youngest, the *bordón* is indistinguishable from his siblings.

I began this chapter with the question why households are occupied by conjugal families, for I was not satisfied that kinship norms by themselves provide the answer. I have tried to show that the shape of the household family is prescribed by certain non-kinship ideals, particularly those concerning the definition of the person. Males and females, adults and children are differentiated from one another. These distinctions are partially expressed through the concept of the household: males are in the fields while women are at home, and adults domesticate or raise children in a house. To be a person, then, male and female, adult and child must be conjoined in a household. Ideally, houses should contain at least one elementary family. Further, most of the ideal rights and obligations between members of the nuclear family, such as those concerning the spouse-spouse relationship or those pertaining to the inheritance system or those relating to the bond of amity between siblings, derive precisely from the fact that the conjugal family is localized. They would make little sense otherwise. Thus, the concept of the individual, the idea of the household, and their interconnection dominate or have a critical impact on the realm of the family. However, I have provided here only part of the answer to my original question, and next we shall see that, by extension of these very same concepts, households ideally should not contain more than one elementary family.

8   From natal to conjugal household

Families in all societies pass through an irreversible but repetitive sequence of changes: a couple marry, have children and their family enlarges; the children grow to adulthood, leave and/or marry, and the elder couple die. Conventionally, this developmental cycle in the family is said to be the cause of the growth and fission of domestic groups. At one level, this thesis cannot be refuted, for without growth changes in the family there would be no need for modification in domestic and spatial organization. However, it is quite different to argue that kinship norms themselves explain the form and timing of this sequence. For example, in a seminal essay on the subject Fortes states:

> We know that they [residence patterns] provide a basic index of the boundaries of the internal structure of domestic groups. But they are not a primary factor of social structure of the order of kinship, descent, marriage and citizenship. The alignments of residence are determined by the economic, affective, and jural relations that spring from these primary factors .... Residence patterns are the crystallization, at a given time, of the development process (1958: 3).

I reject this view that residence rules can always be reduced to or explained by principles of kinship. If anything, in Panama the reverse is true. Among the *campesinos* a locality concept, a rule about properly formed households, has an effect on the residential arrangements of kin groupings. The household idea itself, as we have seen, is used to express concepts about the individual.

My purpose in this chapter is to finish answering the question posed at the beginning of the previous one: why are elementary families identified with household groups? Specifically, why does no more than one nuclear family occupy a household? The answer can best be approached by viewing the life cycle of junior household members from adolescence to the point of a conjugal union, or fission of the domestic group. My argument is simply that these natural processes of growth in the family and of the individual are shaped and governed by a single rule: two conjugal couples are prohibited from occupying the same household. This proscription itself may be understood as a codification of those ideas about the person we have already examined. The kinship domain, again, is moulded by concepts about the individual and household.

The co-residential couples prohibition

According to the people each conjugal couple must have its own home and, in particular, maintain its own bedroom. No two adult couples may occupy the same bedroom or even the same house, although single offspring and, for short intervals, widowed parents may share a bedroom with a couple. The countrymen explain that the couples would hear each other (having sexual relations) and neither, therefore, would be able to respect the other. The rule is rigidly observed; there are no cases of two couples residing together.[1]

This proscription is not a norm of kinship. For example, it would be correct to state that residence in Los Boquerones is neolocal as opposed to virilocal, avunculocal, uxorilocal and so forth. But to formulate the residence rule this way would be to place it within the framework of kinship, and this would unduly narrow the concept; the rule is that no two couples, regardless of their kinship connection, may reside together. The prohibition does bear a similarity to the interdiction against incest. However, the two are not equivalent, and an examination and juxtaposition of the incest prohibitions may bring into sharper focus the difference between the household and family frames of reference.

The people use no word to refer to incest, although the term does exist in Spanish. Nevertheless, they do have such a concept, for sexual relations with certain kin are considered to be a mortal sin. The community applies no sanctions other than gossip to known offenders. But it is felt that in God's eyes there is no remission of the sin and that the offenders are punished in the after-life. In the people's terms the range of prohibited kin extends to second cousins.[2] More formally, we may say that incest restrictions apply between an individual and the persons in each of the stocks composed of his great-grandparents and their descendants through three generations. Slightly more distant kin are permitted but not considered to be proper partners. The people note, however, that with dispensation second cousins may marry in the church (although this would not be needed for common-law partners), and they sometimes cite one case in the community where this type of union occurred. On checking I found that the two partners were first cousins once removed (because of their age equivalence they were labelled second cousins.).[3]

The incest restrictions apply only to kin and not to affines. For example, the spouse of a parent's sibling or of a first cousin is not included in the category of prohibited persons. But engaging in sexual relations with such people is thought to be incorrect, for it shows a lack of respect for one's kinsmen who are or were joined in a conjugal union with them.

One of the crucial differences between the co-residential couples interdiction and the incest prohibition lies in the fact that the former has implications for more than just family members. It is a household-focused prohibition. Like incest it is a negative norm but has the positive effect of forcing every couple to inhabit a separate home.

Adolescence

At the onset of puberty the growing individual enters a new and important stage. This social transition is gradual, and no community-wide *rites de passage* indicate decisively when a child has reached adolescence. However, certain labels mark important changes in the life cycle of the individual.

Girls normally reach puberty from the ages of twelve to fifteen years. Until puberty a girl is known as a *niña* (girl) or *muchacha* (child, girl). After the onset of puberty but before she has had experience with men, a girl is termed a *señorita* (miss, young lady). *Señoritas*, are young, virgin women. Females who have never entered a conjugal union but who have had or are thought to have had sexual relations with men are termed *mujercitas* (diminutive of women). A *mujercita* is capable of or has reached the age when she feels she can leave her mother for a man. Fully grown women or ones in a conjugal union are referred to as *mujeres, señoras,* or adults. Boys reach puberty at the same or a slightly later age than girls. Until puberty they are called *muchachos* (boys). At puberty they become *hombrecitos* (diminutive of men). When they achieve the status of adult males, they are termed *hombres.*

These terms reflect the concepts the people hold concerning the life cycle of the individual. From baptism until the age of from seven to nine children are considered to be *angelitos* (little angels). They are thought to be unknowing in the sense of being incapable of distinguishing right from wrong and of controlling their behaviour and respecting others. They have not yet reached the age of reason.[4] Because they are not responsible for their acts, *angelitos* are incapable of sinning.[5] Therefore, when a little angel dies, his or her soul goes directly to heaven. Since the *angelito's* soul needs no aid from human society to ascend to heaven, the normal nine nights of the wake are abbreviated to one night, and other significant deviations from the normal adult funeral rites also occur.[6] Several years before puberty, children cease to be considered *angelitos*. They have acquired the capacity to reason and their quality of innocence has slowly gone away. The people often express this by saying a child is a little angel until he has a bad mouth. About the age of ten or eleven most children take their first communion and confession. Since children of this age have learned to sin, the purpose of the communion and confession, according to the people, is to cleanse them of their guilt. Finally, it is thought that confirmation should take place when a child is ten or eleven, but in fact it is taken at any time following baptism until this age.

The physical changes of puberty, then, are matched by changes in the definition of the individual. Until shortly before puberty a child is thought to be in a morally and sexually neutral state. His actions may have good or ill effects, but he is too young to understand the difference; he is still an *angelito*. The period from baptism to shortly before first confession and confirmation is one of gradually diminishing latency. By the time an individual reaches puberty he is thought to have absorbed the essential moral rules and to have acquired a sense of shame. The young adult, therefore, is held responsible for his social and sexual behaviour. Moreover, since sexual relations are thought to involve a loss of control and may be sinful, the onset of sexual prowess must mark an end to the morally neutral state.

The physical and social maturing of the adolescent is reflected in his relation to the household and in his new set of interaction patterns. At puberty children emerge from the confines of their natal households (mothers no longer forbid them to visit elsewhere), seek sexual partners and are judged by others according to the respect they exhibit. Just as the process of raising a youngster integrates him into the household, the movement into adolescence takes the child beyond this group into the larger social network. The way in which growing children must learn about sexual matters succinctly illustrates the fact that adolescents must turn their affective attentions away from their natal households.

As noted, children do not learn about sex in the home, and consequently boys, and to a lesser extent girls, are forced to learn about sexual matters in the street. In most gatherings of males a good deal of joking about sex takes place. Whereas a father or close kinsman will never jest with or ask a young man about his women, another older man will not hesitate to do so.

Although adolescent boys and girls both begin to turn their interests out from the household, they do so in divergent ways, and this difference is a reflection of the contrasting male and female roles they are assuming. After reaching puberty young men tend to leave the house in the late afternoon and evening to visit girls or peers. Sometimes they spend an evening gambling at cards or dominoes.

Significantly, both sexual relations and gambling cost money. By this age, however, young males are working and receiving cash. Thus, the point at which a young man has reached puberty, has ceased to be an *angelito,* has been confirmed, has taken first communion, has become capable of respectful and sinful behaviour, and has begun to participate in the social and sexual life outside his home, is linked to when he begins to earn his own money. As a working person the young male demonstrates and gains the wherewithal to prove that he is a man. Paradoxically, the custom of getting an interest first binds a child to his home and then enables him, through the economic independence it provides, to separate himself from his domestic family and to have sexual relations outside the home. The affective, social and sexual characteristics of the young male, then, are indicative of, indeed they are based upon, his growing economic independence from the household.

In contrast, adolescent girls are kept at home, and ideally they are more innocent of sexual matters. Information about the menses is not imparted in advance to girls, and many gain only rudimentary knowledge from their mothers when they first experience menstruation. Compared to boys, young girls also have less economic independence and the new role they are assuming is radically different. If girls go visiting at night they are accompanied by a family member, and if they go to a dance their fathers also may attend. Those who do wander about by themselves or with other girls are considered to be loose and shameless.

Thus, the contrasting expectations for male and female adolescents are an aspect of the broader role contrast between men and women, for it is at this age that the sex role is supplanting the child role. These concepts about the growing individual are manifested in his relation to the household. In this respect, then, the relation of the young person to his natal family is not dictated by kinship imperatives alone but by broader cultural ideals concerning the individual as these are worked out in relation to the household.

Courtship

The people have no term for courtship, and though from adolescence to conjugal union males and females do meet each other, there are no formal courting patterns. Most meetings between young men and women are clandestine and often occur at night. A girl may lie to her parents, by stating that she is going on an errand, leave the house, and meet a boy at a predetermined spot. A favourite time for assignations is at all-night wakes when people can slip away from the praying congregation without being noticed. But encounters also occur during the day. A girl carrying food to men in the fields may arrange to meet a young man who is working nearby. The physical layout of the community is an aid to secret meetings, because there is ample privacy in seldom-used paths leading to dense *monte,* and in abandoned houses and large fields.

Courtship patterns, however, are not chaotic and young people must respond to two forms of restraints. Parents exercise some control over the courting behaviour of their children. Fathers and brothers are not overly worried about protecting the virginity of a daughter or sister, but they do want others to know her as a person with a sense of shame. If a boy visits a girl at her house, the girl's parents may not even retire to the bedroom. For a girl to leave her house at night she must lie to her parents, and if she does this frequently, she risks angering them. As long as a boy still lives in his natal home, his father feels a responsibility for his behaviour.

Nevertheless, though parents may wish to influence the behaviour of their grown children, they have few material means by which to do so, since there is no valuable property from which young people may be alienated. On the contrary, both boys and girls contribute valuable labour to their natal households. Except by virtue of the respect owed them, parents have little control over the sexual and social behaviour of their growing children.

Given the weakness of household authority and given that young people are focusing their attentions away from the household and upon other members of the community, it is fitting that the most powerful restraints are exercised by village members and are non-material. The courting behaviour of adolescents is guided by the differing expectations for the sexes and is regulated by the sanction of respect. A girl keeps her respect by keeping her virginity or at least by being circumspect in her actions. She knows that although most meetings are secret, young men share their experiences. And the pregnant single woman is both talked about and has difficulty in finding a spouse. A boy wants to appear to others as being serious and responsible, characteristics which can be undermined by unregulated sexual behaviour. In this context, respect and shame are elements of a person's character which can be contaminated and lost through indiscriminate actions.

Both sexes, then, to live up to the ideal of keeping respect must be judicious about their behaviour. Courtship patterns are regulated not so much by natal households but by the individual in his relation to the community. On a broad level this is congruent with the fact that the individual is a unit within the social structure, while more narrowly it is consistent with the pattern of adolescent males and females moving away economically from their natal homes, focusing their affective attentions elsewhere and beginning to exhibit respect in their social behaviour.

Moving into conjugal unions

By the age of nineteen or twenty a young man usually focuses his attentions upon one or a few girls. Young women begin to consider conjugal unions at a slightly younger age. The people notice immediately when two young people have paired off, but no term is used to denote the fact, and unless a pair are married in a church there is no engagement period. At most two young people may say that they are *novios* (fiancé, sweetheart), but each may continue to see members of the opposite sex, and their relations may be sporadic directly up to the time they join together in one household.

In return for her affections and to demonstrate his own independence and serious intent, a young man usually supplies his *novia* with small gifts, such as clothes, shoes or cosmetics. He does not normally give her cash or food items. Since a girl may have several *novios,* each may give her gifts but this is within her rights. However, a *novia* does live in her father's house, and it is important to note that her position is structurally different from that of a female spouse or a woman household head, who provisions her home by selling her sexual services. On

the one hand, the payments a man makes to his *novia* are more diffuse
and less obligatory than those he makes to a prostitute. On the other,
since the relationship is not founded on economic co-operation, gifts
handed to a *novia* are more sporadic and specific than the total set of
cash and goods payments given to a mate.

By the time two young people become *novios,* both probably will
have had some sexual experience, particularly the man. Most couples
also cohabit together before they enter a conjugal relation, and many
believe it is better to do so to see if they are congenial. However, if a
woman is serious about a man she also may refuse him or limit his
sexual advances in order to force him into a union; her power to do so
is an important aspect of the contrasting roles of the sexes.

Partner choice

The decision concerning whom to select as a conjugal mate is made by
the individual himself, which is congruent with the fact that unions are
never arrangements between groups. I consider consort selection from
the standpoint of an inner circle of prohibited partners, an outer range
of possible mates and the values used to select a spouse within these
parameters.

An individual is prohibited from choosing three categories of persons. First, sexual relations and therefore conjugal ties are forbidden
between kinsmen within the range of second cousin. Second, as I
explain in chapter 10, kinship relations can arise between non-kin
(excluding spouses) who reside together in the same household. Persons
in such relationships are prohibited from having sexual relations or
joining together in a connubial bond. Third, individuals who are linked
in a *compadre-compadre* or godparent-godchild bond are prohibited
from having sexual and therefore conjugal relations.

The range of partner choice effectively is set by the area in which a
man works or visits, for it is principally through these activities that he
meets new females. In this respect there is a complex interconnection
among conjugal choice, kinship ties and locality. Where a man works or
visits is often dictated by who and where his kin are. Often, two
persons meet through kin or kin and affines, and kin themselves beyond
the second-cousin range may intermarry. Consideration of partner selection, then, takes us beyond such choice itself to an examination of the
bilateral kinship network and its relation to locality. I only wish to
stress here that each individual or group of siblings has a unique

constellation of recognized kin. Since relationships may be traced to the third-cousin level, the range of kin relationships is quite large. Active relations are not maintained with all these persons, but they present a large circle of people to whom and through whom practical relations may be established. It is, then, usually within and through this circle of kin plus their affines and personal friends that conjugal partners are found. Most individuals eventually select a partner from within the community or a neighbouring one where kin and friends are located.

To illustrate the kinds of kinship and affinal connections found between conjugal partners I present one example. Almost at random I have picked nine adult persons, eight of whom are now living in the village. Figure 2 shows the links among them. For simplicity I have eliminated all the ties they have with others, for clearly the stocks of which each is a part stretch in other directions, and I have not even included all the spouses each has had.

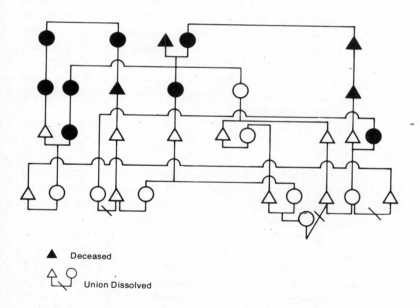

FIGURE 2   *Kinship and affinal links among nine adults*

As I shall explain in a later chapter, not all the kinship relationships are recognized. Nevertheless; it is true that each person in Figure 2 is related to his conjugal partner either directly through a kinship link or indirectly through a combination of kinship and affinal connections. Since Figure 2 is a statistical result which reflects conjugal choices made by individuals, one conclusion which may be drawn from it is that an individual's network of kin and affines presents a framework through which and within which conjugal partners may be found.

Within these external and internal limits the people use, implicitly at least, a set of criteria to evaluate potential partners. A man's primary goal is to secure a girl who knows her *compromiso*. In this context the term refers to how well a woman knows her role and carries out her tasks. If a female knows how to manage a house and will not get involved with other men, she knows her *compromiso*. Women have comparable standards for men. They want a partner who has a good *fundamento*, that is, one who is serious, works hard, provides well, does not drink or joke too much, and does not spend too much money on other women or *fiestas*. In short, each sex desires a partner who will be able to live up to the demands of being a mate. The primary criteria individuals use to judge potential partners, then, are based upon the needs of household organization. Furthermore, an individual's *fundamento* and sense of *compromiso* derive from the way he was raised in a household. In some respects, therefore, parents endow their co-resident children not with physical property but with a sense of shame and respect, and these are the valuables others attempt to maximize in choosing a household partner.

Building a house

The movement from natal to conjugal household is a two-stage change for a boy and a one-step transition for a girl. A young man constructs a home and moves into it before taking a wife. A young woman moves directly from her parental to her conjugal household.

The sexual difference in the transition from natal to conjugal household is related once again to the male/female role contrast. Males have the ability to support themselves. Females are not expected to be independent; their role is to be part of a household group. When a boy builds a new house it is evidence of his growth to maturity, for it shows that he has separated himself from his natal household and is ready to assume the responsibilities of household headship, and it is symbolic of the shift a male must make from his role as son to his role as head, a change more marked and fraught with tension than the daughter-mother shift.

Theoretically when a boy builds his own house, he moves in and becomes completely independent, although in practice the residential shift may work out in variant ways. For example, a young man may build a sleeping house on a site near his parents, carry on separate agricultural work but not construct a kitchen. In return for contributing aid to his father, he may eat in his parent's home and have his washing done there. The pattern is of some theoretical interest in that it is the only case in which the production and consumption group does not coincide with the residential unit. Alternatively, if a boy falls in love with a girl and wants to live with her immediately he may build a house and move directly in with her, skipping the stage of separate residence.

Whatever the details of the transition, the young man should not accept the house from the girl or her family; by doing so he would lose respect. As one person stated, 'No woman carries off the man.' A man joins a woman in her house only when the woman herself has previously separated in the appropriate manner from her natal home and then has dissolved her union with her mate, thus leaving her head of her own household.

Houses are built wherever the man or couple desire or are able to find land. Usually, a male tries to locate his house near where he intends to work and where his or his spouse's kin and friends are situated, for these are the people to whom a couple turn first for aid in an emergency. In particular, siblings often live in close proximity.

Even if a young man is not thinking about a union it is thought to be better if he eventually moves away from his parents' house. Those who are capable of living on their own but remain in their natal households are said not to think well, and they are certainly less respected. As long as a boy remains in his father's house, girls know that he is not seriously looking for a mate.

The realignment of household groups

Although dowry and bridewealth are not exchanged between family or household groups at a conjugal union, property rights are transferred between co-resident parents and children. Before a union, as seen, a young man usually has in his name some forest land, sugar cane and rice. If he leaves his natal house directly to enter a union, his father also may give him chickens, cows and household items. If the household has only a limited supply of these goods but does have money, it may help by purchasing such items. A girl brings less to a union because the man is responsible for her. If her father can afford to, he may give her such household goods as chickens, pigs or even cows, but she never has sugar cane or rice in her name, and the amount of property given to her is usually less than that given to her male siblings. Roughly, a woman brings only movable, partible items while a man may bring both movable and immovable property. It should be re-emphasized, however, that the actual wealth a new household family receives is minimal. The daughter of the wealthiest man in the community brought to her union three cows and some household items. While this property gave her new household some security, it was not sufficient to provide a living nor would it have lasted long if her spouse had not worked.

Property is given to a child only for his first union. Natal households have no responsibility to provide for a second union. If a conjugal pair separate, each takes with him the property he brought. The strength and importance of kin bonds are linked to this ideal form of property distribution. After he builds a house or enters a conjugal union, a child is on his own. Property is no longer held in common with his natal family and the inheritance in the form of gifts *inter vivos* has been transmitted. Therefore, close kin have little other than sentiment to link them together.

Given this context, we can see more clearly the importance of the custom of getting an interest. As a son grows up, the practice of giving him an interest binds him to his natal home. Later, strains arise between co-resident father and son because they inevitably have a clash of authority over the control and partition of the son's earnings. When the son does move to a new household, the break is a major one, for in practice the formula of getting an interest apportions to a child, when he leaves his natal home, the totality of what he will receive of the household property. As he forms his own family the son repeats the process with his progeny. Getting an interest, then, is not only a reflection of the non-corporate or individual nature of property rights, the independence of households, and the importance of manliness, it is also an important dynamic behind the developmental cycle in household groups.[7]

The household and the co-residential couples prohibition

The co-residential couples prohibition codifies an entire set of expectations about the person and his relation to the household and family. On one level the rule refers simply to ideas about sexual relationships. All sexual relations are shameful if not sinful; therefore, conjugal pairs must be segregated since it would be embarrassing for two couples to overhear one another. I refer again to the tale of God, St Peter and the two cohabiting couples in which the unmarried copulating pair are exonerated because they hide their actions and exhibit a sense of embarrassment. But the following ethnographic facts also should be noted. The bedroom is a private chamber to which other adults are not normally admitted. Even the household dogs and chickens, which have the run of the household area, are always kept out of the bedroom. Conversation in the household about sexual matters is avoided, and adolescents must learn about sex outside the home. Even in cases of polygyny each woman at least maintains her own bedroom. The residential ban is consistent with, indeed it epitomizes and sums up, beliefs concerning respectful sexual relations between persons.

The proscription, however, refers to more than sexual relations. To be truly manly a male must be independent; a woman exhibits her total set of female qualities by being the centre of and running a home. In this respect the co-residential couples ban is simply the inverse of those characteristics which draw males and females together into conjugal unions. 'The man is in the fields, the woman is at home' implies not only that the tasks are complementary but that the unit formed is and should be independent. Only one adult male and one adult female are required to form a household; should there be more, the independence created when founding the household would be undermined. Hence, the shame two co-residential couples would feel in overhearing one another refers not only to sexual relations but to a total set of role expectations. The locality proscription encapsulates a constellation of beliefs concerning the individual and male-female relationships.

I began this chapter by asking why no more than one conjugal family occupies a household. The simple answer is that the rule segregating conjugal couples assures that this must be so. But I have been concerned also to delineate the cultural beliefs which underlie this rule and to show how kinship relationships are shaped by values and ideas emanating from other domains. All the concepts concerning the growth of the adolescent, courtship patterns, the selection of conjugal partners, the building of a new house by the male, the female moving directly in, catching an interest, the inheritance system and the structural rearrangements which occur at a conjugal union — all these familial patterns — are acted out by the person in relation to the household, and ultimately these kinship patterns express ideas held about the nature of the individual. At the same time, all these familial patterns which lead to a total movement from natal to conjugal household are condensed and contained within the rule about locality which prohibits two conjugal couples from occupying the same household.

9   Forms of conjugal relations

The people recognize and practise several forms of mating relationship: church marriages, civil or state marriages, co-residential common-law unions, polygyny, extra-residential liaisons, transient affairs, and buyer-prostitute connections. Statistically, their choices are as follows: (1) Of the total of 91 household heads 66 (73 per cent) are in a conjugal union. (2) Of those united by a conjugal bond, 97 per cent (64) are in a co-residential monogamous union. (3) Of those in a monogamous co-residential relationship 30 per cent (19) are united by a church marriage which includes a civil union, 5 per cent (3) are joined by civil marriage alone, and 66 per cent (42) are linked by common-law bonds. My purpose in this chapter is to explain these diverse connubial forms and to account for their different frequencies of selection. I shall show that the choice of conjugal form is influenced primarily by the definition of what a proper male and female is and by the manner in which these ideals are made manifest in the household.

This range of permissible male-female relationships, however, raises the fundamental problem of defining what constitutes marriage and legitimacy in Los Boquerones; and this issue in turn takes us back to the relation between family and household. A classic definition of marriage, can be found in *Notes and Queries on Anthropology* (Royal Anthropological Institute, 1951: 110): 'Marriage is a union between a man and a woman such that children born to the woman are the recognized legitimate offspring of both partners.' Leach (1955) criticized this definition for being too restrictive and suggested that marriage be viewed in terms of the different types of rights it serves to establish. Gough (1959: 32) in a rejoinder to Leach suggested an expanded version of the preceding *Notes and Queries* definition he proposed:

> Marriage is a relationship established between a woman and one or more other persons, which provides that a child born to the woman under circumstances not prohibited by the rules of the relationship,

is accorded full birth-status rights common to normal members of his society or social stratum.

In spite of its utility, the Gough definition, like that of *Notes and Queries,* assimilates affinity to kinship by linking marriage in a one-to-one relationship with birth-status rights. And in both definitions it is assumed that legitimacy is a discrete concept. However true these assumptions may be for some societies, they make little sense when applied to the ethnographic facts of rural Panama.

The Panamanian situation is rather complicated. On the one hand, church and civil unions are considered by both the state and the countrymen to be marriage. In fact, the people reserve the term 'married' *(casado)* for such bonds. Further, the offspring of a church or civil union are considered by the *campesinos* and the state to be truly legitimate *(legitimo).* Therefore, the *Notes and Queries* and Gough definitions do apply to these situations. (Following the countrymen I use the terms 'legitimacy' and 'marriage' only for such religious or state unions.) But a complication arises when we turn to a consideration of common-law unions. Although the state does not recognize these relationships as a form of marriage, the *campesinos* do.[1] Common-law unions are named *(juntado),* are distinguished from affairs in the street, and resemble church and state marriages in that the duties between the partners are essentially similar in all three types. A common-law union differs, however, in that recognition of the offspring issuing from the relationship is not thought to be a right or duty of the male partner. To understand the rationale behind this we must return to a consideration of the people's notion of kinship and filiation.

The mother-child bond, as explained, is thought to be basic in that it is founded on biology and cannot be hidden. Similarly the father-child bond is said to be based on a genetic link but is more tenuous since it is not so easily recognizable. A man will claim or deny a filial link under various circumstances. Normally a male will claim the children born to his co-resident common-law partner and presumed to be his genetic offspring. If he does not acknowledge the children, he will not be seen as a truly responsible man with a sense of honour and independence. However, various circumstances may lead to a deviation from this pattern. Recall the case of Clemente and Edilsa. Several of her children clearly are not genetically related to him, but Clemente steadfastly claims his paternal status. If he did not claim the offspring, he would be shamed for he would be openly admitting to his status of cuckolded spouse. Conversely, Jacinto in his periodic fights with his mate denies his paternal link to her offspring. His children certainly resemble him genetically — several of the people pointed out an unusual formation of the eyelid which was distinctive to him and his spouse's children. His periodic denials, then, are attempts to shame his partner but involve no loss of honour for him. In yet different cases men may deny what they presume to be their children 'in the street' in order not to incur a responsibility toward them. And some men acknowledge children 'in the street' who may not be biologically related to them. At times a man's claims, such as Clemente's, or denials, such as Jacinto's, may stretch the credulity of the people, but this does not mean that his assertions are fictive. Such filial bonds are not a deviation from a 'true' pattern. Rather, since kinship is not only biology but biology plus claims about genetic relationships, it is flexible. Once the premise is accepted that not all genetic relationships are kinship nor kinship relations genetic, it follows that patrifilial recognition and common-law unions are partly independent.

This brings us back to the definition of marriage. On the one hand, if we restrict our use of the term 'marriage' to situations of true legitimacy, common-law unions remain undefined. On the other, if we specify as conjugal unions those relationships from which flow full birth-status rights, then religious, state and common-law unions are not themselves distinctively characterized since birth-status rights may be recognized outside a conjugal bond. I conclude, therefore, that conjugal unions in Los Boquerones are not defined by birth-status rights or legitimacy of the offspring.

In place of proposing a new, universal definition of 'marriage' I shall follow Leach's suggestion and view each conjugal relationship in Los Boquerones as a unique package of rights and obligations. But I am still left with several questions. What defines a conjugal relationship for the people? What influences the paternal claims which are made? And why are conjugal unions and recognized patrifilial relationships normally linked? In the course of this chapter I shall argue that recognized conjugal unions are characterized by co-residence of the partners, and that recognition of a filial bond is normally a function of this co-residence. In this respect, then, I shall be suggesting once again that the domain of familial relations incorporates ideas about the household and the individual.[2]

Common-law, civil and church unions

The three most common types of mating relationship are the monogamous, co-residential forms: *juntado,* civil marriage and church
marriage.

Forming 'juntado'

The word *juntado* is derived from the verb *juntar* which means to join,
unite or connect. The people use the term when referring to a male and
female who are in a co-residential common-law union.

A generation ago the process of becoming *juntado* was more formal
in that a young man had to ask the girl's father for permission. Today
such unions are formed casually. No public ceremony is held and the
couple normally are secretive. Rarely are the parents asked for permission and they may even learn of the union only when confronted by
the *fait accompli.* The boy and girl may inform a few close friends of
their intentions, but the community as a whole seldom has advance
warning.

The partners in a *juntado* union say they are married by *El Padre
Matojo* or *Mata* (Bush Priest), *El Padre Chumico* (*Chumico* is the name
of a leaf used for scrubbing dirty dishes) or *El Padre Monte* (Forest
Priest). To join they simply leave 'fleeing for the bush'. If a couple have
become *juntado* in a first union with the good wishes of their parents,
the morning after their first night together the parents may send them
some food. However, a *juntado* union usually begins with an elopement
which frequently angers the girl's father; his rights over her, which are
legally transferred at her marriage, are usurped. In one case a father
heard in the evening of his daughter's elopement, traced the couple
during the night, and brought his offspring back home before she had
arisen for breakfast.

The fact that *juntado* unions are not formally marked can lead to
difficulty in distinguishing between them and extra-conjugal affairs.
According to the *campesinos,* to be *juntado* a pair must be co-resident;
sometimes they add the qualification that the house must be the male's.
But co-residence, while a distinctive attribute of a common-law union, is
not its only defining characteristic. For a relationship to be considered
a conjugal bond all the sexual, economic and domestic rights, described
earlier, must obtain. Such a co-operative patterning of activities is
manifested only over time, and not every co-residential bond lasts long
enough to be a common-law union. Couples rarely become co-resident

at the male's house unless they plan to form a conjugal union. But limiting cases occur where such unions fail after two days or even several weeks. Were the couple companions — the term used for common-law spouses — or friends — the word used for lovers? The answer varies according to the community's perception of the couple's intentions and their past reputations. A relationship, therefore, which is not co-residential cannot be *juntado*, but not every co-residential bond lasts long enough to be a common-law union.

Forming civil marriage

Civil marriages, obtained in Santiago, also are performed with a lack of ritual. The couple present themselves before a judge with several witnesses and pay $20. A *fiesta* in the community need not and usually does not follow the formality.

Few, if any, men express a desire to have a civil marriage. Such marriages usually are initiated when the man would be liable to legal action. By Panamanian law males and females are minors to the age of twenty-one. Marriage cannot be contracted if the male is less than fourteen or the female less than twelve; should such a marriage take place it legally could be nullified by any of the parents. Marriage also is prohibited to minors above these minimum ages without the consent of the person who exercises paternal power over them. But if such minors above fourteen or twelve do contract marriage, the marriage is considered valid, subject only to certain restrictions concerning rights to property. Also, a child of eighteen may be emancipated by his parents in which case he has the legal rights of a twenty-one-year-old, including the right to contract marriage. Conversely, marriage itself produces emancipation of the minor.[3]

The countrymen are not totally conversant with these laws, but they do hold that a father cannot prosecute a man for eloping with his daughter if the pair have been legally married. Thus, it is primarily for situations in which a girl is below the age of twenty-one, or even eighteen, and in which there is a likelihood that the father would oppose a union, that men resort to civil marriage. In effect, a civil marriage often acts as formal recognition of a couple's elopement. The people rather cynically state that the government does not care about the possible consequences of a youthful marriage and is only interested in the money it can make: 'He who has twenty dollars can rob a woman.'[4]

Forming church marriage

A church marriage is quite distinct from the other two types in the way it is formed, although legally it has the same effect as a civil marriage.[5] Religious marriages normally are performed in Santiago; however a few have been enacted in the community by travelling priests. Church marriages are announced in advance; family and close friends attend the ceremony, and afterward a large *fiesta* is held in the village.

The costs of a church marriage are borne by the groom, not by his family or household group, and though the expense of the ceremony itself is minimal, the attendant costs are large. The groom must provide food and drink for the *fiesta,* purchase clothes for himself, buy a ring for his bride, and meet a number of incidental expenses, all of which may cost from $150 to $200. The bride and her family have only the expense of supplying her clothes. Sometimes the bride's father helps bear the cost of the food, but he is under no obligation to do so. The people point out that he gives the girl, and what more could be expected? The fact that the groom must pay for the major portion of the expenses is illustrative of the value placed on male independence as well as the relative unimportance of the natal family in the formation of conjugal unions and new households.

A religious marriage is said to be pleasurable for everyone. Unlike a *juntado* union or a civil marriage it never involves robbing a girl, and nearly all fathers would be pleased to have their daughters married in the church.

The three compared

The three co-residential monogamous conjugal forms are chosen with different frequencies: 30 per cent church marriage; 5 per cent civil marriage; 66 per cent *juntado*. In all three forms the relationship is based upon an exact division of duties between male and female, and in considering the reasons for their differential selection other factors must be examined, including age of the partners, prestige of the union, juridical relation of the spouses and of the parents and children, financial cost, and religious significance of the bond. A critical, though not the only, difference among the forms is that a church marriage imposes a sacred tie between the partners. Many males and some females wish to avoid this enduring bond, and for this reason primarily the majority of the unions are common-law alliances.

The developmental cycle of the family and age of the individual have minimal impact on the choice of conjugal union. Generally, the people do not progress age-wise from *juntado* to civil to church unions. No one speaks of such a progression as an ideal, and statistically age and duration breakdowns of the unions bear out the point. In Tables 5 and 6 the current unions are displayed according to the average age of the couple. An inspection of Table 5 shows that *juntado* and church unions

TABLE 5 *Types of co-residential monogamous union by age*

Average age of couple	Juntado	Civil	Church
20^+ – 30	19% (8)	33% (1)	10% (2)
30^+ – 40	26% (11)	33% (1)	32% (6)
40^+ – 50	21% (9)	33% (1)	26% (5)
50^+ – 60	26% (11)	–	26% (5)
60^+	7% (3)	–	5% (1)
Totals	99% (42)	99% (3)	99% (19)
			n = 64

have approximately similar distributions throughout the age brackets. Similarly an examination of Table 6 shows that within each age bracket

TABLE 6 *Types of co-residential monogamous union by age*

Average age of couple	Juntado	Civil	Church	Totals
20^+ – 30	73% (8)	9% (1)	18% (2)	100% (11)
30^+ – 40	61% (11)	6% (1)	33% (6)	100% (18)
40^+ – 50	60% (9)	7% (1)	33% (5)	100% (15)
50^+ – 60	69% (11)	–	31% (5)	100% (16)
60^+	75% (3)	–	25% (1)	100% (4)
	66% (42)	5% (3)	30% (19)	64

the percentage of unions is roughly equivalent to the overall percentage of that type of union. In Tables 7 and 8 the duration of each type of union up to 1967 is displayed.[6] On the average, current church unions have endured for 15.6 years while common-law unions have endured 14.6 years and civil unions have lasted 6.67 years. The median duration is 13 years for church unions, 12 years for common-law unions and 8 years for civil unions.

TABLE 7   *Types of co-residential monogamous union by duration of union*

Duration of union to 1967	Juntado	Civil	Church
0 – 5	20% (8)	33% (1)	5% (1)
5^+ – 10	22% (9)	33% (1)	26% (5)
10^+ – 15	20% (8)	33% (1)	32% (6)
15^+ – 20	10% (4)	–	–
20^+ – 5	10% (4)	–	16% (3)
25^+ – 30	4% (2)	–	16% (3)
30^+ – 5	7% (3)	–	5% (1)
35^+ – 40	4% (2)	–	–
40^+ – 5	2% (1)	–	–
Totals	99% (41)	99% (3)	100% (19)

TABLE 8   *Types of co-residential monogamous union by duration of union*

Duration of union to 1967	Juntado	Civil	Church	Totals
0 – 5	80% (8)	10% (1)	10% (1)	100% (10)
5^+ – 10	60% (9)	7% (1)	33% (5)	100% (15)
10^+ – 15	53% (8)	7% (1)	40% (6)	100% (15)
15^+ – 20	100% (4)	–	–	100% (4)
20^+ – 5	57% (4)	–	43% (3)	100% (7)
25^+ – 30	40% (2)	–	60% (3)	100% (5)
30^+ – 5	75% (3)	–	25% (1)	100% (4)
35^+ – 40	100% (2)	–	–	100% (2)
40^+ – 5	100% (1)	–	–	100% (1)
	65% (41)	5% (3)	30% (19)	63

Although I think it is fair to conclude from these statistics that the unions are not entered progressively by age, let me add some explanatory remarks. First, the statistics only include current unions. I shall note later *juntado* unions are less stable than church unions. I was unable, however, to obtain data on every prior union which each adult had entered. Were all these unions to be included then common-law unions would turn out to have a much lower average duration than church unions. This hypothetical statistic might then be interpreted in various ways. One explanation might be that church marriage is the ideal toward which the people aim. At a young age they enter common-law bonds and switch partners; at an older age they enter religious marriages and do not separate. From this pattern it would result statistically that church marriages last longer than *juntado* unions. In support of this possible argument I should also point out that in perhaps five or six unions the partners did take out church marriages after having been in *juntado* unions, and that one man in a civil marriage spoke of his intention of marrying his wife in the church. Nevertheless, the statistics presented in Tables 5 and 6 generally do bear out the point that age is not a factor in connubial choice. Second, for reasons already mentioned, civil unions usually are between younger couples or are the first union for a girl. In this respect age does have an effect on which form is chosen, but the reasons for the choice are not directly a function of ideals which are held at a particular age. Young people do not enter a civil union with the intention of later forming a church bond; usually they are forced into the state marriage. In sum, the life cycle by itself does not account for the selection of type of conjugal union, and the statistics collected at a particular time illustrate that the people prefer common-law unions to the other forms.

In terms of social standing or status a church marriage is said to be preferable to the other forms. A religious union is the ideal of the church and Panamanian society, and as members of these larger units the countrymen also feel that a church marriage is better, more respectful and more prestigious than a civil or common-law union. Church-married partners also may take mass. Within the community itself a church-married couple gains some respect in the eyes of others: their children are fully legitimate, and only church-married couples together may sponsor a godchild. Religiously married spouses are said to respect one another more than civil or common-law mates; they use the formal 'you' for one another. But it is females who gain most from a church union. A woman is supposed to receive more respect from a church-married husband than from a common-law spouse, and she binds him more strongly to herself religiously and legally. It is said that only a man who has great respect for his mate or wants to tie her down desires a church marriage. Usually the suggestion and impetus for such a union come from the woman. That 30 per cent of the co-residential unions are church marriages attests to the strength of the values of the church and larger society and to the desires of females.

Civil marriages, in addition to providing legal protection, are undertaken sometimes as compromises between the woman who wishes a church marriage and the man who wants a *juntado* union. State marriages have a little more status attached to them than common-law unions but less than church marriages.

Financially, the major difference among the three is the initial expense of forming the bond. A *juntado* union costs nothing, while the charge for a civil marriage is $20.00. A church marriage may cost ten times this amount. Given the relative poverty of the people it would appear that on the basis of financial cost alone *juntado* unions would be preferred. Although this is true on the individual level, it is important to look at the social reasons for the financial impediment. The church charges nothing for performing the religious ceremony; indeed the clergy would be delighted if more countrymen entered sacred bonds. All the monetary outlays are made in fulfilment of social requirements. A church marriage entails a lasting commitment on the part of the two mates, and by lavishing money on the ceremony a man shows publicly that he is undertaking and is committed to this obligation. To some extent he is also paying for the measure of status which accrues to a church-married couple. By requiring the financial outlay, then, the community re-enforces the importance of the step. Thus, financial expenses do deter individuals from entering church marriages, but the costs themselves are a reflection of the enormity of the transition in the *campesinos'* eyes. In this respect expense is an immediate but not the ultimate reason for the preference for common-law unions.[7]

The form of conjugal union chosen also has a juridical impact on the relations of a man to his mate and to his children. The data concerning the legal status of the children are complex, and the situation has been made more complicated by a relatively recent change in the application of Panamanian law. Prior to the 1940s, as recognized by the state, there were three legal categories of offspring: legitimate, recognized and natural. Offspring of church- or civil-married parents were (and still are) legitimate. They always carry their father's surname. For the country-men the advantages of bearing or being a legitimate individual are few. Within the community the legitimate person has no greater status. Some claim that the legitimate individual, by showing his identity card, can receive a little more attention in government offices, but the *campesinos* have little commerce with the larger society, and their personal reception in a government office is not very important in their lives. A legitimate offspring also has prior rights to an inheritance over an illegitimate one, but the people have no continuing estates or offices, and from the perspective of property rights there is no need for legitimate offspring or civil or church marriages.

In the past, offspring of a common-law union were in one of two juridical statuses: recognized *(reconocido)* or natural. At the birth of his child a father could choose to recognize or not his offspring. If he wished to recognize the child, he put his name down in the civil registry of births. The offspring then carried his surname. If a father chose not to recognize his child, the offspring carried only the mother's surname and was natural.[8] Both recognized and natural, then, were categories within the larger Panamanian society, and in total three legal classes of individuals were distinguished: legitimate, recognized and natural.

The countrymen, in the past, had a similar but slightly different set of 'legal' classifications. Like the state, they utilized the categories of legitimate and recognized for legal and non-legal unions. They differed, however, in their use of the category natural. Within the community a man, who supposed himself to be a genetic father, had the choice of acknowledging whether or not a natural child was his; that is, a presumed father might or might not acknowledge his biological father-hood before the village.[9] In a majority of cases in prior generations children were legally natural. Yet, most of these natural children were acknowledged before the community by their fathers. Therefore, the question arises: if males usually accepted responsibility for their pre-sumed natural children, why did they normally refuse to recognize them before the state? This issue is linked to the people's conceptions about males and females.

Men have always valued their freedom. They would not be *facultado* in the street if they could be indelibly linked to their children. And just as a woman retains the weapon of cuckolding her spouse, so a male in counterbalance may deny paternity of her children. Men explain that because a woman can never be trusted to be sexually constant and because other men always take advantage of sexual opportunities pre-sented, they can never be certain who the true genetic father of their children is. By Panamanian law, however, men have always been obliged to support their legitimate and recognized children and have always been liable to legal sanctions if they failed to do so; they have never been obliged to support their natural, acknowledged children. Thus, the males' reasoning concerning the uncertainty of paternity is in part a fiction to justify their freedom from their spouses, their spouses' children, and their lovers' children. In the past, therefore, a man's decision to recognize children or not hinged upon his willingness to make a binding commitment to them and, by implication, to their mother. Whether they were legitimate, recognized, or natural a father usually supported and raised his children. But by only acknowledging his children, a male avoided the lasting commitment to care for them. He maintained the right to deny his natural fatherhood and responsi-bilities and to sever kinship ties at any time.

According to recent application of the law, all children must be either legitimate or recognized, whether their father's relation to their mother is a legal one or is based upon a common-law union. Children cannot be natural. All offspring in the present generation, therefore, bear both a matronym and a patronym. At birth a mother must name the putative father and the father must register his name in recognition of his paternity. The law is relatively easy to enforce since most babies currently are born in hospitals and until signed for are not released. If a putative father refuses to sign, the mother must find another male who is willing to be named as the father.[10]

This legal change was made because of the prevalence of common-law unions and separations. Now all children must be provided for whether or not they live with their recognized fathers, since their mothers can always sue the recognized father for child support. The result of this change in the legal status of children has been to limit though not extinguish a man's right to negate his familial relations. A putative father may still deny his children, but only at birth and not later.

In present times, therefore, the legal status of the children still has an impact on which conjugal form is chosen. Whether his children are legitimate (i.e. issue from a civil or church union) or recognized (i.e. issue from a common-law union) is unimportant to a father. But by entering only a common-law union a man preserves the right to deny 'his' children when they are first born to his spouse. Normally a man recognizes the children who are born to his co-resident common-law partner in order to establish and preserve his own sense of honour. But if he wishes to shame or leave his spouse, or to avoid the continuing financial obligation of raising her children, he may refuse to recognize the offspring she bears. This pattern of men preserving the opportunity of denying paternity is consistent with the value concerning the independence of males. The related part is that the mother-child bond is thought to be durable; mothers are said to be respected above all other persons, and there is a greater emphasis on matrifiliation than patrifiliation.[11]

Once again, then, the conceptions the people hold about kinship relationships and their choice of conjugal unions are influenced by concepts which encompass more than the familial domain. Further, how a male puts these ideas into practice depends very much on whether he and his sexual partner are co-resident.

The juridical statuses of the two partners also differ by type of connubial union. The difference among the three forms concerns separations. A *juntado* union is dissolved by physical separation of the partners. I heard of no cases of civil divorce, but they are possible to obtain and, according to the people, cost about $80.[12] Normally two partners married by the state who wish to separate do so without legal formalities. A valid religious bond may not be dissolved, although a few people feel that such a divorce may be obtained at great expense. One tells of the time she asked a priest about a divorce. He responded: 'When you can take a cup of coffee with cream and separate it into two cups with coffee and cream in each, you can have a divorce.'

The males' interpretation of these rules is as follows. It is said that a church-married wife always retains certain rights over her husband. If a man, married in the church, leaves his wife and lives with a second woman, his first wife retains full rights to his property and labour. For example, if a deserted wife falls sick, by going to the mayor in Santiago she can compel her husband to care for her, even if she too has a second partner. More importantly, when the man dies, all his wealth, even if it was built up by his common-law mate, can be claimed by his church-married wife.

According to the men, then, the legal rights concerning separations do influence which type of union is chosen. A *juntado* union, unlike a church marriage, leaves a man legally free. But a male rarely has a sizable amount of property in his name. More important, a civil-married wife has exactly the same property rights as a church-married one, but this aspect of the law is not recognized by the men. The only difference between the church and state forms is that a civil union may be legally dissolved; yet no one had even heard of cases of state divorce.[13] Thus, the legal statuses of the partners in a church and civil marriage are equivalent and in practical terms not much different from their statuses in a *juntado* union.

The argument proposed by the men concerning the legal rights of church-married wives is valid but not convincing since it omits the facts concerning the legal rights of civil-married spouses, since civil divorces are never sought, and since men rarely have fortunes which can be lost. In sum, it is not only the juridical rights of a church marriage which lead males to prefer state or *juntado* unions, but what these rights represent. This leads us to an examination of the specifically religious aspects of the marital bond, for it is these which lie behind the folk reasoning about the legal rights.

Fundamentally a church marriage differs from the other two forms in that it adds a lasting, sacred bond to the relationship, and it is primarily this enduring spiritual tie which is avoided by the countrymen.

The people, on the one hand, do feel that it is better in God's eyes to be married in church. Just as they are baptized and confirmed, and make a first confession, so they feel they should be married before God. Marriage is the 'ultimate mystery' and church-married persons die in God's grace. (Because God's forgiveness is valued, some religious marriages *in extremus* have occurred, although it is considered a great joke if the dying spouse recovers.) But unlike baptism or confirmation which affect only the ritual status of the novitiate and his sponsors, church marriage commits two individuals to a tangible relationship.

A married pair are expected to respect each other more than are other conjugal partners. Church-married spouses should not fight, for quarrels between them are sinful. Yet since they live together, it is inevitable that such mates will fight. Moreover, the devil is thought to be especially angry when a man and woman are married before God. He is said to pursue such a pair relentlessly in order to provoke fights and cause sins. Because they fear the influence of the devil — not respecting, losing control of themselves, fighting and sinning — the people avoid the danger and the responsibility by not marrying in church.

In contrast a *juntado* union is said not to be correct in God's eyes: it is a relation the devil rules. But a common-law union does not involve spiritual obligations and the consequent possibility of a fall from God's grace. In this context, the sacraments are seen as a ladder; it is thought worse to ascend them and regress than to stop when one can go no higher. Once the obligations of a church marriage are undertaken the failure to comply with them brings castigation.

Juntado unions may be dissolved by physical separation. Effectively civil and church divorces are impossible to obtain. However, while civil-married partners may separate and join in *juntado* unions with others without receiving the disapproval of the community, church-married partners who separate become the subjects of severe criticism and are even thought to be living in spiritual danger.

The sacred tie in a church marriage also hinders a man's ability to be *facultado*. The onus for having illicit sexual relations always falls on the woman, for it is her responsibility to refuse the man, but the one who becomes involved with a married man is considered to be especially sinful. (A church-married woman who has an affair with another man is thought to be even more sinful and scandalous.) Also, since church marriages are seldom dissolved, a woman who is approached by a church-married male knows that she has little chance of forming a conjugal union with him. Thus, it is more difficult for a church-married man to find women, his rights are diminished, and this strikes at the conception men have of themselves. Indeed, it is sometimes said that church-married men are *pendejo,* the term used for a dependent and sometimes cuckolded spouse. A man, as the males point out, can never rid himself of his spiritual wife; he can never marry again.

Finally, a church marriage ties the partners down by the very fact that it adds a perpetual spiritual obligation to what is fundamentally a material and tangible relationship. A church-married spouse like a *compadre* is a sacred and perpetual partner. However, unlike the *compadre-compadre* bond the marriage tie entails definite material duties. The people's view of themselves as evading *compromisos,* as being independent persons, does not fit with the enduring demands the sacred tie involves.[14] An old maxim is 'married — tired' *(casado — cansado).*

To sum up, the statistical preferences (66 per cent common-law, 30 per cent church, 5 per cent civil) are an outcome of individuals choosing in accordance with the pulls and stresses of different values. To be a man a male must be independent and without *compromisos,* and one way he can exhibit this manliness is by having sexual freedom. Precisely because it adds an unbreakable sacred bond to his conjugal mate and a tie to her children, a church marriage is the antithesis of this ideal. Also, as a manifestation of the sacred tie a church marriage is expensive and requires that a man pay more respect to his wife. On the other hand, a religious marriage is the ideal of the church and state, and such a bond is respected within the community. Men also exhibit their financial independence by undertaking a religious marriage.[15] Additionally, a church union is desired by most women in that it represents a commitment to them. An obligated husband legitimates his wife's sexual powers and implies that he considers her an embodiment of the feminine ideal. The more than two-to-one choice of common-law over church marriage, then, attests to the relative weight of these ideals and the dominant male position.

Civil marriages stand somewhere between church and common-law unions. Normally they are undertaken when the female partner is young and her father would object to her leaving, when the woman wants some legal protection in the union, or more rarely, as a compromise, when the female wants a church marriage and her mate wants a *juntado* union. In terms of legal rules a state marriage is like a church union in that it jurally binds a man to support his wife and children. Nevertheless, civil unions are entered somewhat more readily than church marriages and the people paradoxically consider them to be almost equal to *juntado* unions.[16] The sole difference between a church and state union is the enduring religious bond. The comparative acceptance of state marriages, then, re-enforces the point that it is primarily the conceptual obligation — the perpetual sacred tie — which the males and some of the females wish to avoid.[17] And this desire itself is a product of the countrymen's ideas about what the male and female person are.

Polygyny, extra-residential liaisons and prostitutes

In addition to the co-residential types, other forms of mating relationship are practised. Polygyny is considered to be a kind of conjugal bond. Extra-residential unions and relations with prostitutes in the community also resemble connubial ties but both these relationships stretch the male-female bond too far to be considered conjugal unions. To gain a better understanding of what constitutes a conjugal relationship it is useful to examine these mating forms and the reasons for their infrequent selection.

Polygyny is found in various forms. One man travels back and forth between a spouse in the community and a mate in a neighbouring village. Each has her own home and is supported by the man. Except for possible occasional paramours, the women reserve their attentions for him and do not receive money from other males. Each is spoken of as his 'companion', the term used for a spouse. Similarly, in one reported case a man maintained five women simultaneously. The houses of his spouses were located on the same plot of land, but each female had her own kitchen and bedroom. The five co-operated in some of their domestic functions; while some cooked, others washed. In yet another case of polygyny, three women shared a single kitchen but had separate bedrooms.

Although the three cases of polygyny differ, they have a common factor: all conform to co-residential couples prohibition. The women in a polygynous union may have complete houses in separate locations; they may have complete households on the same site; or they may be located on the same plot and share a kitchen while maintaining separate sleeping quarters. But the rule that only one conjugal couple may

PLATE 5   *Listening to lottery*
             results at midday

PLATE 6   *Sweeping the patio*

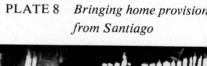

PLATE 8   *Bringing home provision*
             from Santiago

LATE 7   *Sorting and cleaning rice*

PLATE 9 *Making one's own leather sandals*

PLATE 10 *Washing clothes a brook*

PLATE 11 *Near an old-style fireplace at grandmother's house*

occupy a house is observed in that each female has her own sleeping quarters. The distinctness of each matri-unit is maintained, and each polygynous spouse is mistress of the internal domain of her home.

Polygyny, therefore, is a conjugal variation which is consonant with the rules governing connubial relations and the values of being a man. Why is it infrequently practised? In the first place, the economic demands on the polygynous male are heavy, and it is often difficult for a man to work out the interrelations of his polygynous spouses. Furthermore, a man is not considered to be more masculine if he has several mates. Moreover, if his women live in separate locations, a man runs the constant risk of being cuckolded, since he cannot keep watch over all of them.

Plural unions are not attractive to most women. The female does not have the full backing of her mate, and this is a reflection on her womanhood. The polygynous female is also is in a precarious position, for she can easily slip into being classed as a prostitute, if her mate does not visit her frequently.

An extra-residential liaison, although resembling a polygynous union, stretches the male-female tie too far to be considered a conjugal bond. Extra-residential partners are not thought to be in a *juntado* relationship and are not called 'companions'. No term is used to refer to an extra-residential bond but several factors differentiate such liaisons from other heterosexual ties. The relationship involves some reciprocal aid; to some degree the man provisions the woman's house, and she fulfils some but not all of his domestic needs. The male focuses his sexual attentions upon the female, and she maintains sexual constancy to him. Offspring normally are recognized as being descended from both partners; they are not accidents from affairs in the street. The children, however, usually live with the mother. Although extra-residential relationships are not considered to be common-law unions, they are not far different. Indeed, if 'birth-status rights' were considered the attribute of a union, extra-residential ties would be a type of conjugal bond.

The one case of an extra-residential relationship occurs in a household which contains three generations of females and a baby male. The eldest woman had several spouses, some of whom were extra-residential mates. Her fifty-year-old daughter maintained an extra-residential liaison with a now dead man of a neighbouring community. The daughter's daughter, Delmira, is a recognized offspring of this relationship. She, in turn, maintains an extra-residential liaison with a man who lives outside the community, but he helps support Delmira and her son, who is his recognized offspring.

A comparison of Delmira's situation with that of Antonina, a single girl, illustrates the people's recognition of and expectations about an extra-residential bond. Antonina formed a relationship with a man by whom she had a child. Shortly after, the man departed and Antonina returned to the home of her parents. She, then, proceeded to meet a number of men in the community and left her child to be partially raised by her parents. At one point she formed a brief co-residential union with another male. Throughout, Antonina spoke of her distant mate as if she still had a continuing relationship with him, and, at times, he did send her money. The people, however, classify Antonina and Delmira quite differently. It would be difficult, they say, for a male to get Delmira to leave her house, and she is the head of her own home. Antonina, by contrast, lives in her father's house. She 'does it for a cigarette' with anyone, and is therefore 'valueless'. Delmira has a recognized extra-residential union; Antonina meets none of the expectations and does not.

The low frequency of extra-residential relationships is a result of several factors. Occupation and demographic circumstances do not necessitate the formation of such ties. The men usually are farmers, and a man's work normally does not require him to live outside the community. Delmira's mate does have a salaried job some distance from the community, but there is nothing to prevent her from joining him. Conversely, few men in the village would wish to be supported by a woman who has a job in Panama City. Thus, demographic and occupational factors alone do not account for even the relatively infrequent extra-residential liaisons which are found.

The extra-residential relationship offers few advantages. Some men and women do prefer the greater freedom which an extra-residential relationship affords, and it is a respectable bond which permits them to live independently. On the negative side, the man is obliged to undertake some of the responsibilities of a *juntado* union, while he must forgo having all his domestic needs satisfied, and the male is unable to ensure his spouse's constancy. For her part the woman loses having the full material assistance of a *juntado* union, and she must always do some provisioning herself. Yet, if she does not want to be classed as a prostitute, she must refrain from using her most valuable resource. The women in an extra-residential relationship, like polygynous spouses, find themselves in a precarious role and few choose this course.

Some women in the community subsist by selling their sexual services. I term such females 'prostitutes', but their role is slightly ambiguous. On the one hand, they are not equivalent to urban prostitutes. On the other, though they do sell their services, their position borders upon that of the extra-residential, polygynous and even *juntado* mate. It is precisely because relationships with such women contain but attentuate many of the elements of a conjugal bond that they are of interest.

Prostitutes in the community collect for their services, charging from $0.25 to $1.00, less than in Santiago. They entertain men in their own homes but do not have a specific locale set aside solely for business use. A village prostitute is called *la zorra* (fox, prostitute), or *la camaronera* (shrimp), the latter term applied because 'like shrimps they do not have a specific place for doing it'. Lower price, lack of a special room and independence are three of the factors which distinguish prostitutes in the community from those in Santiago.

The prostitute role need not be permanently affixed to a female. Some assume the role after they have been separated from or lost a spouse; several in *juntado* unions were prostitutes in the recent past. The role is taken on because single women in the community have few other lucrative opportunities open to them.

The ambiguity in the prostitute role arises for several reasons. First, because the prostitute has many kin ties in the village, she is not strictly a businesswoman. Certain partners are sexually prohibited. In addition, because recognition of the filial bond is not linked to a conjugal relationship, sexual relations alone can give rise to kinship ties. Moreover, because having sexual relations always implies that a couple could form a conjugal union, a relation with a prostitute can give rise to quasi-ties of step-parenthood. Further, a man's relations with a prostitute can be sporadic or regular to the point of monogamy, and since residence can be an ambiguous marker of the conjugal bond, the prostitute can easily slip into the role of conjugal spouse. At times, therefore, it becomes difficult to distinguish between the statuses of prostitute and spouse. Some examples illustrate the ambiguities.

One of the community's prostitutes had a man living in her house for a period of about ten days. The man performed the normal domestic duties of all mates, such as bringing home firewood. One day as I was sitting with Jaime at his store, one of the prostitute's young daughters was playing in front. The prostitute's 'spouse' came to make a purchase, and as he was leaving he turned to the daughter and told her, in the tones of a father, to come home. After he left, Jaime jokingly turned to the daughter and told her to obey her 'papa'. In a similar vein he referred to the man as a 'transitory husband'. The prostitute herself had never previously acquired a mate, so Jaime's designation of the man as transitory was based on the expectation that he would leave shortly, which he did. In contrast, other couples who formed co-residential relations lasting no longer were considered to have been in true *juntado* unions. In the case of this woman, then, there was no clear way to distinguish between her roles as prostitute and as *juntado* spouse, and the lack of definition gave rise to joking.

Two other examples concern the nature and definition of step-parenthood. Filiation, as seen, is not necessarily linked to a conjugal bond, but step-filiation is. A step-child is the prior offspring of a spouse, and a step-parent is a succeeding spouse of a parent. Unlike filiation, then, step-filiation is an indirect and involuntary relationship which is dependent upon the recognition of a conjugal bond. The connubial tie in turn is characterized by co-residence of the partners.

Many years ago Virgilio used to visit Josefina, a single woman. While maintaining his own household he carried on a steady relationship with her. Some time later Virgilio's eldest son, Crispin, went to Josefina to purchase her services. But she refused him, saying she felt she could be his step-mother and relations between them would be incestuous. Technically Josefina would be Crispin's step-mother only if she had participated in a recognized union with Virgilio; and as I shall explain sexual relations would be prohibited between her and Crispin only if he had grown up in a house with her. In her eyes, however, the prolonged affair she had had with Virgilio bordered on, or was equal to, a recognized conjugal bond. Josefina did not distinguish between the relation of prostitute and that of affinity.

In an earlier chapter I cited the case of Carlos who some years previously carried on a prolonged extra-conjugal affair with Luisa. In one sense Luisa was a prostitute, and Carlos was purchasing her services. It should be recalled, however, that their relationship became a diffuse exchange. After a time Carlos did not directly and immediately pay Luisa but allowed her to run up a credit bill in his name at a local store. In essence he partially provisioned her home just as a male spouse provides for his mate. At the time of fieldwork Luisa was in a co-residential relationship with another man. Her eldest daughter, Aminta, who was a pretty, young woman, lived with her. Carlos, somewhat jokingly, used to make advances toward Aminta. She would tell him, however, to respect her, for she could be his step-daughter. Carlos would retort that it meant nothing that he had visited her mother's house. Strictly speaking, Carlos was not Aminta's step-father and sexual relations were not prohibited between them since he and Aminta had not lived in the same house. But there was some ambiguity as to whether a familial or business link had been formed, and again the ambiguity of the borderline case produced joking.

My central concern in this chapter has been to describe the types of connubial relationships which are recognized and to show how these are connected to the concept of the household. This theme, however, raised the problem of defining a conjugal union. My approach has been to view connubial arrangements within the broader domain of all male-female bonds. Each of the ties distinguished by the people may be seen as a particular configuration of rights and obligations ranged along a scale of man-woman relationships. A conjugal bond consists of one such package; its distinguishing mark is co-residence. But the elements which comprise it do not always occur together nor are they exclusive to it. Furthermore, the differences among the relationships are not always discrete. The different types of bonds are summarized schematically in Table 9.

All of the male-female relationships, including courtship, are distinguished from other bonds by the fact that sexual and economic services are exchanged. In courtship a man may provide gifts or even money to his 'friend' but there is no stated obligation concerning the amount. The relationship is diffuse, enduring and is balanced in the long run. A friend usually lives in her father's house, although she also may be a household head if she already has had a conjugal union and separated.

A prostitute is clearly labelled. Conceptually, prostitute-buyer bonds are distinguished from courtship by the precise economic duties involved. A relation with a prostitute is short-term and contractual; the male must provide a specified payment for the services he receives. Also, a prostitute is a household head. Both courtship and prostitute-buyer relationships may result in offspring being born to the woman. If children are born, the man may or may not recognize them, but even if he does so, this fact does not transform the relationship into a conjugal union. Nevertheless, despite their differences, since a man does pay something to his friend, and since she may have several lovers and even be a household head, the real difference between the friend and the

TABLE 9 Forms of heterosexual relationship

Rights and obligations	Type of Bond							
	The unrelated	Courtship	Prostitute-buyer	Extra-residential liaison	Polygyny	Common-law union	State marriage	Church marriage
Woman provides sexual services		X	X	X	X	X	X	X
Man has specified economic obligations			X	X	X	X	X	X
Sexual constancy expected*				X	X	X	X	X
Partial co-residence: partial division of labour					X	X		
Complete co-residence: woman undertakes domestic functions; man provisions completely							X	X
Legal bond							X	X
Sacred bond								X

* With the provision that the man is free to find women in the street.

prostitute may be only in the mind of the lover.

An extra-residential liaison is distinguished from a prostitute-buyer relationship in several ways: a degree of sexual constancy is expected of both partners, there is some economic co-operation between them, and the offspring of the woman normally are recognized by the man. An extra-residential female mate, then, is something more than a prostitute but not quite a spouse. She is not called a companion. Nevertheless since both the prostitute and the extra-residential mate are separately domiciled as household heads, a relationship which begins as a prostitute-buyer exchange can easily shift into an extra-residential liaison and vice versa. Or it can contain elements of both as in the case of Carlos and Luisa. Further, the actual difference between the extra-residential mate and the friend may not be great as in the cases of Delmira and Antonina.

A polygynous union is considered by the people to be a conjugal relationship as signified by the fact that the partners are termed companions. The distinguishing characteristic of the relationship is its residential basis, although the partners are not continuously co-resident. It is thought that the man should provide the house for the woman. The fact that the partners are at least partially co-resident means that the man must totally provision the home, the woman must provide domestic and sexual services when required, and the children normally are recognized as being the offspring of both. Nevertheless, since common-law unions have no community rites to mark their inception or termination, the partners in a polygynous union are in ill-defined roles, especially if the females reside in separate locations (and perhaps have even provided their own homes if they had previous spouses). With a slight shift in emphasis on the obligations, one of the polygynous spouses may easily come to be considered an extra-residential mate or even a prostitute.

Juntado or common-law unions are based upon complete co-residence; there is only one household and one locus of authority. The unitary residence implies total economic and sexual interdependence, with the proviso that the man is free to seek sexual partners in the street. The male usually recognizes the offspring of his female mate, although he is not required to do so. Both partners are termed companions. None the less, *juntado* unions can resemble the other forms if they are of short duration.

State marriage differs from the *juntado* union in that it adds a legal bond to the relationship. The primary consequence is that the children are legitimate and at birth are indelibly linked to the husband-father, if he and his wife are co-resident at the time. Legal divorces are never sought, although separations are common.

A church marriage adds an unbreakable sacred tie to the legal obligations of a civil marriage. Separations of church-married couples are neither expected nor common. The male's extra-marital sexual adventures are limited by the bond. Only church and state unions are termed 'marriage'; the partners are 'companions', and husband and wife.

Male-female relationships, then, always consist of the exchange of economic and sexual services. In a conjugal union the exchange is co-residential. Food and sex, the kitchen and bedroom, together comprise a connubial relationship and a household. The conjugal tie is not defined internally with respect to the family alone; its distinguishing characteristic derives from the domain of locality.

Given this range of recognized relationships, I have been concerned to account for the varying frequencies of selection. Only one tie is an extra-residential liaison. Of the conjugal bonds only one is polygynous, the rest are *juntado,* civil or church unions. I have argued that this preference for co-residential relationships is an outcome of the values defining the male and female person. These ideals require that a man and a woman be co-resident. A man has to exhibit his *fundamento,* his basic ability to be financially independent, and he does this by maintaining a household. A woman must have shame for her sexual powers, and she manifests this by being under the authority of a male and by being a mother, which legitimates her sexuality. In the proper household a man is in the fields and a woman is at home. Other forms of household and mating relationships are recognized and permitted but are difficult to maintain.

Within the category of co-residential relationships the *juntado* form is overwhelmingly preferred, although church and civil unions also are practised. This statistical fact is the outcome on a different level of a compromise between the values held by men as ideally independent, unfettered beings and by women as creatures of shame. Given that a man exhibits his foundation by being in a co-residential relationship, then he maximizes his independence by choosing the *juntado* form. I have not yet answered, however, why only three-quarters of the household heads are in a conjugal union. Does this statistical fact undermine the proposition that the man is in the fields, the woman at home? It is to a part of this question that the next chapter is devoted.

10 Conjugal instability

Within the community there were twelve temporary or permanent conjugal separations during an eighteen-month interval. Of the co-residential unions 19 per cent were unstable. Does this statistical fact contradict the assertion that households consist of a conjugal pair plus children? The topic of this chapter is the relation of conjugal separations to family structure and household organization. The material is divided into three sections. In the first I show how conjugal instability is a reflection of ideas which are held about the person, that is, the contrasting definitions of the sexes. I then explain how a separation affects and fractures an entire household group. Finally, I show how households, after a separation, are re-constituted in accordance with the ideal patterns described.

The material in the final section, however, brings to the foreground again the theoretical issue concerning the relation between kinship and residence. The problem here is as follows. In addition to the parent-child and spouse-spouse bonds, more distant family ties may be utilized to gain and justify entry into a household. Once a distant kinsman is admitted to a house, however, his recruitment relation normally is reformulated and supplanted by a nuclear family bond. Grandparents, for example, may raise a grandson; under certain conditions they may refer to and call this child 'son', and he may reciprocate with 'mama' and 'papa'. Thus, a grandparent-grandchild link may be transformed into a parent-child one. In the orthodox view such a custom might be interpreted as an instance of fictive or metaphoric kinship. The explanation might be that since nuclear kin live together, anyone who enters a household must be a nuclear kinsman. If in fact a new entrant is not a member of the elementary family, then his real relationships must be juggled to match the ideal ones.

Such an argument rests uneasily in the Panamanian context. In the first place, the countrymen do not consider any of these reformulated bonds to be 'fictive'. On the contrary, for them such ties are nothing less than real kinship bonds. As one of their proverbs expresses it, 'He who raises is more a father than he who begets' *(Más padre el que cria que engendra)*. Furthermore, in the orthodox argument it must be assumed that kinship is 'prior' to residence, and that there is a real kinship grid after which other relationships may be patterned. Ultimately, of course, this grid has to reduce to genetic ties or to social ideas about biological relationships. I have already shown, however, that a purely genetic description of the people's kinship system would be incorrect. If, then, we reject the idea that these reformulated bonds are fictive kinship, what are they, and what is kinship? My own view — again — is that kinship in Los Boquerones is formed partly on the idea of biological relationships; but such ties also must be recognized, expressed and made manifest in households: kinship is compounded of both genetics and residence. Therefore, in the case of the reformulated bonds it is quite understandable that common household membership alone may give rise to ties of kinship. The material brings us to one of the extremes in the definition of kinship: the genetic component is submerged and the residential element is stressed.

Conjugal instability

Conjugal separations are unmarked, occurring at a moment's notice. Communal rites are not used to recognize or formalize a separation, and a dissatisfied partner gives little advance warning to the other or to outsiders, although it is usually evident when strains between a pair exist. Most separations occur between *juntado* partners.[1]

Several factors make it easy for two partners to separate, although these factors are not causes. In the first place, given the lack of valuables and property a couple never have to stay together in order to preserve an estate for their legitimate children, and what property there is, easily can be divided. The partners themselves usually have little to gain materially by maintaining their bond, for the essence of a union is that it is an exchange of economic and sexual services. As long as persons shift from mate to mate, they are assured of receiving the requisite services. Second, conjugal unions are not perpetual alliances between two groups, nor does the connubial relationship usually have the enduring sacred bond added to it. Third, the pattern of conjugal instability is related to the manner in which disputes are settled in the community. When non-residents argue, they express their displeasure by not talking to one another; they withhold social recognition. When two mates fight, they often do not resolve their differences through an exchange of views but simply separate.

The *campesinos* provide a number of explanations for why couples separate. Men, they say, leave their spouses when the latter fail to fulfil their tasks. Males have been known to become irritated when their clothes were not mended within a reasonable time or no hot meal was awaiting them upon returning from a day's work in the fields. Such minor grievances may not be the underlying reasons why men leave their mates, but it is appropriate that separations are explained in this idiom. Because the conjugal relationship is built upon an exchange of services, non-fulfilment of these tasks strikes at the foundation of the union.

Men themselves cite various reasons for changing mates. Some like to change women or a man may fall in love with another female and wish to change partners, although if he has children he may be reluctant to do so. Conversely, when a man's spouse is unfaithful to him, he is the subject of mild ridicule. The cuckolded male, who is aware of his spouse's activities, can fight the lover and beat his mate, he can leave, or he can do both. Usually, a man becomes mad and threatens to fight his rival, but then decides to split up with his spouse.

Men also have their explanations for why women leave. They see the love of a woman as being impermanent. A man, they say, always maintains control of his emotions. A woman should, but often does not, look after herself *(cuidarse)*. According to the men, women leave a house because it is in them to wander.

Women, too, express their reasons for leaving spouses, and their explanations also are voiced in terms of ideal expectations. A woman may decide to leave if her spouse is irresponsible and does not provide well. Sometimes a female decides not to countenance the amorous behaviour of her mate. (It is added, however, that if a man spends money in the street but fulfils his obligations at home, a woman has less right to desire a separation; and often a woman will suffer much in order to provide a home for her children.) If a man becomes excessively protective and jealous, he may force his spouse to stay at home, to see few other people and to fulfil all her obligations in the house to the letter. This, too, can drive a woman to leave. Women, like men, also fall in love with others and depart.

If one looks not at the voiced reasons but at the pattern of leaving, an important statistical fact emerges: it is the women who initiate and carry out the separations. Of the twelve separations that occurred while

I was in the community, eleven were originated by females. A generation ago, before the highway was built, women left their spouses and
either returned to their natal homes or went to nearby towns and
sought work. Today a frequent pattern is for them to flee to Panama
City, contact a friend or relative there, and find a domestic job. The
pattern of women leaving has not changed over time, but better
transportation has given them more choice about where to go, and the
lure of the city draws them there. Why is it, then, that it is the women
who usually leave?

The pattern becomes comprehensible when viewed in the context of
the opposing male and female ideals. Men are *facultado:* by right they
are not tied to the house socially or sexually. Furthermore, if a woman
demands too much of her spouse she may be beaten or he may become
even more assertive in his sexual behaviour to reassert his masculinity.
By contrast, a woman is expected to stay at home, raise her family and
preserve her sexual purity. Females view their life within the community as being hard, in the sense that they have an unrelenting series
of demands placed on them. Against her spouse, however, a woman has
two offsetting powers. She may cuckold him, or she may leave him; of
the two, women most frequently choose the latter course, departing
either temporarily or permanently. In the city a woman can redefine
her role; at the same time her leaving may serve as a lever upon her
spouse, for a female may make her return contingent upon certain
concessions. Indeed, even when they are not going, women often
discuss the possibility of moving.

Economic factors, it is true, do play a part in this pattern. Both the
Canal Zone and Panama City populations provide women with opportunities for domestic work. By contrast, men have many inducements
to stay in the community and few to attract them to the city. Occasionally some males do go and find jobs working for a construction
firm or selling ice cream in the streets, but few openings are available,
and men do not spend much time speculating about finding work in the
city. However, this economic context provides only a support structure
for the basic concepts which orientate males and females in their
respective directions. A generation ago women did not have such
lucrative opportunities, yet they too would flee their mates.

The case of Eufemia and Jaime provides a graphic example of a
temporary separation and illustrates clearly how some of the ideas
about the person affect and sometimes are in opposition to a stable
conjugal bond. Jaime is hard working and energetic. He owns a store

and continually tries new ventures including a large fowl project. As a result of his endeavours Jaime provides well. In addition, he is one of the few leaders of the community. He is president of the school committee, assists in running the chapel, is the spearhead of the small agricultural co-operative in the village, and helps administrate the overall organization of co-operatives which reaches into several communities of the province. With all these interests he is often away from the house for over a day.

Eufemia, Jaime's spouse, is the oldest of nine siblings and half-siblings. Because her father, who is now quite old, has so many children to support, and because she and Jaime have no children of their own, they have taken in three of Eufemia's half-siblings. Jaime supports the children and treats them with affection; he also pays for the eldest to go to secondary school in Santiago, an act few can afford and one that is scarcely expected of a foster parent.

In other respects, however, Jaime is not a model spouse. He is quick-tempered and at times drinks heavily. He can be stubborn and dictatorial. He is co-operative but also independent. Eufemia often has had to run the store from morning to night, feed the 500 chickens, and undertake all the normal domestic duties, including providing her brother with a fresh white shirt for school each day. Eufemia was pushed by her natal family to accept these duties because Jaime aided her father. But she was not happy. She was jealous of Jaime, resenting the fact that she had to care for the chickens and store, while suspecting him of spending money on other women and alcohol.

One New Year's morning Jaime returned drunk from a gathering of his friends. Eufemia, who was at the store, commented publicly to Jaime about his late hours, his drinking, and his spending money. Jaime grew angry, asserted he would not be bound by any woman, and then hit Eufemia in the mouth and knocked her down. Almost immediately he fell asleep, and Eufemia fled to her parents' house, taking her belongings. Her father tried to convince her to return to Jaime as she was his only hope. But early the next morning Eufemia departed for Panama City where she immediately found domestic work with an ex-employer.[2]

Over the next few months while Eufemia was away, Jaime's household deteriorated. His agricultural work fell behind and he had to hire labourers to work in the fields while he stayed at home, cooking and tending the store. Even then Jaime did not have time to stock his store well. His plans for the coming agricultural year became more modest.

Jaime drank more and looked haggard. He admitted to some that his head hurt. He made discreet inquiries about Eufemia to find out if she had another man and if she intended to return, but he did not contact her directly. If passers-by asked about Eufemia, Jaime would say that she was visiting elsewhere. Significantly, Eufemia's half-siblings remained at Jaime's house and the relationship between Jaime and Eufemia's family was unaffected. In fact, Eufemia's father hoped that she would return. He did not castigate her but his sympathies lay with Jaime. After a time Jaime secretly went to a *yerbero* (herb doctor) in a town some fifty miles away and requested him to make up a potion that would work on Eufemia from a distance and entice her to return. Jaime ridicules those who believe in native curers, and it was symptomatic of his position that he was forced to resort to such aid. He is a proud man and it would have been at considerable cost to himself had he fetched Eufemia from the city.

More than two months after she left, Eufemia returned; she announced immediately, however, that her belongings were still in Panama City and that she had come only for a visit, for she had grown lonely for her friends in the village. Her employer had told her, so Eufemia said, that he wanted her to stay and that if Jaime were brusque with her again, she should return.

Shortly after her return Eufemia extracted some concessions from Jaime. One activity which falls in the domain of women's work is the sorting of the peeled rice. The man who is found doing such an activity may be laughed at for being under the domination of his spouse. Nevertheless, one day shortly after Eufemia's return, I came across Jaime sorting rice; and others also remarked upon seeing him doing this work. Later Jaime took more part in caring for the chickens and tending the store. Temporarily, at least, Eufemia was able to extract concessions and negotiate a re-allocation of duties. As time went on she stayed and sent for her belongings in Panama City.

The means which Eufemia used to achieve a better domestic situation were extreme, although she did not go so far as to cuckold Jaime, and of course some women leave permanently and do not use the separation as a lever against their spouses. None the less, the case illustrates how as persons live up to the ideals of being a male and a female the conjugal bond can become polarized. Both Jaime and Eufemia are in some respects 'models' of the male and female, but their maleness and femaleness conflicted with their connubial tie. The reason why it is women in particular who run away can be better understood by viewing more closely the position of men.

Men rarely leave their homes angrily for more than a few hours. Only if his spouse has been having an affair with another man is a male likely to initiate a breakup, and even then she rather than he will leave the household, for she will join her new mate. Men have other means for handling conjugal difficulties. Dissatisfied males can increase their activities in the street, or they can provoke their spouses to leave. For example, Edilberto and Matilde were *juntado* for a number of years and together accumulated some agricultural and household property. Matilde, everyone agrees, was an exceptional spouse. Edilberto, however, fell in love with a young woman, Ceferina, who was living with another man. Ceferina agreed to leave her mate, and Edilberto set about giving Matilde a difficult time. He began to fight with her and to hit her with a strap. Finally, one *fiesta* day he locked her in the house. Eventually, Matilde left for Panama City, leaving behind her common property. She is still bitter about the treatment she received, while Edilberto is happily settled with Ceferina and his property.

Regardless of who leaves, the woman often ends up with the original house. If the couple separate and the woman takes the children and has no place to live, then she may go to the legal authorities in Santiago to enjoin support for her offspring. The law invariably sides with the female, forcing the man to leave the home to his spouse and to build a new one for himself.

Thus, the pattern of women running away from and then returning or not to their mates is not indicative of 'disorganization' in the conjugal relationship but is an aspect of the tendency toward opposition which is built into the bond. Women leave when they wish to end a conjugal union, whereas men incite their mates to go when they want to terminate the relationship. But it is the female who feels the pressure most and the need to flee. Yet, those who do go and then return explain that they came back because they missed their children; and those who do not go claim that they stay only for the sake of their offspring. Men have a weaker tie with their children, but they do not flee from the conjugal bond in the same way. This pattern of separations, however, poses a paradox. Normally a man, to preserve his sense of independence, wants a common-law union, while a woman desires a sanctified bond. It is the women, however, who can take advantage of the non-formal tie. If a man is willing to be married in the church, then his very commitment lessens the likelihood that his wife will want to leave him.

Children, money and property

The severance of a conjugal tie results in more than the physical relocation of the two partners, for rights concerning the children and property also must be re-allocated. It is considered better if the children stay with their mother. Nevertheless, there is no absolute rule that the children must accompany their mother, and, in fact, various options exist. For each child there is a series of eligible guardians. The mother has the principal responsibility, followed by the father, then the two sets of grandparents and finally more distant kin. Who raises a child depends upon the specific situation. One case may illustrate this.

Artemio was *juntado* with Aminta for several years. Aminta already had borne a daughter to a prior mate, and together she and Artemio had a son. Aminta's daughter lived with Aminta's mother, the child's grandmother. When Artemio and Aminta separated they returned to their respective natal homes. The question arose: where would their baby son go? Because Aminta wanted to keep her liberty, and Artemio wanted to avoid making monthly support payments for his child, Artemio took their son with him to his own parents' home where, in effect, it was raised by his parents.

In other situations a child lives with one parent during the school year and stays with the other for the summer months. Or, a child may live with one parent while he is young and live with the other when he grows older. Siblings also may be split up between the ex-partners.

Statistically, of the 185 junior household members in the community, 132 or 71 per cent live with both their recognized parents.[3] Of the rest 28 (15 per cent) live with their mothers, while seven (4 per cent) live with their fathers. Nine children (5 per cent) live with their maternal grandparents, and 1 (0.5 per cent) lives with his paternal grandparents. Eight children (4 per cent) live with other persons. The statistics reflect the strength of the matrifilial as opposed to the patrifilial bonds (20 per cent vs. 4.5 per cent).

If his children do not live with him, a father legally is obliged to support them if the mother requests. Support payments are made monthly and are usually $5. The father delivers the money to a judge in Santiago and the mother collects it there. A man may find this obligation hard to fulfil during the winter months. In a few cases, after several months of default the authorities summoned the father and imprisoned him for a short time. If both the parents live in the community and there is no discord between them, they may reach an informal agreement concerning the father's obligations. At intervals the father may deliver some money directly to the mother or take a child for several months of the year. Ordinarily a father's obligation to support a non-resident child does not cease until the offspring is fifteen to eighteen years old, the age at which he can support himself.

When a separation occurs, whoever remains in the house keeps with him the major portion of the household goods, such as cooking utensils, benches, stored rice, and even the chickens. The internal domain stays intact. Crops in the field and rights to use the *monte* remain with the man. The goods that each brought to the union mostly go back to the original owner. If the woman had brought some cattle, the original animals as well as most of the progeny would be returned to her, but the man would keep a few of the issue as payment for raising them. This partition of goods upon a separation is consonant with the pattern of endowing children with property when they first leave their natal households. Property is held individually and is parted when households divide.

Household re-formation

Concepts about the individual and the household, I have argued, lead to the idea that houses should be occupied by elementary families. Yet, in this chapter I also have suggested that these same concepts lead to conjugal instability. Surely, if households are so easily and frequently broken up, most households cannot consist of nuclear families. Does my argument contradict itself? The answer is no, but a further facet of conjugal instability must now be considered: after a separation households are re-constituted in accordance with the concepts concerning the individual. This re-formation of households may be seen in two ways.

In the first place, the remnants of an old household do not long remain an incomplete group; they join other units or bring in new members to form a complete household. Thus, although there was a relatively high degree of conjugal instability in the village during eighteen months, in this same interval the total number of household groups remained almost constant. Numerically, of the twenty-four persons involved in the twelve separations, sixteen rejoined their original partners or combined with new ones. Four affiliated themselves with other households. Only four people constituted household remnants, and all four were actively searching for partners to complete their units. Household remnants have difficulty existing precisely because they lack the appropriate economic organization.

In the second place, when households recruit new members and reconstitute themselves, their new organization is patterned after the model of the nuclear family according to the ideal specifications. Indeed, ties within a household are not only likened to those of the elementary family, they are sometimes deliberately re-formed to be nuclear family bonds. Common residence can lead to the recognition of new kinship ties. To show how households and kinship bonds are re-formed, I examine the institutions of adoption, fostering and step-parenthood, and the forms of sibling relations and extensions of the incest prohibition which result from them.

Adoption and fostering

I use the terms 'adoption' and 'fostering' to refer to those situations when a child is raised by one or more older persons as if he were an offspring but is not the legitimate, recognized or natural child of either adult. The people use the term adoption *(la adopción)* to describe the institution when it is legally recognized by the state. Fostering, which is more common, describes the practice when it is not legally sanctioned. The two institutions are similar but not equivalent.

The occasions which give rise to adoption and fostering are various. Adoption and fostering occur when children are left as orphans. In addition, if a house has too many children and they cannot all be maintained, some of them may be sent away to be raised in another home. Fostering most frequently occurs when conjugal partners separate and between them cannot maintain all their children.

Household groups which adopt or foster children usually do so when they have no children themselves, for a childless couple often wants children to make the home 'happier'. Children run errands and provide company. Being 'little angels' they help keep the devil away, and the house itself gains more respect in the eyes of others when it is a complete unit. Most importantly, children bring an 'interest' to the adults; the new parents have something for which to work. Children are said to give a household faith and greater stability.

Adoption and fostering are not practised to provide a man or woman with an inheritor or successor, nor are they practised to forge a bond between two unrelated household groups. Indeed, the fostered child may sever his ties with his old household, and between a child's recognized parents and his foster parents there is no special relation-ship; the two couples only should pay a little more respect to one another. Also, children are not adopted in order to increase the size of the household, for larger families gain no more social or economic benefits than smaller ones. Statistically, of the 185 children in the community there were 21 cases of adoption and fostering, or 11 per cent of the junior members were adopted or fostered.

Legal adoption itself is infrequently practised; only one child in the community was adopted. In order to adopt a child, one or both of the adopting parents must go to court and register the child in their names. The parent(s) giving up the child must, of course, cede him. Through legal adoption the adopter expresses his obligation to raise the child and assures that the original parent has no further claims to the child. The surname of the child is changed to that of his adopting parent. If there is an inheritance, adoption gives the child rights to the property equal to those of his recognized siblings. In one case two adults said that they intended to adopt their granddaughter who lives with them so that she could inherit their cinder-block house instead of their own grown children.

In fostering one or two adults take a child into their home without jural sanction from the state. No ceremonies announce or distinguish the institution. Nevertheless, in the countryside it is considered perfectly legal. The people refer to this practice as 'raising' *(criar)* a child.

In cases of fostering it is necessary to distinguish the recruitment relationship from the ensuing one. The recruitment bond is the link used to justify bringing a person into a household. Almost invariably it is a kinship tie. Different types of such links are used: sibling, grandparent or parental sibling ties. Which option is utilized depends on the circumstances of the case. Of the 20 fostered children, 13 were with grandparents, 3 with a half-sister on the paternal side, and 2 with more distant kin. One was a godchild, and only one had no relation to the members of the fostering household.

Once a child has been admitted to a household, the link used to justify his entry is overlaid by an elementary family tie. The uncle-nephew bond, for instance, is transformed by common residence into the father-son one. The new link supplants but does not obliterate the old. This reformulation of kinship ties derives from the people's concept of raising. I have explained that the verb 'to raise' is used in reference to things which are brought up in the household area. With respect to children, the term 'raised' is employed in both a general and a particular sense. In the general sense a child whom one brings up, regardless of whether he is a blood offspring or not, is called 'a raised child' *(un hijo criado)*. Normally, however, the people reserve the term *hijo criado* in order to refer to a child who is not the recognized offspring of the adult(s) raising him. This category, then, includes both foster and, as we shall see, step-children. Such raised children also are known as *los hijos de crianza* (breeding children), and the adults who raise them are termed *los padres de crianza* (breeding parents). By contrast, a child who is raised by his recognized parents usually is termed simply an *hijo*. (However, if a recognized child, living with his parents, has recognized siblings who do not in fact live in the same household, then the qualifier *criado* may be added when referring to him in order to distinguish him from his non-resident brothers and sisters. Recognized children who are not brought up in their parents' house are not raised children.) In direct address the terms *'crianza'* and *'criado'* are not used. A fostered child addresses the people who raise him as 'papa' and 'mama', and they reciprocate with 'son', 'daughter' or more normally the child's first name. All *criados,* whether they are genetic offspring or fostered children, have equal rights in the house-hold. As remarked, a frequently voiced proverb is, 'He who raises is more a father than he who begets.' The *crianza* or residence relationship is more important than or supersedes the genetic relationship.

An important qualification must be added to this rule. The age of the child when accepted influences the relationship he forms with the fostering adults. If a child is taken in before his puberty, the new tie is viewed as one of child to parent. He calls his new parents 'mama' and 'papa'. Older children who are fostered — ones who have begun to mature sexually and whose period of primary socialization is complete — usually do not consider the new relationship to be a child-parent tie. In this respect there is a raising period during which time a foster parent may take the place of a recognized parent. After a child has been raised, a fostering adult cannot supplant a recognized genitor who has raised his own child. The dividing point is not a specific age but the time at which a child begins physically and sexually to move away from his natal home.

A fostered child occupies a double kinship position. Fostering or raising, unlike adoption, does not entail the renunciation of one set of kinship bonds and the recognition of another, although a fostered child like anyone else may choose to deny his recognized parents.[4] Normally the fostered child carries at least one if not both of his recognized parents' surnames, and he may even call them 'papa' and 'mama'. The fostered child, then, recognizes both a constellation of genetic kin and a group of household kin. These two sets of kin are not equal in extension or importance. Household kin are limited to the roles of the elementary family. With reference to fostering the people only recognize and have terms for raised children, raising parents, and raised brothers. In addition, the newly recognized kin are further restricted in that they include only those persons who actually live in the new household with the fostered child. In practical terms which set of kin turns out to be more important depends on such factors as time spent with them, age at which fostered and so forth. Since persons normally are fostered by kinsmen, this double recognition usually presents no conceptual problems. Grandparents, for example, may become parents in addition to the 'real' parents. The rest of the recognized genetic kin, except those actually living in the grandparents' home, do not change their statuses. When queried about a fostered child's kin, the people will respond with either or both of his kinship positions, depending on the context and the particular case. In relation to his grandparents who are raising him a fostered child may be said to be a grandchild and/or a raised child.

Two conclusions may be drawn about this dual kinship position occupied by the fostered child. A fostering relationship never furnishes a child with a complete kinship personality; fostering provides a set of bonds which partly change but which also are added to an existing constellation of kin.[5] Yet, because a new set of kin becomes recognized by the fact of co-residence, because this role set is conceptually limited to those who occupy a household, and because the persons actually recognized as new kin are restricted to those who occupy the household with the fostered child, it can be concluded that co-residence may give rise to a bond of kinship.

Since the parent-child raising relationship, like the common-law conjugal tie, is based on residence, problems arise concerning recognition of the bond. In the abstract the rules are clear: the practical applications may vary. For example, many children live for a time in one household and then another. Sometimes a mother leaves her children with close relatives while her own position is uncertain and later takes them back. In such cases the children may end up having lived in the households of several different adults. A complication then arises from the social recognition of these bonds. What length of time must pass before the *crianza* relationship is constituted? In one case which occurred during the collection of census materials, a child (aged three) was living with his maternal grandparents. His mother had been living there too but at the time of the census had been away in a neighbouring community for some weeks. The grandparents referred to the child as their son. Other informants, who perhaps were not fully conversant with the situation, were emphatic that the boy was only a grandson of the old couple; there was no *crianza* relationship. In cases such as this diverse people may legitimately define a relationship differently.

Step-parents and step-children

The step-parent—step-child relationship is formed when one of a child's parents forms a co-residential union with a mate who is not the child's recognized father or mother. The new spouse and child become step-parent *(el padrastro, la madrastra)* and step-child *(el hijastro, la hijastra)*. To be a step-child an individual need not be co-resident with his parent's spouse. A child, therefore, may live with one parent and one step-parent but have another parent and step-parent in a different house. A young fostered child is always a *criado;* a step-child may or may not be a *criado*. Often the step-parent—step-child tie is the result of a conjugal separation, since the relationship is formed on the re-union of a parent. Thirty-two (17 per cent) of the junior members are step-children.

Once formed the step-parent—step-child relationship is deemed always to exist, even if the child's parent and step-parent separate. Nevertheless, the relationship may vary in importance. If a child is not resident with a parent who has entered a new union, the tie with the parent's partner may exist but never be utilized. If a child is in the same house as his step-parent the relationship with him may become a raising one.

The tie between step-parent and step-child is also a justification for bringing a new member into a household. When a conjugal bond is formed, either partner has the right to bring his children to the new home, and the other should assume parental responsibilities for his step-children. However, if a spouse brings too many children, the conjugal relationship itself may suffer; and some men refuse to raise their partner's children.

An example of step-parenthood and its relation to breeding is provided by the following case (see Figure 3). Eloisa (no. 1) and Modesto (no. 2) formed a common-law union. By a previous union Eloisa has a son who lives with his paternal grandparents. Eloisa also has

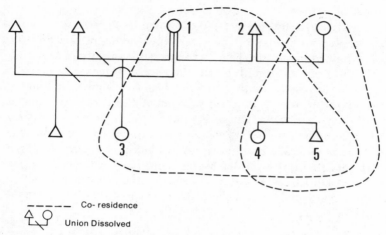

- - - - - Co- residence

Union Dissolved

FIGURE 3   *Step-parenthood, raising and the household*

a daughter (no. 3), aged fifteen, who lives with her. Modesto separated from a civil married wife by whom he has two children (nos 4 and 5), aged six and seven. Modesto's ex-wife lives in a different community which has no school, and, therefore, his two children live with him during the school year so that they can attend the school in Los Boquerones. The three children, then, live in a home with one parent and one step-parent; from this standpoint Eloisa's daughter, and Modesto's son and daughter are in symmetrically opposite positions. But their actual relationships are not equivalent. Eloisa's daughter was eleven when Eloisa joined Modesto, so she is not his raised child; she calls him by his first name. By contrast, Modesto's children, even though they live part of the time with their recognized mother, are very attached to Eloisa and she is affectionately raising them as daughter and son. For reasons we shall examine below, there is no prohibition on sexual relations between Modesto and Eloisa's daughter, but there is between Eloisa and Modesto's son.

Step-parenthood is defined by co-residence in that the step-parent must be or has to have been in a co-residential conjugal union with one of the child's parents. Given this folk definition it would appear that the concept of step-kin is both distinct from and derived from that of recognized kin. However, in some circumstances the distinction between the two may become fuzzy, and an examination of such situations sheds light on the nature of kinship for the people. Ordinarily the step-father—step-child tie is easy to define. For example, if a girl, past puberty, is taken into her step-father's house to be cared for, she is a step-daughter but not a raised daughter. If she has not reached puberty, then the girl is both a step-daughter and a raised daughter. The distinction, however, between step-parenthood and parenthood becomes blurred in the case of a man who forms a *juntado* union with a woman who is pregnant with a child that is not his biologically. Is the child his step-child or 'real' child? Invariably, because the man was co-resident with the mother, he would want to preserve his own honour and therefore would claim the child as his own. Also, as one informant put it, 'The daughter is yours really, because you raise it.' Even at the age of one, the child is almost 'yours'.[6] In such situations, co-residence of male and female or of parent and child dominates known biology in the definition of kinship.

Types of sibling bond

A correlate of the various modes of recruitment to households is that several types of sibling bond are recognized. Full siblings are offspring of the same set of parents. Half-siblings are distinguished from full siblings and from each other .according to whether they are matri- or patri-siblings *(los hermanos por la madre, los hermanos por el padre)*. Full siblings are said to be closer to each other than are half-siblings, while siblings by the mother are said to be closer than those by the father.

Two children whose parents form a conjugal union are termed 'political brothers' *(los hermanos politicos)*. They have no recognized kin tie themselves. Their relationship derives from the fact that each has a parent who is united with a parent of the other. Even if their parents split up, the bond between the political siblings endures. Political siblings are expected to respect each other, but they are not so close as either full or half-siblings. Because there are so many conjugal separations and re-unions, many individuals have several step-parents and political siblings spread throughout the community.[7] Step-relationships are not recognized beyond parents and siblings.

The word 'political' is employed in two other contexts. First, a godchild and the children of his godparent are termed 'political brothers'. Second, siblings of a parent are a person's 'carnal' aunts and uncles; their spouses are 'political' aunts and 'political' uncles. According to the people the word 'political' is used in the three relationships because in all three the partners are expected to respect each other like close family, yet there is no prohibition upon sexual relations between them. Political relationships, therefore, are thought to be desirable, for they combine the advantages of kin with the advantages of non-kin. Occasionally out of consideration an elder person is referred to as a 'political aunt' or 'political uncle'. The usage is intended to convey a closeness and lack of strain between the two, and makes clear the affect which underlies the bond.

The full-, half- and political-sibling relationships are not directly defined by co-residence. Such siblings need never occupy the same household in order that their relationship be recognized. A final sibling category, however, differentiates between co-residential and extra-residential siblings. Two children who were raised at the same time by the same parents are 'raised brothers'. They may be completely un-related, or political, patri-, matri-, or full siblings. Raised siblings are said to be closer to each other than are non-*crianza* ones. For example, two half-sisters or two political sisters who were raised together are closer than two full sisters who were not. Common household member-ship is the most significant factor in determining the importance of a sibling bond.

An example of the different types of sibling relationship is the following, Emilio lives with Amada in a common-law union (Figure 4).

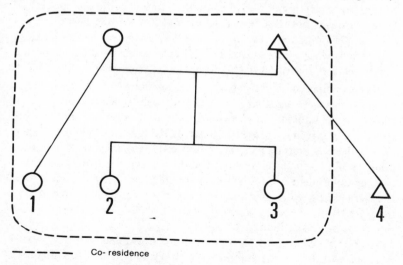

————— Co-residence

FIGURE 4 *Types of sibling bond*

Together they have two daughters (nos 2 and 3). Emilio also has a son (no. 4) by a previous union, who lives in a different community with his mother. Amada has a daughter (no. 1), born before Emilio and Amada joined together, who lives with them. The girl was born outside a conjugal union, but is recognized by another man who now has entered a church marriage. The daughter of Amada (no. 1) is a step-daughter and *criada* of Emilio, but the son of Emilio (no. 4) is only a step-son of Amada. The two children (nos 2 and 3) of Amada and Emilio are full siblings and *criada* sisters of each other. They are matri-siblings and *criada* sisters to Amada's other daughter. With the son of Emilio they are only patri-siblings. Finally, the daughter of Amada (no. 1) and the son of Emilio (no. 4) are political but not *crianza* siblings. The important distinction lies between the three co-residential sisters and Emilio's son, for the three girls are being raised in the same house. Few distinctions are made between the two full siblings and Amada's daughter by a different father.

Incest re-examined

The range of persons with whom sexual relations are prohibited is defined not only by bonds of kinship but also by ties of common residence. As explained, sexual relations with kin who are second cousins or closer is prohibited, although coition with the spouses of these persons is not. But the incest prohibition is based also upon ties of common household residence. Sexual relations are barred between two persons who are raised together or between one person and another who raises him, regardless of their original kin link.

Raised siblings should not have sexual relations with each other. It is worth re-emphasizing that this category can subsume full siblings, half-siblings, children of two parents who unite (political siblings) and completely unrelated persons. If two individuals are raised together, even if there is no traceable kin tie between them, they must treat each other as if they were close kin. The only exception is if two persons become co-resident after at least one of them has reached puberty and has learned how to respect others. In such a case, there is no bar upon sexual relations between them, but the two also would not be con-sidered to be raised siblings.

A child who is raised by a non-kinsman also may not have sexual relations with his raising parent. Manuel raises his sister's son. Manuel's spouse, Laudelina, is a political aunt to the boy and ordinarily, therefore, would be permitted to have sexual relations with him. However, since she is raising the child, sexual relations between them are prohibited, even though he does not call her 'mama', as his recognized genetic mother lives nearby.

Similarly the prohibition upon sexual relations between a step-parent and a step-child depends upon whether or not they were co-resident, but the issue can be complex. If the parents become co-resident while the offspring is young, and if the child lives with them, he is a *criado* and the interdiction is in force between child and step-parent. If the child never becomes resident in the household of his step-parent, he is not a *criado* and there is no prohibition. If the child lives in his step-parent's house but has already reached puberty when the parents join, he is not a *criado,* and sexual relations are permitted between him and his step-parent. But this last case, although clear in principle, is ambiguous in practice and is not entirely free of disapprobation. For example, one older man is living with his middle-aged step-daughter. No one is certain whether they are having sexual relations, and if they are whether or not it is proper. Years ago, the man was in a common-law union with his step-daughter's mother. At that time he helped raise two of his step-daughter's younger full siblings, and sexual relations with them are prohibited. The step-daughter, however, did not have her step-father as a breeding father, and technically sexual relations between them are permitted. But since two of her full sisters are prohibited partners, the situation is ambiguous. In any case the people point out that it is up to the woman as a female to decide whether to refuse or to accept her step-father as a sexual partner.

The ambiguity of the raising relationship and its relation to coition is further brought out by a proverb which the men recite with relish: 'Raise your own pigeon so you can eat it' *(Crié su paloma que se la come).* One level of the expression (bird = girl, eating = sex) is transparent and consciously recognized by the people. However if one can joke about raising a female in the house to eat, it can only be because her kinship status is ambiguous. The expression contrasts with the other dictum that, 'He who raises is more a father than he who begets.' Raising alone creates kinship, but admittedly there is something equivocal about it.

The key concept in this discussion of incest is *criar* (to raise), and *criar* is a concept about domesticity. As a child is raised in a home he learns to control and to direct his sexual impulses. Therefore, persons in the household group where he is raised become prohibited sexual partners. The incest prohibition is determined in part by residence.

I have focused in this chapter upon the form, reasons for, and consequences of conjugal instability. On the one hand, conjugal instability
is not evidence of a family system which is breaking down; it is linked
directly to the concepts of what a male and female are and to the
strains which follow from these complementary and sometimes opposing ideas. On the other, the fact that conjugal unions often dissolve
does not undermine the general argument that elementary families
ideally should and do live in households. Household remnants quickly
re-form themselves, and when they do their new organization is patterned
on the nuclear family. To show how this re-formation process occurs I
described the institutions of fostering and step-parenthood, and the
sibling relationships and incest prohibitions which follow from them.
This discussion led to a further examination of the links between
kinship and locality. From one perspective, residence acts upon a
pre-existing set of recognized genetic bonds: normally it is kin who are
fostered. From a second perspective, residence and genetics become
interlocked in the definition of kinship: (1) whether a fostered individual becomes a son or daughter depends on whether he or she is
raised in the household by the fostering adult; (2) whether two persons
are raised siblings depends on whether or not they were co-resident
while young; (3) two persons who have the prohibition of 'raised incest'
between them have lived in the same home. From a third perspective
residence penetrates even more deeply into the definition of kinship, as
in some cases of step-parenthood. In the situation of a step-father who
raises a child from birth, residence acts upon biology before it becomes
filiation and thus is the sole component of kinship. ·

This chapter concludes my consideration of the relation between the
family and the household group. In Appendix A statistical facts concerning households and families are presented, and the relation of the
statistics to the principles outlined is discussed. In general, households
do in fact conform to the ideal pattern of two adults plus children
living together. Not all households contain 'true' elementary families,
but most are variants of this ideal.

11 Extra-domestic kinship and affinity

Beyond his immediate household family each individual recognizes a range of bilateral kin. Genealogies are remembered to a depth of three to four generations, and the scope of recognized collaterals reaches roughly to the third-cousin level. Both lack of mobility and the fact that kin 'look' for one another lead to a connection between kinship and locality at the community or area level. Each *campesino* village consists of a dense network of kinship and affinal ties, and these bonds spill beyond the borders of a community into adjacent hamlets. Therefore, within a locality each individual bears a complex and total kinship status. Yet, paradoxically, in everyday terms, this complete system of relationships determines little of an individual's actions. Except in cases of renunciation, an individual must recognize his kinship bonds, but the relationships themselves need not be activated. In this respect, the broader kinship network provides a marked contrast to intra-household bonds. Households are largely self-sufficient and independent; within the context of the home, family ties are of utmost importance. Co-residents must fulfil their mutual obligations. By contrast, kinship and affinal links outside the household are sporadically utilized. The broader kinship network is characterized by 'ascribed optation'.

Parents and grown children

The most significant kinship bonds that a grown individual recognizes outside the household are those with his parents (or children). These relationships are flexible in that they may be increased or decreased in importance as the participants wish; they have few binding obligations attached to them.

When two young persons leave their natal homes to form a conjugal union, there is a complete realignment of authority structures, power to dispose of labour, and property ownership. A portion of each natal household is completely removed, and three independent units are formed where previously there were two. This total separation does not sever the parent-child link; parents and children always bear some responsibility towards one another. But the tie is based on the volition of the parties. At one extreme a parent or child may renounce the other and recognize no bond; at the other a parent and child may work together in a range of economic activities. Normally parents and children continue to recognize, visit, assist, and send gifts to one another. For example, one woman was given some cattle by her father at her marriage. Now, she is allowed to pasture the animals free of charge in her father's field with his herd. Ordinarily pasture rights cost a dollar per month for each head of cattle. One man, who owns a sugar-cane press, allows his daughters and sons-in-law who live nearby to use it for free. Parents state that they feel their responsibility for their children never entirely ceases, and most do keep an eye on the welfare of their offspring even when they have no common economic interests.

The flow of aid also goes from children to parents, and older people often can count on some aid from their children, although normally they do not become entirely dependent upon them for sustenance. Occasionally, however, children renounce their parents and vice versa. Several aged men who are too old to work appear from time to time in Los Boquerones. They do have friends and distant kin in the community, but they have even closer kinship ties elsewhere. Their families, however, refuse to aid them. One of these men comes to the community and passes from house to house, begging food and sleeping a few nights on a kitchen bench. In return, he makes some attempt to perform menial jobs, but he is basically dependent on the goodwill of several household groups. Another, who is lame, set up house under a crude lean-to. He obtains vines, to weave carrying baskets for cash, but he too is dependent on some food gifts from people. His sons live in a not-too-distant community, but they came to the point of refusing him further aid, and then his entire family ceased to recognize him as a relative. His case is unusual but is within the bounds of possible kin behaviour.

Affinal relationships

The only affines who are labelled are parents-in-law *(el suegro, la suegra)*, brothers-in-law *(el cuñado, la cuñada)*, and sons-in-law *(el yerno, la yerna)*, although in address the relationship label need not be used before the proper name. No general word is employed to distinguish this set of persons in contrast to others and they are not considered to be family in any of the senses of that term. Between the parents of two individuals in a connubial union there is no named relationship.

Affines are said to stand between kin and non-kin in importance. One is associated with them and owes them consideration, but one is not expected to respect them in the way one should respect parents. The lack of strong ties between in-laws is correlated with the independence of households and the instability of conjugal unions.

Strains do arise between parents-in-law and children-in-law, although many have amicable relations. In the first place, if the partners in a conjugal union give aid to their parents, each spouse wishes to favour his family over the other's, and this can lead to bad feelings between all the households. Then, authority problems often arise. A mother, for example, keeps watch over her son's welfare. If she sees that he is not being served hot coffee to begin the working day, she may say something to his spouse; but as mistress of her own household, the daughter-in-law resents the intrusion. Also, because in-laws sometimes do co-operate economically, they may be brought into close contact, which can lead to quarrels. Yet, because they are affines, they feel obligated to settle such fights.

Being the reciprocal of relations with family members, affinal bonds also hinge upon the volition of the parties. A man in particular seldom has strong economic ties with his spouse's parents since his basic productive resources theoretically come from his own natal household, and the resources of his mate's natal home go principally to her brothers. Sometimes affinal relationships are used to advantage, but such bonds are not perpetually reliable.

Keeping up sibling ties

The ties between grown non-resident siblings may be sustained for many years. As a group, siblings have few common duties. Individual siblings may co-operate over a range of activities, consult each other for advice, or simply remain friends; usually 'raised siblings' have the strongest ties. An example is provided by Virgilio and Benigno. Virgilio, who is relatively poor, sometimes receives small gifts from his wealthier maternal half-brother, Benigno. In the course of a year he received half a sack of cement, some galvanized tin roofing, some chicken wire and the use of a shovel. These gifts were relatively minimal, and Virgilio incurred no obligation to return them in value. But, he is careful not to ask Benigno for a monetary loan, for he is aware that he might be unable to repay it, thereby rupturing his relationship with his brother.

Some members of a sibling group frequently live near each other, their proximity making it possible to call upon one another to run an errand, to watch the house when it is empty, or to help out in an emergency. Inter-house favours of this type are small and no precise accounting is kept, but the people are aware of the demands of reciprocity. In any case, non-kin neighbours can and do perform these same minimal favours.

Siblings also express and maintain their bond through visits. If two siblings live in the same community they may drop by each other's house, although, of course, not all the members of a sibling group are equally close. If they live in distant communities, siblings may visit one another several times a year on *fiesta* days. An individual's entire household family ordinarily accompanies him on such journeys, and the group may stay overnight or for several days. Friends also visit one another, but they seldom have such protracted stays or partake so freely of someone else's food.

If a man's sibling is fighting an outsider, whether or not the two are still co-resident, he should aid his sibling. It is considered better, however, not to join a brother's row but to calm his temper and prevent a fight. (The rule of support follows more generally for any family member. A father, son or cousin should be defended or calmed in a fight. Friends, also, may be aided. The more distant the kin relationship, however, the less obligated a person feels to join the fight. First cousins, for example, have only a minimal duty to support each other in a quarrel, and fights never involve the mobilization of opposing kindred.)

The relationship between grown siblings is considered to be less important than that between parents and children. Siblings are less obliged to help each other than they are their parents (and children). As a result the tie normally has fewer tensions. I recorded no cases of siblings renouncing each other. In most cases the relationship between grown siblings lies dormant, activated only on certain occasions.

The two situations in which siblings, offspring and parents become most involved in one another's lives are births and deaths. Immediately after a woman has given birth her sister or mother may help her with her domestic duties for several days. But just as frequently the new father pays a non-kinsman to do this work while friends also may give assistance. At a death, the deceased's family members are expected to and do congregate, even if they must come from some distance away. The principal task of parents, children, siblings and other close kin is to attend the funeral proceedings and to mourn. Close kin should not handle the body or carry the coffin to the grave,[1] but during the nine nights of the wake, they may contribute and prepare food and coffee for visitors, or help care for the young children of the deceased. Occasionally they may foster some of the deceased's children. Close kin, however, have no binding material obligations to the deceased's family. Kin help a bereaved family in the period immediately following a death but then re-focus their interests on their own household families.

The obligations and use of these close kinship and affinal ties are well illustrated by the case of a woman with three children whose spouse suddenly died from overdrinking during a *fiesta*. The positions of the relevant kin were as follows. The parents of the widow lived at one end of the community; her father was semi-crippled and scarcely able to provide for himself and his mate. The widow had several younger sisters, but they either had their own families or, while living part-time with the parents, were looking for work in Panama City. The deceased's own mother was dead, and his father, who was slightly deranged, lived alone in a neighbouring village. He also had a sister who lived with her spouse and children near the widow. In addition, by his mother the deceased had in the community five uncles and an aunt, each of whom had a family. Of the deceased's kin, his sister had been the closest to him and his family.

In the days immediately after the man's death, most of these people aided the widow. One of her sisters came to the house and helped with the cooking; some neighbours cared for her children; the uncles stopped their work and aided in various ways. But soon the primary problem came to the forefront. How would the widow be able to survive with her three children? (In addition, the woman was pregnant, although two months later she had a miscarriage.) The only resources the widow had were the sugar cane and rice fields her spouse had planted. The problem was discussed extensively. The uncles of the deceased suggested that the widow sell for immediate cash the rights to her next cane harvest. Others pointed out that this would leave her in debt to the mill and suggested that the uncles were trying to avoid having to help her. Still others proposed that the men of the community form a co-operative *junta* (one without obligation to return the labour) to weed and harvest the seeded rice and sugar cane. Eventually the problem was resolved by having the deceased's father come to live with the widow and her children. The father was not able to perform all the tasks of a male, but the household group was able to survive. However, within a month and a half another tragedy occurred: the father was hit by a small bus on the highway and died shortly thereafter. At this point the situation became quite complicated. The widow wished to keep her house where it was. She hoped to subsist by selling the sugar cane and by performing odd jobs herself. The five uncles made clear in private and public that there was little they could or would do; they had their own responsibilities. In fact, in the early morning following the final all-night wake for the father of the deceased, one of the uncles stood up and began to ask people to help carry the widow's house to her parents' house site. The neighbour who had aided with the children began to have designs on the widow's plot of land and also encouraged her to move. The sister of the deceased continued to play the primary role among the kinsmen,[2] but she began to talk of leaving her own spouse and going to Panama City. She made clear by other means also that her own obligations towards her dead brother's family were ending. First, she suggested that the widow find work in Panama City and leave her children with her parents. Then, she became more and more critical of the widow, pointing out that she was not raising her children well and that they would be better off with someone else. She would tell others that the widow had been hitting her children; she accused the widow of being lazy, and of abandoning her children. The sister was concerned about her dead brother's children, but her ambivalences about her own obligations received clear expression. Finally, almost without the widow's consent, a small *junta* was organized and her home was moved to her parents' house site. Her old site was immediately occupied by the neighbour, preventing her return. The widow was not happy in her new location, and she made plans and requests to move back to a spot near her old site, but nothing happened. She survived by taking on odd jobs, lovers, and by receiving some aid from my wife and myself.

In this case, then, a variety of kinship bonds were activated at the death of a person. The ties brought into play were bilateral in that both the widow's and her deceased spouse's kin were involved. The members of the dead man's family explained their role not in terms of the widow but in terms of their interest in and tie to the surviving children with whom they were kinsmen. The deceased's father came to live with his son's family, not because his obligation was primary, but because the easiest solution was for him to move into the house. Nevertheless, the kinship network provided emergency help only. This aid was important, but the widow had no right to call upon her own or her spouse's kin for permanent help to keep her household solvent. Thus, close kin — parents, children, siblings, and parental siblings — by the fact of their kin ties have obligations toward one another. Yet, once they have established their own households, their responsibilities and interests become focused on their own domestic groups.[3]

The problem of the aged and the single

Elderly and single persons often have difficulty surviving. An older couple usually are able to subsist because their needs are so few they can provision themselves, and their children may send them food from time to time. However, if either of the older persons dies, survival becomes an acute problem for the remaining partner. Several possibilities are open to the aged single person. Theoretically, it is the *bordón's* task to care for his parent; in fact, a child aids his parent depending on sentiment and ability. Such help can take several forms. Sometimes an elderly person will live next door to a sibling or child and offer household help in return for his sustenance. In other cases an aged parent is affiliated more directly with the house of a child. He cannot share their bedroom, but he may sleep in the kitchen, in the loft above the kitchen, or in a separate hut. The son or son-in-law is still the household head; although he does not have the right to order the aged person to work, he may ask him to perform such minor tasks as feeding the pigs or leading a horse to pasture. In total, eight households in the community have elderly persons affiliated with them in one of these variant ways.

To a lesser extent the aged or even younger single person can ally himself to a sibling. In several cases men who live alone reside near their sisters, who offer occasional help by washing clothes or cooking food. One man who separated from his spouse reverted for a time to eating, although not living, at his mother's home. Finally, if the aged individual's children renounce him or if he has no offspring, the older person becomes dependent upon others for assistance in return for menial work performed. However, such a dependent individual nearly always has at least one kinship link to someone in the community where he lives. Nevertheless, it is probably true that the death of many of the elderly is hastened by undernourishment and lack of care; help is given, but it is not sufficient.

Kinfolk beyond the nuclear family

Depending on the context the word 'family' may refer to the nuclear family, to 'close' kin or to all kin. All the descendants of a pair of great-grandparents, second cousins, are considered to be close kin. Third cousins approximately are distant kin or 'relatives' *(el pariente)*. Beyond this level kinship relations are not recognized.

Relatives or far-off family have no obligation to one another and feel that only a minor link unites them. They have 'something family-like, but distant'. One man used to work occasionally in a semi-distant community, and he encountered there several families who bore the same surname as himself. After some discussion, he and the families found a distant kinship bond between themselves; the families then began to call him 'cousin'. He, however, thought it was senseless to consider them relatives, and made no practical use of the recognized bond, although it should be added that he also had no need to activate the relationship.

Grandparents and great-grandparents are distinguished terminologically by gender and degree (grandfather: *el abuelo*; grandmother: *la abuela*; great-grandfather: *el bisabuelo*; great-grandmother: *la bisabuela*). Usually, they are addressed by the kinship label. A child seldom knows personally his great-grandparents. With his grandparents he is expected to have an affectionate but respectful relationship; the frequency of interaction between a child and his grandparents is largely a function of where his parents live. By the time a child leaves his natal home to enter a new household, his grandparents are either dead or his own interactions with them are rather minimal.

Cousins also are distinguished by gender and degree (first cousin: *el (la) primo(-a) hermano(-a); second cousin: el (la) primo(-a) segundo(-a)*). First and second cousins are addressed by name, kin term or both. It is considered polite to use the kinship label but since close cousins, especially first cousins, know that they are cousins they need not reiterate their relationship. More distant ones stress their bond.

Aunts and uncles *(la tia, el tio)* are distinguished according to whether they are parental siblings or their spouses. A *tio carnal* (carnal uncle) is a sibling of a parent; a *tio politico* is the mate of a parent's sibling.[4] The affinal is always distinguished from the genealogical kinsman, although in ordinary usage the qualifiers are dropped. Nephews *(el sobrino)* and nieces *(la sobrina)* also may be distinguished as carnal and political relatives, but the qualifiers are not employed in direct address. Sexual relations with one's carnal aunts and uncles is incestuous, but coition with political aunts and uncles is not.

The kin terminology is not employed in precisely the same way as in ordinary English. The label 'once removed' is not used, and in its place relative age is stressed while generational distinctions are suppressed. Thus, an individual who is a first cousin once removed and who is older than the speaker normally is labelled 'second uncle' *(el tio segundo)* and is addressed as 'uncle'. The term for a parental sibling is used to stress the age difference between the two cousins, for it is a more respectful label than 'cousin' which implies equality. In return, the 'uncle' considers the speaker to be a 'second nephew' and calls him 'nephew', for he owes less respect to his age junior. By contrast, first cousins once removed who are of the same age, call each other 'second cousin'. They stress the equality of their ages and suppress their generational difference. And an uncle and his nephew who are of the same age often call each other 'cousin'. Finally, the sibling of a grandparent is a 'second uncle' (aunt), and the grandchild of a sibling is a 'second nephew' (niece), although occasionally a second aunt or uncle is called 'grandmother' or 'grandfather'. In direct address these more distant kin terms usually are employed without the modifier or personal name.

Kin terms also may be used metaphorically. If a man has a young, nubile daughter or sister he may be addressed jokingly by his male friends as 'father-in-law' or 'brother-in-law'. 'Brother-in-law' sometimes is used as a pleasure between two age cohorts who have no sisters, while an older person sometimes will call a younger one 'my son' or 'my daughter'. The term expresses both affection and age difference.

Thus, the total range of kinship bonds is continually recognized terminologically; the nomenclature itself is said to be a reflection of the consideration which should obtain between kinsmen. Yet, in everyday life the terminology is often the extent of the recognition of the bonds.

The kinship network and locality

Genealogies of about five generations, including the youngest living, may be elicited and constructed for the entire populace. In the first place, the depth of such genealogies is related to the scope of persons recognized as kinfolk. As noted, the range of close kin extends to second cousins which means that genealogies need be recalled only to the level of great-grandparents. Second, such family histories underscore the fact that each individual bears a total kinship status. He is the offspring of both a male and a female, and through them and a succession of other filial links he is related to others. The total system of relationships is bilaterally symmetric, and although it is sometimes said that a person is closer to his maternal than paternal kinsmen, in fact, relations to the two sides are equal in importance, and the differences that do exist are a function of proximity and common interest which vary by family. Underlying the system is the 'amity' (Fortes, 1969: 232-49) of kinship.

The fact that an individual not only recognizes a network of kinsmen but usually lives in the same or a neighbouring community with a number of these kin indicates that there is a connection between kinship and area. The reader is now referred to Figure 5 in which almost one-half the population and household groups of the community are displayed. Exhibited at the same time are kin ties between persons, kin ties between household groups, and kin and affinal ties between conjugal partners. Before turning to the problems raised by Figure 5 I had best give some explanatory notes. First, the figure is provided only as an example. Nearly everyone else within the community could be linked on to the figure through a kinship bond, affinal tie, or a combination of such links; solely for the sake of comprehension have I omitted these ties. For simplicity also I have omitted a few of the connections between persons which would unduly complicate the figure and I have not included all the conjugal relationships which each individual has had. Correlatively, I have not displayed all the cases of step-parenthood and fostering. A final omission requires more extended explanation. I have not in every case included all the descendants of a conjugal pair. I have focused primarily upon those who now live or did live in the community. For this reason alone the 'stocks', i.e. descendants of a conjugal or sibling pair, which appear in the figure, should not be considered to be discrete groups. At each generational level some siblings in a stock have left the community and 'founded' new stocks in other villages. (Aside from this consideration a stock or set of stocks would never form a discrete group anyway, since only full siblings have the same constellation of kin, and stocks always overlap. These are ego-focused calculations only.) Thus, in Figure 5 I do not present all the kinship connections among all persons in the community, but the omissions have been made only for clarity, and to

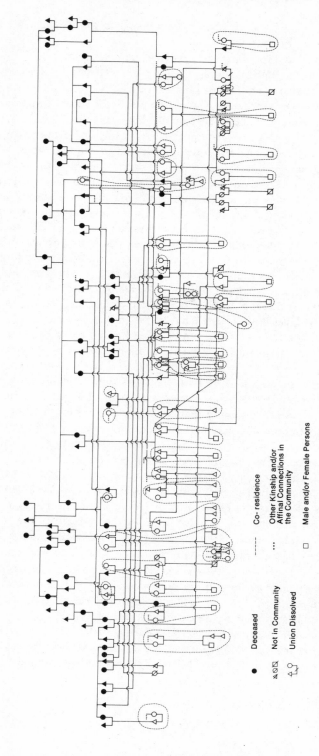

FIGURE 5 *The kinship network and locality*

Co-residence ------

Other Kinship and/or Affinal Connections in the Community .....

● Deceased

◁⊘⊠ Not in Community

⟨⟩ Union Dissolved

□ Male and/or Female Persons

my knowledge no important facts have been obscured.

Even with these qualifications, Figure 5 brings to the forefront the problem of the relation between kinship and locality at the community level. On the one hand, even a quick perusal leads to the conclusion that the community members are enmeshed in a complex set of kinship and affinal links, and it would appear that kinship and affinity some-how provide an ultimate structure for the village. On the other, the figure itself was pieced together from separate family histories, and each individual carries in his head only parts of the total picture. Family relationships are not a common topic of conversation, and genealogies sometimes are remembered with difficulty. An extreme case of genealogical amnesia is provided by the example of a man whose recognized father died when the subject was still a boy; he had diffi-culty remembering his father's first name. Furthermore, I never heard any statement of this order: 'We are all kin here.' No one consciously, at least, thinks of the community as a conglomerate of kinship and affinal bonds, and I, too, was not fully aware of this tangle of ties until they were all placed on paper. What, then, are the factors which give rise to what is clearly a connection between kinship and community? Why does the village consist of such a dense network of kinsmen and affines?

To answer the question, we must first view the community not as a grouping of families but as one localized segment of a vast network of kin spread over the countryside; kinship relationships do not, as stressed earlier, stop at community borders which are themselves flexi-ble. Within this context we must next distinguish the impact of three interrelated factors: kinship, conjugal unions, and mobility.[5]

Generally the men have had few economic opportunities to do other than work the land. Only within the last generation have access roads and means of transportation improved. Mobility, therefore, has been primarily a function of the search for fresh land to work, and in their movements the people usually have spread amoeba-like across the countryside. The countrymen have not been known to make mass migrations or to move to new areas great distances away. The result is that a dense network of kinship bonds obtains within and between neighbouring villages. Lack of mobility leaves a person close to his parents' families; propinquity re-enforces genealogical links.

But it is also true that low mobility itself is partly a function of the desire to live near kin. While no one asserts, 'Here we are all kin', the people do say that they 'search for family'. If an individual moves to a new community or to a new area within the village he looks for kin; he uses the link to justify his presence and to give him an initial security before new friends are acquired, for a kinship relation can — if the parties are willing — provide a framework on which other ties may be established. A few individuals within the community have only a few close kinsmen. Significantly, of all the people, they are the most able to recite the various but distant links they have to other community members, and they often call their distant kinsmen by kin terms, although the practice may not be reciprocated. Nevertheless, a person's move is not contingent upon his finding kin, for he can move to a new area and after a short time develop other ties. Close relatives often become neighbours, but neighbourly bonds are not contingent upon kin ties. Further, an individual always has a range of kinfolk both within and without the community among whom he may choose for friendship and help. Choice is a characteristic feature of the system.

Thus, a typical pattern — and evidence of this can be seen in Figure 5 — is for a conjugal or a sibling pair to move to a new area, to have progeny, and for the stock descended from the couple or siblings to expand. Some of these descendants leave for a new village while others remain in the area. Kinship ties spread beyond the community while in a locale stocks of kin also develop over time.

If low mobility and kinship amity were the only factors leading to the localization of kin, and if conjugal partners were always sought from outside the village and its environs, then each stock descended from a sibling or conjugal pair would be a discrete unit. It is clear from Figure 5, however, that stocks are not distinct units even on paper, and in this respect conjugal unions also have an impact on the kinship network. Thus, examples in Figure 5 may be found of two stocks linked simultaneously by several conjugal unions: two cousins may unite with a sibling pair. Cases of unions between persons within the same stock also may be found. (The closest unions displayed are one between a man and his father's sister's daughter's daughter, and another between a man and his mother's sister's son's daughter.) And, there are many examples of persons joined in a conjugal union who already have a diversity of kin and affinal ties between them. What, then, are the factors which lead to this pattern of connubial unions?

Again, the pattern is partly a function of mobility. Given that both males and females are, relatively speaking, not mobile, and given that kin do occupy a local area, then the probability of uniting with someone who already is a kinsman or affine is high. In the second place, kinship and friendship ties provide a network through which conjugal partners may be found. To illustrate, if a man leaves a village, he often goes to work with a kinsman or a friend. In this new community he may meet a young woman and decide to set up a household with her. In turn, some of his kinsmen may come to visit or work with him, and they too may meet a person of the opposite sex and decide to settle in the new community. The third factor in this conjugal pattern is the idea, sometimes expressed, that it is good to unite with kinsmen. And fourth is the related notion that it is good for two kinsmen to unite with two kinsmen, although connubial unions are never contracted between specified categories of kin. Thus, kinship, affinal and friendship networks help organize a geographic area in which conjugal partners are found. These factors, incidentally, re-enforce the bilaterality of the kinship system. If a conjugal partner is selected from within a relatively small area, then the offspring of the union will not only recognize but be able to activate both their maternal and paternal kinship ties. At the household level residence is neolocal; in this higher-order sense, too, residence is neolocal in that neither the maternal nor paternal line is built up locally at the expense of the other.

In total, low mobility, the amity of kin, and conjugal-partner selection all result in a dense concentration of kinsmen living within a locality. But this network is not of great importance in a person's everyday life. The broader kin ties are activated and manifested only in times of death and church marriage. Close kin may be called upon to help in an emergency, to do small favours, and occasionally to lend money. Kin links do not provide a person with rights to property, although they do give him some right to settle and work in an area. An individual may gain entry to a household on the basis of a close kin tie he has to one of the principal household members; and thus kinsmen do provide some security for both young and aged persons. But close kin are not the only sources of credit and there is a limit to what one may ask of a kinsman. Also, the range of recognized kin is rather restricted, family relations and histories are not commonly discussed, and the kinship system by itself does not present a framework of enduring groups. Thus, in practical terms kin outside the household are not of paramount importance. This characteristic undoubtedly is related to at least two factors. First, since there is little property, kinsmen never hold an estate in common which might unify them. Second, kinfolk have no right or need to exercise political or legal functions together since only outside agencies are vested with political-legal power. A kindred, for example, is never activated to redress a murder or settle a dispute.

Outside the household group, family ties are recognized but sporadically activated. Elementary family members keep up their bonds once they live in separate homes, but their offspring do not rely upon one another. On the one hand, the larger kinship network is congruent with the nuclear family in that the bonds may be utilized or renounced. When the ties are activated, as in the nuclear family they are used for material, practical affairs. On the other, there is a disjunction between the co-residential family and more distant kin. Members of a household are family; members of the community need not be related. Relationships within the household are constraining; all must live up to the demands or be extruded from the group. Broader relationships of kinship are optative. Kinsmen ordinarily are recognized as being kin, but they can impose no duties on one another. And an individual's relations with his kinfolk are progressively de-activated from near to far. The broader kinship system, not vested with jural functions, is based on sentiment.

12   Forming the 'compadrazgo'

In the preceding chapters we have considered the ways in which the person as a natural being is engaged in a system of kinship and conjugal relationships. Here we turn to another aspect of his character. As a sacred being he becomes interlinked in a complex of spiritual relationships, the *compadrazgo*. In both systems the individual is enmeshed in ego-centred networks of bonds, but while the first, represented by the surname, continues through time, the second indicated by the Christian name has no perpetuity beyond one generation.

The *compadrazgo* is formed at three church rituals: at baptism a baby acquires two godmothers *(la madrina)* and one godfather *(el padrino)*; at confirmation a young person assumes a godparent of the same sex as himself; at church marriage the marital couple together receive a godmother and a godfather. In each case the parents of the novitiate and the godparents become co-parents *(el compadre, la comadre)* with each other. The godchild is termed *el (la) ahijado(-a).* Each rite, then, brings into being two new relationships: godparent-godchild and *compadre-compadre.* In addition, over a fourth ritual outside the church, the breaking of a rice stalk, two individuals may become *compadres,* but no godchild is involved.

An examination of the *compadrazgo* raises an analytical problem similar to that confronted by descriptions of the hot/cold and male/female concepts. The analysis must entail two levels of explanation. On the one hand, the *compadrazgo* is a cross-cultural institution which has its immediate roots in sixteenth-century Catholic theology. On the other, it is a functioning part of the community and has there a distinctive configuration. The analysis, therefore, must have validity on both levels. My own solution to this problem is to view the *compadrazgo* in Los Boquerones as one among many variants (Gudeman, 1972). The total system of permutations includes the past religious and folk versions plus the current variations. All are united by their historical connection to the church and to the spread of Christianity in the

New World. Among these variants there is no 'true' *compadrazgo*; even the church formulation has undergone considerable change over time. Nevertheless, the church version at the Council of Trent (1545-63) marked a watershed in the development of the *compadrazgo*: few changes in church law were made following this council, and the rules enunciated by it provided the pattern for the development of the *compadrazgo* as it spread throughout the world. My understanding of the *compadrazgo*, then, is based primarily on an interpretation of the theology of the Roman Catholic Church as elaborated at the time of the Council of Trent.

The *compadrazgo* is connected to the family through the concept of the natural and spiritual person. At birth a child is born to a set of natural parents. He is marked with original sin from Eve and must be cleansed of this sin through baptism. Since the natural parents transmit original sin, they are prohibited from sponsoring their own child. Thus at baptism the child is reborn spiritually to a second set of parents, the sponsor and minister, and just as the child contracts natural relationships with his natural parents, so he contracts spiritual bonds with his spiritual parents. In effect, the natural parents must give away rights over a portion of their child to others, and this act endowed with religious significance creates spiritual relationships between them and the spiritual parents (Gudeman, 1975).

Formed in the image of the family, the *compadrazgo* is linked to the kinship and marriage systems. Conceptually, the family is composed of mother–father–child; the *compadrazgo* contains parent–godparent–godchild. The two stand in the opposed relation of the natural to the spiritual; as birth is to baptism, the family is to the *compadrazgo*.

The *compadrazgo* is a system of spiritual relationships, and its participants are bound together by spiritual affinity, just as kin are linked by a series of 'natural' ties. These spiritual bonds are no less 'real' or 'factual' than natural kinship. Within a society the sacred ties may become encrusted with other, more strictly social, obligations, but these material manifestations of the bonds are effective precisely because the *compadrazgo* is ultimately and irreducibly a system of spiritual links.

In the pages which follow I shall be presenting one variant of this total system. But the continuity with my previous argument concerning the nature of kinship should be noted. In both cases I am viewing the relationship structure as a system of ideas and in terms of its connection to broader cultural conceptions.

In this chapter I shall be concerned with the rites of formation of *compadrazgo* ties, leaving to the following one a discussion of the patterning of the bonds and of the rules of selection. In looking at the formation of the ties I shall consider their significance in terms of the growth of the person. The godparents play a crucial social role with respect to the changing relation between the individual and the society. The *compadrazgo* is part of the dynamic of the individual life cycle. By means of baptism and confirmation children and adults both acquire public and institutionalized ties outside their homes. However, at base the ceremonies have a spiritual significance, for when a youngster enters into these recognized and valued relationships, he becomes endowed with a sacred character; and this spiritual quality makes the individual into a total social person within the community.

The first sections of this chapter are primarily ethnographic; in the last I consider the rites in terms of their significance for the individual.

From birth to baptism

Until a newborn is baptized, it is not considered to be a Christian; it is known as a *moro* (unbaptized, Moor) and is thought to be like an animal. The unbaptized baby is in a ritually dangerous state. He is susceptible to harassment or pursuit by the devil who might take him away to inferno, to molesting by witches who also can carry him away, and to the evil eye, an involuntary eyeing by others which can give him certain forms of sickness. At baptism the devil ceases to be a source of danger, but witches and the evil eye, although with less likelihood of causing harm, can be dangerous to a child in his early years.

Various precautions are taken to protect a child from these perils. Some or all are put into effect immediately after birth in the case of a home confinement, or as soon as the baby arrives home when born in hospital. To keep the devil away a large, hand made wooden cross is hung on the wall of the house or a small one is suspended by a chain around the baby's neck. Against witches several precautions may be taken. A pair of scissors may be opened in the shape of a cross and tacked to the wall above the bed of the mother and child. The house broom, made anew each week of short leafy branches, may be turned upside down at night outside the door to the sleeping room. And the notched pole, used as a ladder to reach the loft or storage area above the kitchen, also may be turned upside down when the family goes to sleep. Witches are thought to be more active at night, and these measures stop a witch from approaching the kitchen or bedroom. Less frequently incense is used. From the Indians who live in the mountains of the province but who come into Santiago to sell goods, a log containing a resinous gum can be purchased. The wood is cut open and heated over the kitchen fire and a grass *(la paja de nata)* is placed on top of the log. As the incense begins to fume, the log is picked up and passed beneath the baby in counter directions, representing the cross. The smoke is said to pass upward through the child. The smoking incense then is carried around the inside of the house, so that it penetrates into all parts of the interior, and around the outside as well. As the log is carried, the sign of the cross is repeatedly made. Wherever the odour of the incense lingers, witches do not approach. Protection lasts at least twenty-four hours, and the process may be repeated every three days or so until the child is baptized.

To combat the evil eye one red band of cloth or beads is placed on a child's wrist and another on his opposite ankle. The two bands are thought to cover him from one end to the other. When visitors come to the house their eyes and attention are attracted to the bright red bands instead of to the baby, and the chance of their giving him the evil eye is reduced.

Since the unbaptized child is considered not to be a legitimate human being, if a baby is born sick or falls gravely ill, an effort is made to baptize it promptly in the church in Santiago. Should the child die or be in imminent danger of dying a special baptism is held in the community at the parents' house.[1]

For such a baptism the parents of the child select one godfather and one godmother. The godfather, who should have some knowledge of prayers or be a local prayer *(el rezandor)*, acts as godfather and as priest. He obtains *agua socorro* (help, succourance water) to use in place of the *agua bendita* (blessed water) of the church. Only a small amount is required; it comes either from the first rain of the year, which is collected as it falls from the house roof and is stored in a bottle, or from a type of vine *(bejuco de pedorro)*. With a branch the priest/godfather sprinkles the water on the sick or dying child and recites whatever prayers he knows.

This ceremony presents a number of departures from the normal baptismal rite. Used only for dying or dead children, it is performed in the community at a house and not in Santiago in the church. The godfather normally serves not only as *padrino* and *compadre* but also as priest, although it is permissible to find a separate individual to act as the cleric. If a man who knows how to recite cannot be found, then a woman may substitute for him in his role as substitute priest.[2] In either case a normally secular individual acts as if he had sacred powers. A godmother may be in attendance but her role, if any, is unimportant. By contrast, at a normal baptism there are always two godmothers one of whom is as important, if not more so, than the godfather. As with a normal baptism the godparents of the child become the *compadres* of the child's parents.

The people do not agree whether this ceremony may be performed over a dead child or whether he must still be alive. I learned of one abortion and one miscarriage in the community. In neither case was the mother in an advanced state of pregnancy. The first occurred at home and the other in hospital. The ceremony utilizing *agua socorro* was not performed over the remains of either child.[3]

The countrymen speak of the rite as being 'not very legal'. It is performed only as a last measure and because God prefers that children die baptized. It is thought that the soul of an unbaptized child probably goes to heaven anyway. If the rite is performed and the child lives, he later is taken to Santiago for an official baptism, for, though the infant is no longer a *moro,* he still needs the official sanction of the church. As one person pointed out, a child baptized by *agua socorro* is like a cow without a brand.[4]

Baptism

Nearly all baptisms are held during the sugar-cane harvesting months in the summer, for money is more plentiful then. There is no set age at which a child must be baptized, but he should be baptized by his second birthday at the latest. Normally, if a child is well he will be baptized within from six to eight months after birth.[5] Baptizing a child later than this incurs no penalty other than the prolonging of his ritually impure and dangerous state.

Baptisms are performed on Sundays in Santiago.[6] Several weeks ahead of the planned baptism the father and mother discuss whom they want for the godparents and decide on suitable choices. The father then approaches the man they have chosen and asks him to be the godfather. If the date set is not convenient with the *padrino*, they agree upon another time. Then the father asks the two godmothers and, if necessary, yet a different date may be arranged. Later, the guests for the baptismal party are invited. They may include friends, family and other *compadres* of the parents, although there is no obligation to ask any of these persons. No prescribed ritual accompanies the verbal invitations.

On the day of the baptism a small group of people makes the trip to the Santiago church. The father goes, but sometimes the mother does not. The *padrino* and the two *madrinas* always go. In addition, family, friends or other *compadres* of the parents, if asked by the father, may accompany the group; however, their presence is not necessary. At most ten to twelve people travel to Santiago.

The unbaptized baby is carried to Santiago by the *madrina de pila* (godmother of the baptismal font). The *madrina* comes to the child's house and dresses him in a new suit of clothes and shoes, which she will have purchased for the occasion. This is the child's first complete outfit of clothing. Prior to this most children go about nude or with only a shirt. Hardly any children have shoes until they are baptized. Then, the godmother makes the sign of the cross over herself and the baby, utters several prayers, and leaves the house carrying the child. The devil, it is said, particularly pursues and tries to harass the baby on its journey from house to church, and it is for this reason that the *madrina* takes these precautions before leaving the child's home. In addition, as the godmother leaves, some parents have her remove the scissors and straighten the broom and ladder that were previously used to ward off witches. (Others wait and do so themselves a week after the baptism.) The group of family and friends takes a bus to Santiago and there waits outside the church in a small park. Because she protects the child during this dangerous journey, the *madrina de pila* is considered by some to be the most important of the godmothers.[7]

At the park the child is handed to the *madrina de la puerta de iglesia* (godmother of the church door) or *contra-madrina*. Infrequently this *madrina* also purchases garments for the child, and if so, she then dresses the child in these. It is considered mandatory for the *madrina de pila* to provide clothes and shoes but optional for the *madrina de la puerta de iglesia* to do so.

As the group waits outside, the father and godfather enter the church and register the child. They also specify who the child's parents and prospective godparents are and whether or not they were religiously married. The *padrino* pays a $2 fee. Since baptisms are held *en masse* each Sunday, it is not necessary to sign up in advance for a place. The father and godfather exit and rejoin the entire group which then waits outside. At this point the *padrino* may buy coffee or purchase a bottle of liquor to begin the day's drinking.

When the hour for the baptism arrives, the *madrina de la puerta de iglesia* carries the child to just inside the church entrance where she hands it to the *madrina de pila*. This completes the duties of the *contra-madrina*. According to the people a saying summarizes her task: 'From the lodging to the church door' *(De la posada a la puerta de iglesia)*.[8] Because she has fewer responsibilities, the *madrina de la puerta de iglesia* is considered to be less important than the *madrina de pila*. Indeed, some say it is merely a luxury to have a second godmother. In taking a census of godparents and *compadres* I found cases in which the *madrina de la puerta de iglesia* had been omitted or had been found at the last minute from among strangers in Santiago.

Inside the church the *madrina de pila*, accompanied by the godfather, carries the baby to the baptismal font. Facing the font the *padrino* stands to the right of the *madrina* and holds the baby's head; the *madrina* holds the child's feet. The parents stand to one side or behind the *padrinos*.[9] The priest baptizes the baby in accordance with church regulations and, as the *campesinos* point out, bestows upon it a first name.[10] At the conclusion of the church procedures the godmother, sometimes saying prayers, carries the child from the font to the church door, where she hands it to the mother if she is present. This concludes the ceremony. But, upon emerging from the church a final practice usually is enacted. The godfather stands on the church steps and throws out one or two dollars in pennies and nickels to unknown youngsters who have assembled at the entrance. The practice is said to bring good fortune to the baby. If the godfather does not throw out the money, the children chant 'Penniless godfather does not take a godson' or 'Penniless godfather does not get anything when he does not throw anything' *(Padrino pelado no saca ahijado; Padrino pelado no saca nada quando no echa nada)*. The stingy godfather is embarrassed by the shout but incurs no further disapproval.

The newly baptized child is kept in his baptismal vestments for twenty-four hours following the service. The clothes are left on him so that the mystery and sacredness of the sacrament may become more firmly implanted in him.[11] In older times, the baptismal garments were then kept unused and unwashed in a box. If a child caught certain diseases his clothes were put on to combat the malady. When the child was grown, his mother would give him the vestments and the child might give them away to someone else. Today, the tendency is to use the clothes for everyday wear, but they still are preserved and considered to be special.

When the baptismal group returns to the community, a *fiesta* is held, its size and elaborateness depending upon how much the father and godfather wish to spend. The party is held at the parents' home. While the group is in Santiago, family members or close friends stay at the house to prepare a meal. Often the mother herself stays home and does most of the work. Sometimes the house is decorated with streamers and favours, other times not. More people come to the *fiesta* than go to the baptism. Although the guests are invited ahead of time, should an acquaintance pass by, he may be invited to join, though more for the drinking than for the food.

After the food has been eaten and toward the end of the *fiesta,* a final custom is occasionally performed. The godfather lines up the children present and hands out a few pennies to each. This is considered to be a nice gesture and is not thought to be comparable to the practice of throwing money from the church steps.

Expenses vary by the baptism, but they usually fall within a range for each of the principals. The *madrina de pila,* who buys the clothes and shoes, spends from $5 to $10. If the *madrina de la puerta de iglesia* buys a suit of clothes, she spends about $2.50. But usually her expenses are nothing. The *padrino* pays $2 at the church, throws money from the church steps, and sometimes (depending on the father) pays the transport costs for all the participants to and from Santiago, which can amount to several dollars. The *padrino* also buys several bottles of alcohol, each of which costs from $1.50 to $2. Thus, expenses for the *padrino* may amount to $20 but usually are nearer $10 and can be less. The food costs are paid for either by the godfather or, as is more likely in present times, by the father. They amount approximately to between $10 and $15 for a normal sized *fiesta.*[12] The father also may purchase a few bottles of drink. Extras such as serving fried pork or having live music are spoken of but infrequently indulged in. Despite the fact that baptismal parties vary in size and cost, they are not competitively compared. An exceptionally private and small *fiesta* might draw comment, but a large affair brings no enduring prestige.

Should the parents of the child have split up before the baptism, the father may send some money for the *fiesta* or the mother may go ahead as well as she can but in a more simple manner.

Confirmation

Confirmation is less elaborate than either baptism or church marriage. It usually is received between the ages of eight and ten, although it can be performed later and sometimes is conferred directly after baptism.[13] Confirmation is seen by the countrymen as being another step or grade in fulfilment of the complete Christian life, and almost everyone is confirmed. But should an individual die before being confirmed his burial and after-life are not affected. For the people, confirmation is not so important a theological event as baptism.[14]

At confirmation an individual acquires one godparent of the same sex as himself.[15] A boy, therefore, normally has a total of two godfathers and two godmothers while a girl has one godfather and three godmothers. The godparent of confirmation usually is considered to be of less importance than those of baptism. In the census the least remembered godparents and *compadres* were those of confirmation.

As with baptism, confirmation is received in Santiago,[16] but it is not followed by a *fiesta* nor does it involve elaborate ritual. The adults involved may celebrate afterwards with a few drinks.

Church marriage

The final religious occasion upon which individuals may acquire godparents is church marriage. The marital couple obtain a *padrino* and a *madrina,* and both these godparents become *compadres* with the couple's parents. For the people, as seen, the most significant aspect of a church marriage is that it implants a sacred bond between the two partners with all the special obligations that this tie implies. The religious link is made public and legitimated by the godparents. By church law, however, the sponsors are considered only to be witnesses, their appellation as godparents and *compadres* being a custom of the people. As witnesses, the two must swear that the marital couple are not close kin, although, as noted, dispensation may be obtained for second cousins to marry. Since the majority of the people are joined in common-law and civil unions, only a limited number have marital godparents.

As with the baptismal and confirmation *padrinos*, the parents of the novitiates ask the chosen individuals to be the godparents. However, it is the couple themselves that usually make or agree upon the selection.

Rice 'compadres'

In addition to the three forms of the *compadrazgo* which originate in sacred rites, there is a fourth type formed outside the church. Two individuals may become *compadres* over the breaking of a rice stalk. Absent from this form are church rites and sanctions and the idea of a novitiate's spiritual progress.

Rice *compadres* are linked by means of a rice stalk rather than by a child. Two people who wish to become rice *compadres* find a rice stalk in which the rice grains have not yet emerged from the stem or leaf.[17] The entire stalk is cut off at its base. The rice spigot, that is, the grains and their stem inside the larger outer leaf, is considered to be the child or godchild. One of the prospective *compadres* holds out the stalk, base end towards himself, and the other pulls out the rice spigot. The first is left with the outer leaf, while the second has the grains and inner stalk. The second is said then to have pulled or taken out the godchild. The expression is the same as that used for a regular godfather who also 'takes' *(sacar)* a godchild. Some claim that after seven years of respectful behaviour towards one another the two become enduring *compadres*, while others state that the relationship is permanent from its inception. Rice *compadres* are considered to be full *compadres,* equal to those formed over baptism, confirmation or church marriage, although now a few express disbelief in the custom.

The prospective *compadres* may be of the same or opposite sex. They are usually people who do not have children but who wish, for the sake of affection and respect, to become *compadres*. This form of the *compadrazgo* is infrequently practised today and probably occurred more often in the past. It is said that young men who worked together in the fields used to form the bond.

'Compadrazgo' rites and the spiritual person

These rites and concepts concerning the formation of the *compadrazgo* are reflections of the people's view of the individual as a religious person. Each ritual adds a new layer of spirituality, transforming the novitiate into a more complete being. Baptism is the most important of the rites followed by confirmation. Socially also it is these two ceremonies which set in motion the primary role contrasts of age and sex. I turn now to a consideration of the significance of the rites.

The church's theology concerning baptism is to be distinguished from the people's notions, although the two are related. Officially, baptism is said to remit original and all actual sin. To obtain salvation, reception of the rite is necessary, and through it there is a spiritual regeneration. Baptism imprints an indelible character which is the sign of the supernatural union of the baptized with Christ. This indelible character makes the baptized a juridical person within the church with all the privileges and duties of a Christian.

The countrymen are not well acquainted with the church doctrine, and their verbal statements concerning the theological significance of baptism are rather sparse. The unbaptized is said not to be a Christian, he lacks some of the mystery of the church; he cannot grow up with faith in God. Nevertheless, the importance of baptism is expressed in other ways. Basically, for the *campesinos* baptism adds to the natural being a spiritual character, and this makes the individual into a total social person within the community.

The unbaptized is said to be a 'little animal'. Children and animals are, of course, distinguished but in this instance they are thought to be alike in that they both lack grace, God's mystery and a supernatural character. Also, to label the unbaptized a 'Moor' is to state not only that he is not a Christian but that he is outside society as well.[18] At baptism the individual is officially given a first or Christian name, and this name classifies him with other humans bearing the same first name while it distinguishes him from family members. The first name as a saint's nomen also allies the person with a saint and collocates him within the calendrical cycle and the round of religious celebrations. Should a person remain unbaptized, he would not have a first name, and, it is said, would have to be referred to by some other means.

Prior to baptism the infant is thought to be in a special, dangerous state. Being an incomplete member of society he is especially susceptible to attacks from extra-human agents, and special measures must be used to ward off these dangers. At least some of these practices are modelled after religious customs — the incense, cross, and scissors in the form of a cross. In addition, the upside-down broom and ladder mimic the baby's own 'reversed' state. Symbolically both broom and ladder are appropriate items: at one time the people did sleep in the loft to which the ladder leads, and the broom is used everyday to clean and thereby define the limits of the domestic area.

The type of burial used for dead unbaptized infants further reflects their lack of a complete social and spiritual status. An unbaptized or natural child must be buried outside the community cemetery.[19] A dead animal similarly is either buried in the fields or left above ground to decompose. Cemetery burial, then, signifies that an individual was baptized and that, unlike an animal, he was a whole social being with a full jural personality. If the being has never been integrated into the social grid, he remains forever outside society and is disposed of accordingly.

If it is true that baptism provides a natural child with a social personality, might an animal be transformed from his natural to a social state by the rite? There is no agreement concerning the answer. Under no circumstances may a cow, horse, or cat be baptized.[20] However, some maintain that dogs, which are kept as domestic pets, may be baptized.[21] Should a dog be baptized he would become equal to a person, he would have the mystery of a human, and he would be a son of God. Moreover, humans would have to respect the baptized dog just as they do other human beings. The baptized dog would be given a human or Christian saint's name and would not be called 'Blackie' or 'Cinnamon' or by some other non-human dog name. And a baptized dog would have to be buried, like a human, and not be left out for other animals to eat. At the death of a baptized dog the ordinary death prayers would not be said, but this would be because a dog neither sins nor knows how to sin. As with an *angelito,* the prayers would not be necessary.

Admittedly, I never had the pleasure of meeting a baptized dog, and not everyone would maintain that dogs may be baptized; however, the significance of the custom lies not in the practice but in the idea. To occupy a recognized position in the society the individual not only must be physically generated, he must have a total personality, and the society itself must bear witness to this event. The parallel of a domestic animal and a human being emphasizes the total social nature of baptism.

The baptismal process itself, as elaborated by the *campesinos,* is a typical rite of transition. To shift from animal to social being, the baby must be separated from his house, be taken to Santiago, undergo a sacred change, and then be returned to his home. Ritual specialists from outside the family are used to effect this transformation. The godparents physically carry the child away, just as they remove him from his old status, take over a part of his personality and assume a new set of responsibilities toward him. The godmother opens the rite. She comes to the house, dresses the child in a complete and new set of clothes, utters several prayers, and separates the child from his house. (Before baptism a child goes about nude, like other animals, or in a night shirt; at baptism he acquires human vestments.[22]) The transitional journey from home to church is said to be particularly dangerous and it is the godmother's duty to protect the child in this interval.[23] During the sacred ceremony the godparents hold the child and stand in place of the parents. The ritual itself follows the recognized dogma, but at its conclusion a final folk ceremony is practised: the throwing of coins by the godfather to assembled but unknown youngsters at the church steps. This final ritual act is worth examining in detail, for it expresses clearly the nature of the rite.

The custom, which is quite widespread in Spain and Latin America, is often called the *bolo,* although the villagers have no term for it.[24] George Foster (1967) has already provided one interpretation of this institution, based upon his notion of the 'Image of Limited Good'. Briefly, Foster thinks that the people of Tzintzuntzan, Mexico, conceive of all their resources — natural, economic, social — as existing in limited and insufficient quantities. Therefore, what one individual or family gains must be at the expense of others. Some people, however, inevitably have better fortune than others and are the objects of envy. Consequently, various symbolic devices are employed to neutralize the envy of others. It is within this context that Foster interprets the institution of the *bolo.* Babies in Tzintzuntzan are highly valued goods and precautions are taken to shield a new-born from the envy of others. Eventually, however, a child must be baptized, and the ceremony is a public event. Therefore, after the ceremony the godfather throws out the coins to the assembled youngsters. 'Symbolically, he gives something to others who have not shared directly in the good fortune of the birth' (Foster, 1967: 159).

The rite is understandable in terms of Foster's logic, but my own interpretation of the *bolo* as it occurs in Los Boquerones is different and more structural; to explain it I need to introduce first one further piece of information. The people of Los Boquerones say that if the godfather holds money in his hand while the baby is being baptized and has the priest baptize the money and not the baby, then he will have good fortune and become rich.[25] The money and not the baby gains the church's blessing. One man in the community, who had amassed a number of cattle, was said to have done precisely this, although it should be added that a greedy spouse later drained off all his wealth.[26]

My interpretation of the act hinges upon seeing the substitutability of baby and money. From one perspective, the ceremony is an example of the separation maintained between the secular natural world, as represented by the money, and the sacred world, as represented by the baptized baby. The one must be forgone to enter the other. By scattering the coins the godfather expresses publicly that the baby and not the money was baptized. The money being 'valueless' is thrown away; the baby having received a sacred character is retained. Indeed scattering the coins is said to give the baby good fortune. Should the *padrino* keep the money, it would show that the baby is not baptized and that the godfather held his individual goals uppermost — he kept the good fortune to himself. Thus, by renouncing the money the godfather states that he, the baby, the other godparents, and the parents have all assumed new roles within and subordinated themselves to the spiritual realm of the *compadrazgo*. Throwing out the coins is a negative expression that the godfather did not baptize the money and a positive statement that the child is a baptized being.[27]

From a different perspective, the dispersing of the money is the final act in a series of ceremonial behaviours. The godmother carries the child to the church where it undergoes the sacred transformation at the hands of the priest. During the ceremony the godparents themselves, the intermediaries for the parents, are exposed to sacred powers with which they are not ordinarily equipped to deal. At the church steps, then, the godfather decontaminates himself and returns to a normal state by throwing out the valueless, but potentially magical, coins. In this respect it is interesting to compare the baptismal clothes with the coins. The godmother opens the series of ritual acts and provides the clothes; they are sanctified and then left on the child for twenty-four hours so that their sacredness may penetrate into him. The magical clothes, being beneficent, sacred objects, are preserved. By contrast, the godfather closes the sequence of acts by throwing away the coins which, unlike the clothes, were not baptized. The clothes indicative of domesticity are provided by a female, are sanctified, are given in private to one known child, and are retained. The coins, symbolic of the productive sphere, are given by a male, are not sanctified, and are thrown away to a number of stranger children. The clothes and the coins, symbolically opposed, open and close the entire ritual. Part of the meaning of the coins lies in their contrast to the clothes.

Thus, the *bolo* ceremony, far from being a mere symbolic repayment, is a crucial act. It is the only truly public event in the sequence and it sums up the entire baptismal ritual. By throwing out the coins the godfather proclaims that the ceremony has been successfully completed and that the baby has been baptized. It follows that the journey from Santiago back to the village is not thought to be fraught with dangers and is less stressed than the trip to the church.

Baptism, in sum, effects a crucial change in a person's status. It adds a spiritual character to an individual's natural being. The baptized becomes human-like instead of animal-like, he becomes clothed instead of unclothed, he becomes immune to some extra-human dangers, he may be buried instead of thrown away, he becomes deserving of respect from others, and he obtains a Christian name. The individual's family and Christian names together give him a position in the social fabric and he becomes a complete, natural and spiritual, person. Through baptism, then, the child takes his first public step toward socialization; the fact that there are two baptismal godmothers and only one godfather may serve to emphasize the domesticating aspects of the ritual. The importance of the rite is further underlined by the people's belief that it is a grave affront to refuse to be a godparent. A rebuff removes God's grace from the child and expresses the fact that the requested godparent does not want the child to be a Christian or, even worse, a member of society.

In terms of the growth of the individual confirmation is the second most important transition. Again, the people's view of confirmation must be distinguished from the church's position. Officially, through baptism spiritual life begins; through confirmation it is perfected. Before his seventh year a person is termed in canon law an 'infant'; he is presumed not to enjoy the use of 'reason'. After completion of the seventh year a person is presumed to have the use of reason. Confirmation, as noted, should be postponed until the seventh year; it marks the inception of the age of reason.

For the *campesinos* confirmation adds a layer of spirituality to the person. Although it has not the crucial social importance of baptism, it marks some important changes in the life of the individual. When a child is confirmed he is reaching puberty. Within a short time he will be able to earn money outside the home and to have sexual relations. He no longer is an *angelito,* for he knows how to sin, and by this age a child has learned how to respect others. He is becoming a full and participating member of the community and is beginning to practise his appropriate sex role. That the godparent of confirmation is of the same sex as the youngster emphasizes the fact that at this age the sexual role, as opposed to the child role, is being developed. If baptism gives a child an official place in the home and overall society, then confirmation states publicly that he has a place within the village itself.

Finally, at church marriage the man and woman symbolically move from being under the authority of their parents to being valid progenitors and spiritually bound to one another and their children.

The *compadrazgo* is centred about the most important life changes of the person. In some societies kin, affines or other specialists participate in such status transitions, standing between the novitiate and public. In rural Panama godparents have these key roles. They represent the larger society to the participants, and through the godparents the village witnesses and sanctions a baptism, confirmation or church marriage. More than a religious institution, the *compadrazgo* is a moral system in that it symbolically integrates individuals into the community. This moral commitment, that a child has a jural personality, that his parents are his natural parents, and that the godparents are his spiritual parents, is continually reaffirmed through the public and respectful manner by which *compadres,* godparents and godchildren greet one another. The statuses of all are reiterated continually through expressions of mutual respect.

Baptism, confirmation and church marriage are the principal public ceremonies in the society.[28] They are announced in advance, two of them are inevitable, and they are celebrated with *fiestas.* Hence, there is a contrast between the family and the *compadrazgo.* The family system lacks ceremonies but consists of concrete, visible interactions. The *compadrazgo* is based upon tangible ceremonies, but, as will be seen, consists largely of non-material relationships.

13   The structure of 'compadrazgo'

As a system of relationships the *compadrazgo* is not corporate in the sense of having group continuity over generations. The bonds are freshly formed for every individual, and each person may build around himself a distinctive *compadrazgo* network. However, these relationships, buttressed by a religious legitimation, last for a lifetime, and having an enduring justification, they may be elaborated beyond their original sacred purposes and be put to secular uses. What are of interest, then, are the patterning and tasks which characterize the bonds.

In Los Boquerones *compadrazgo* relationships are expressed primarily through ceremonial acts; ordinarily they are not used for utilitarian purposes. But the bonds are highly valued. Ties of godparenthood and co-parenthood generally are contracted with other *campesinos* within the community or neighbouring villages. Only infrequently are they formed with individuals of a higher social class. Within the community the *compadrazgo* has an impact on several levels. As an extension of the spiritual portion of the person it links each individual in a network of personal relationships complementary to his family ties. As a spiritual image of natural kinship the *compadrazgo* also presents an inverse pattern to that of the family. Further, just as the concept of the home has an impact on the shape of the family, so also the *compadrazgo* is formulated with respect to the household; *compadrazgo* bonds are extra-domestic ties. I describe in this chapter, then, *compadrazgo* relationships, the rules for selecting godparents, and the patterning of *compadrazgo* ties in relation to the individual, the family and the household.

The godparent-godchild bond

By current canon law only one or at most two sponsors may be employed at a baptism. No more than one sponsor may be used at a confirmation, and only witnesses are required for a church marriage. A spiritual relationship is contracted between the person baptized or confirmed and his sponsors. A child is not permitted to marry his baptismal godparents but he can marry his godparent of confirmation. Both baptismal and confirmation godparents, although themselves theologically distinct, have two general functions: they accompany a child to and stand up for him at a religious ceremony, and they are expected to regard the child as being perpetually entrusted to them and to provide for his Christian education as promised in the religious ceremony. Theologically, then, sponsors are parents in the church. A child is reborn to them, and by this act a spiritual relationship is created between the godparents and godchild. The godparents, therefore, bear certain rights and obligations towards the spiritual portion of their godchild's personality.

The countrymen distinguish the godparents according to the rite at which they assumed their roles. In Table 10 the possibilities are set forth. Most individuals have only four godparents since common-law unions are preferred to church marriages. If a baptismal sponsor becomes the confirmation sponsor, or if only one baptismal godmother is used, the total number is reduced to three.

TABLE 10   *Types of godparent-godchild relationship*

	Type of godparent	Sex of godchild	
		Male	Female
Baptism	*Madrina de pila*	cross-sex	same sex
	Madrina de la puerta de iglesia	cross-sex	same sex
	Padrino de bautismo	same sex	cross-sex
Confirmation	*Madrina de confirmación*	X	same sex
	Padrino de confirmación	same sex	X
Marriage	*Madrina de boda*	cross-sex	same sex
	Padrino de boda	same sex	cross-sex

The baptismal godparents are considered to be more important than the confirmation sponsor who in turn is thought to be more important than the marriage *padrinos*. The baptismal godfather, regardless of the godchild's sex, is considered the most important of the godparents. Of the godmothers the *madrina de pila* is the principal one, followed in descending order by those of *puerta de iglesia,* confirmation and marriage. There is a correspondence between the theological significance of the rites and the *campesinos'* concept of the relative importance of the godparents; however, the importance of the godparents is also a direct reflection of the people's understanding of the significance of the ceremonies and of the roles the sponsors play in these rites. In the discussion which follows I treat the godparent-godchild relationship as being of one type; the different forms vary only in the extent to which the rights of the bond are observed and accentuated.

According to the countrymen the godparent-godchild relationship is a spiritual bond, but they do not elaborate upon this idea. They speak of and describe the tie mostly in terms of respect. Above all, a godparent and a godchild must respect and consider one another. Relationships of respect are not limited to the *compadrazgo,* but in the context of godparenthood, respect defines, expresses and re-enforces spiritual behaviour. This respect obtaining between godchild and godparent should be exhibited in various ways, some of the most important being forms of salutation.

A generation ago a godfather and a godchild used a special greeting. The godchild went upon his knees to his godfather and each said a benediction to the other. The godfather then made the sign of the cross over his godchild.[1] Even in the midst of a *fiesta, padrino* and *ahijado* would greet each other in this manner. Such a form of address is no longer used, but adults remember it and speak in mild despair of today's youth who greet their *padrinos* by the lighthearted and familiar, What's new, Godfather?' Nevertheless, three other forms of address between godparents and godchildren are still used. In direct address, proper names must be prefixed by the relationship term. In direct address the respectful and formal 'you' must be used; the informal 'you' is never employed. Finally, if a godparent or godchild is speaking of his reciprocal in indirect address, he prefixes the name with the appropriate title.

The respect that a godparent and godchild must have for one another is exhibited also by a sexual prohibition. Godparent and godchild commit a sin if they join in a common-law union, have sexual relations or even indulge in sexual joking with each other. To engage in these actions with a godparent or godchild is as sinful as with a family member.

A *padrino* is like a father: 'After the parents comes the godfather.' A godchild must be taught to respect his godfather like his own father. When his godfather is near, a godchild should not be drunk, speak bad words, make sexual approaches to or be angry with others, or talk about sexual matters. A godchild should not joke in front of his godfather nor speak ill of him behind his back. And, he should never fight with his godfather. Similarly, in his own behaviour a godfather should respect his godchild, set a good moral example, and observe equal precautions.

The godfather, as a surrogate father, has the right and duty to look after his godchild. Should parents mistreat their child, the child's godfather may ask them why they are doing so, although I never heard of a godfather intruding. A godfather also may counsel or admonish his godson — in a sense be a moral father to him, although, again, it is rare to see a godfather play this role. One of the most frequently mentioned obligations is that if a child's parents die, both his godfather and godmother should raise him as a family member. Yet, again, very few godparents undertake this task.

When a godparent or godchild dies, the other should attend his funeral and offer help to the bereaved family by bringing candles, money or coffee, by finding a reciter for the prayers, or by helping at the cemetery.

A striking characteristic of the godparent-godchild relationship is that it entails no mandatory, material obligations. Godparents and godchildren sometimes do engage in informal, unsolicited material exchanges, but compared to other such ties which each has, this aspect of their relationship is unemphasized. The primary occasion for gift-giving from godparent to godchild is the child's birthday or saint's day. For example, when Virgilio reached the age of three, his principal godmother brought him a dollar bill. On Marcelino's birthdays his godparents have given him clothes and a live chicken to raise. Sometimes a godparent gives his young godchild a little money or purchases candy for him when they happen to meet. It is said that a godparent gives gifts to his godchild to receive his love, but such presents are given only when the child is young and usually are not offered.

A relationship of mutual help also may grow up between a godfather and his godson. For example, Manuel raised one of his godchildren for several years. After the boy reached puberty and returned to his mother in another community, he would return occasionally at harvest time and bring Manuel a little rice or beans. Other times he would bring firewood and fruits. Now, the godson is fully adult, and Manuel has given him 'rights' to a small area of land on which to construct a house. In his old age a godparent can sometimes rely upon his godchild for food or help, just as he may have assisted earlier with gifts of goods or even animals.

Several factors, however, inhibit the formation of a very close and tangible tie between godparent and godchild. First, should a godparent favour one godchild over another, the two godchildren may become envious of each other. Second, and more important, the respect a godparent and godchild owe each other restrains the relationship. Godparent and godchild can loan money to one another. But should a loan not be repaid or be delayed in repayment, and this is often the case, the relationship would be disrupted.

Because godchild and godparent must have mutual respect, they should try to avoid being together when the behaviour of one might cause the other to lose respect for him. Since normal relations among men and women outside the household often do involve disrespectful actions, the presence of a godparent circumscribes a person's behaviour. The respect owed is not consonant with a friendly and close tie.

Thus, the godparent-godchild relationship is deemed to be very important and is thought to endure forever, but the tangible relations it involves are few. As a spiritual tie, the bond requires the payment of mutual respect, involves various modes of address, and entails a number of prohibitions. Godparent and godchild also bear certain moral responsibilities towards each other. In these respects the bond is firm, unending, and continually expressed. But its more tangible aspects are non-obligatory. Material exchanges are unsolicited, sporadic and rather limited. And such gifts and aid are given out of love and interest, sentiment and affection, rather than as jural obligations.

The 'compadre'-'compadre' relationship

The *compadre-compadre* relationship obtains between the parents of a baptized, confirmed or church-married child and his godparents, although the tie has no foundation in the current canon law. The system centred about one person can bring into play twelve *compadre-compadre* bonds, since each individual can have up to six godparents and since both his mother and father enter into the relationship. In the two principal forms of the *compadrazgo*, baptism and confirmation, only one family with its attendant godparents is involved, but at church marriage the godparents become *compadres* with two sets of parents. In none of the forms, however, is a relationship recognized between godparents to the same child; sharing a godchild does not give rise to a bond.

Terminologically *compadres* are differentiated only by sex. According to the sex of his co-parent each calls the other *'comadre'* or *'compadre'*. A number of other possible terminological distinctions also are obscured by use of the general term *'compadre'*. The various types of godparent are not discriminated by *compadre* name, and parents are not differentiated linguistically from godparents.

In relation to the child the godparents have a rank order of importance, but the same people in their roles as *compadres* to the parents are nearly equal. Marriage *compadres* are less important than those of baptism and confirmation, and the *comadre* who is the principal godmother is said to rank higher than the other *comadres.* Otherwise all are equivalent. In addition, godparent and parent are thought to be nearly equal as *compadres,* although some say the parent owes more respect to the godparent than the reverse.

The *compadre-compadre* bond, like the godparent-godchild tie, is deemed to be a spiritual, sacred relationship, but again the bond is most frequently talked about as one of respect. One should respect his *compadres* even more than one's own parents. As expressions of this respect, forms of address between *compadres* are thought to be important. Before becoming *compadres* two friends or kinsmen might have addressed each other by the informal 'you'; after becoming *compadres* they must use the formal form. The title *'compadre'* is used in both direct and indirect address, and the title must precede or replace the proper name. Although no form of asymmetric benediction greeting has ever been used, *compadres* sometimes embrace one another in a manner also used for intimate friends and family who have not seen each other for a period of time: *el saludo con brazos* or *echando el brazo* (greeting with arms or giving the arm). The greeting is effected by holding both arms out and placing the hands on the other's shoulders or arms.

Compadres also call attention to their relationship by invariably greeting one another, even if they are some distance apart. It would have been impossible to trace kinship relations of even the first degree without asking persons who their kin were, but a good approximation of *compadre* ties could have been made simply by noting each day who addressed whom as *'compadre'*.

Compadres should respect and consider each other in all their behaviour. They should never fight; it would be worse only to fight with one's mother or father. *Compadres* should never use bad words with one another, speak of women or swear in each other's presence. One also should not admit to seeing a *compadre* commit an a-social act. If a man were to go to a *fiesta* and see his *compadre* with a woman who was not his spouse, he would not greet his *compadre* or mention the incident to him or others. An individual who was not a *compadre* could be expected to circulate such gossip. Not all these strictures are observed by all *compadres* at all times, and on occasion two *compadres* will be angry with one another, but even then their argument is likely to be muted. Thus, a person can nearly always depend upon a *compadre* yet this is due partly to the refusal to admit disrespectful elements into the relationship.

The bond is also marked by a sexual prohibition. It is a mortal sin to marry, take as a common-law spouse, sleep with or even sexually jest with a cross-*compadre*. The prohibition is an aspect of keeping respect; however, as I shall note, the interdiction has a more important basis to it than this.

A person should attend the funeral and wake of his *compadre* and should offer help to the widow and children. But like a close family member, a man should not dress the body of his dead *compadre*, carry the coffin to the cemetery, help to dig the grave, or shovel on the dirt. These tasks must be undertaken by community members less closely related to the deceased.

As an instrumental exchange the relationship is rather circumscribed, although in this respect intra- and extra-community bonds must be distinguished. Infrequently, the ties are contracted with non-countrymen. When such persons are selected, they come from a higher social class. Labourers from the mountains or Indians are not chosen to be godparents. The outside *compadre* also is almost invariably the godparent to the villager's child, since the *campesinos* themselves are not selected by wealthy outsiders. Such outside relationships tend to be asymmetric in that wealth, political favours or simply prestige are exchanged for respect. For example, Ricardo's wealthy *compadre*, who is a bus driver, occasionally stops in the community and gives him $5-10. From a *compadre* in a nearby town Jacinto was able to raise a loan of several hundred dollars to finance the ploughing of his rice field, although it should be added that he has adequate collateral in the form of several head of cattle. But examples of such help are rare. For most, a *compadre* bond with an outsider would be valuable simply as a source of prestige. Nevertheless, an outside *compadre* often does not meet even the demands of respectful behaviour. With some disdain one woman told how her daughter's godmother, who lives in a city, greets her by slapping her arm and saying simply, 'How are you?'

This pattern of relationships with townsmen fits into a broader context. There is a rather sharp break between the *campesinos* and the larger society. The people are squatters but have never had much to gain by forming special ties with the absentee landowners. The rice mills and sugar-cane mills buy produce from a vast number of country-men at standard prices, and individual ties between *campesinos* and foremen have no special value. Large stores in Santiago do not grant credit to the people. Thus, ties with outsiders are essentially transitory and economic. As part of this complex, it is logical that *compadrazgo* bonds are infrequently used to solidify ties with townsmen. The practice of confining *compadrazgo* links to other countrymen fits with, re-enforces and perhaps helps to create the basic economic and social disjuncture which exists between the people and the larger society.

Compadre-compadre ties within the community are more symmetric and less materialistic. On the one hand, the people say that a *compadre* is like a brother; he can always be trusted.[2] Occasionally, the relation-ship is manifested in instrumental ways. For example, a man may help settle a face-to-face dispute between two of his *compadres*, although he would never serve as an intermediary between them. One older, single woman once asked her *compadre* to count her money for her, to sort the money into piles for paying her workers and to hold the rest in safekeeping. Her *compadre*, however, was an honest man whom others, too, would have trusted with a sum of money. Some years ago when a woman without family in the community, grew old and then sick, her *compadres* and godchildren brought food to her. A woman is more willing to ask her *comadres* for aid than a man is to request help from his *compadres*. Less of a woman's status is linked to her economic well-being, and in particular by asking her child's godmother for food or clothing she shows that she is concerned about her children. Such examples of instrumental relations, however, are rare; the *compadre-compadre* relationship is little used for borrowing money.

Some of the people, while admitting that borrowing between *compadres* is infrequent, claim that a *compadre* should in theory be a potential lender. Others think that a *compadre* should never be asked for a loan. In fact, the two views are not contradictory. *Compadres* must and do trust one another, but lending inevitably leads to problems and thus seldom occurs because it could undermine the mutual respect which *compadres* must preserve.

This pattern of symmetry and mutual respect between *compadres* within the community is congruent with the people's own economic situation. Within the village there are few substantial economic differences, and fortunes can vary on a yearly basis. Therefore, even if desired, it would be difficult to choose a *compadre*/godfather with the hope of receiving endless help. The impact of wealth on the pattern of selection is not entirely negligible, however, for some of the wealthier persons are frequently chosen, partly because they can afford the expenses and partly because if they are storekeepers they will be more likely to grant credit. But a storekeeper does not confine his debtors to his *compadres*, and the people themselves say that they avoid seeking *compadres* for material gain.

Within the community, then, the sacred *compadre-compadre* tie is largely separated from instrumental duties. *Compadrazgo* relationships also are the only ego-centred bonds which have absolute perpetuity; they are never broken, even after death. By contrast, transactions of a political or economic nature are marked by distrust and impermanency. In the one permanent, non-renounceable tie, exchanges of an economic, political, social and sexual order are minimized.

The permanent nature of *compadre* relationships is exhibited in various ways. If the child about whom the *compadre* bond was formed dies, his parents and godparents continue to be *compadres*. This is true even in the case of baptism in the home. The relationship also endures after death of one of the *compadres*. A dead *compadre* is always referred to as 'my dead *compadre*, Juan'. If a man's *compadre* precedes him in death, the first person to greet him at his own death, and he will give the greeting of the arms, is his *compadre*. If in life a man has hit his mother or father his *compadre* will defend him before God in the other world. And, if a man has fought in this world with his *compadre*, he will fight with him in the other. In short, a *compadre* is for ever.

Compadres are a special order of people, and their importance can be seen in a final and explicit way: the people express the desire to have *compadres*. Being of the church, godchildren and *compadres* bring one good luck. The community members know who has many *compadres* and who does not, and because those who are often chosen receive respect from many *compadres*, their position is enhanced in the eyes of others.

It is also true, however, that having too many *compadres* can be cumbersome. A baptism places a financial demand on the godfather and to a lesser extent the godmother. The individual who accretes many *compadres* pays for them. Having many godchildren, while a source of pleasure, places more obligations upon a person; and having many *compadres,* while giving an individual more respect, also formalizes and therefore creates a type of strain in just that many more relationships.

Elaborations

The *compadrazgo* is a clearly defined system in that it is formed over baptism, confirmation and church marriage, and contains the three roles of parent, child/godchild, and godparent. But this structure is also elaborated, and I turn now to these refinements.

The *compadre-compadre* bond, as explained, may be formed over a stalk of rice. The two individuals concerned consider each other to be and address each other as *'compadre'.* Since a number of persons express disbelief in the practice, and no one thinks of it as the paradigmatic rite, I consider the custom to be an extension of the other patterns. Yet, by its existence it enriches the meaning of the three more religious rites, for it nearly inverts their theological basis. In this ceremony the rice stalk is 'taken out' just as a godparent 'takes out' his godchild. From one perspective the *compadrazgo* (in which a bond is recognized between parent and godparent) is but a variation of simple godparenthood (in which no bond is recognized between parent and godparent). The institution of rice *compadres* brings this series full circle by denying the very basis of godparenthood: there is no spiritual rebirth of a human being. The rice is a metaphoric child, but the metaphor is not carried to the extent of recognizing the parent-child and godparent-godchild bonds, and conceptually neither person is distinguished as father or godfather. The institution, therefore, is an extension of other practices; yet because it is modelled on the *compadre-compadre* tie, it stresses the importance of this bond. There is no comparable way for a person to become a godparent without also becoming a *compadre.*

A second elaboration is somewhat different: a godson and the children of his godfather are said to be 'political brothers' *(los hermanos politicos).* As several explained, since the word 'son' *(el hijo)* is a part of the word 'godson' *(el ahijado),* the two are like brothers. Political brothers should give each other the consideration of brothers, but they do not address one another as 'brother' nor greet each other in a special way, and there is no prohibition on their having sexual relations. Unlike the preceding extension, this relationship is not a matter of choice. It is an element in the overall structure and is invariably acknowledged. Regardless, it presents a contrast to the first elaboration. The former stresses the tie of co-parenthood through substitution in the child/godchild position. The latter relies on godparenthood and parenthood to generate fraternity.

The *compadrazgo* also is extended in a more informal and non-prescribed manner. On some occasions when a young adult, who is still living in his parents' home, is chosen to be a godparent, the parents of the godchild use the term *'compadre'* for both the sponsor and his same-sex parent. That is, when a youth is still living in his natal home, the co-parental term of address may be extended to his parent of the same sex. The practice is a reflection of the fact that it was the parent as much as the child who was selected. The godparental term, however, is not extended by the godchild. In this case, then, co-resident parent and child stand in place of each other *vis-à-vis* the natural parents; residence impinges upon the structure of the *compadrazgo*.

On some occasions a completely fictional bond is formed. Virgilio asked Manuel to be godparent to one of his children. At the time, Manuel could not afford the baptismal expenses. Explaining his position to Virgilio, he did not outrightly refuse but begged off. Since that occasion, however, each has called the other *compadre* and there is a certain respect between them, although both are aware that they are not true *compadres*. And this example is related to a further practice. Male friends sometimes greet one another as *'compa'*, a contraction of *compadre*. To greet a true *compadre* in this manner would be improper, lacking in respect and a *'relajo'* (*relajar:* to relax, to weaken the observance of custom).[3] Thus, by use of this truncated utterance individuals signify at once that they are not *compadres* but that their relationship partakes of elements of the *compadre-compadre* bond in that it is durable and trustworthy.

The term *comadre* may be used in place of the word for a female witch *(la bruja)*. It is said that witches call one another *'comadre'*, and that one may address an actual witch who appears at night in this way. Real witches do not like churches and thus rarely become true *comadres*. Of course, to call another *'comadre'* when in fact she is not a *comadre,* is an insult. Like the contraction *'compa'* the word *comadre* (as witch) depends on it being used 'out of context', although the two are employed differently. In context *'compa'* is ugly; out of context it is a term of esteem. In context *comadre* is respectful; out of context it is an insult.[4] Both terms are meaningful only by contrast to their other uses. Conversely, their existence suggests that a co-parent is neither a friend nor a witch, but conceptually he is perhaps not far removed from either. As noted, the godparent is connected to the luck and grace of his godchild.

The rules of choosing godparent/'compadres'

Godparent/*compadres* are selected in accord with certain regulations. In this section I provide an observer's view and explanation of these folk rules. I shall argue that the people's statements concerning choice of a godfather/*compadre* can be described as a body of rules, that this corpus comprises a system, and that the countrymen's application of the rules generates a complex network of ties between household groups in the community and neighbouring villages.

An individual is chosen as both a *compadre* and a *padrino*. If a man will be a good *padrino,* he also will be a good *compadre,* and in reverse.

Rule 1: Parents may not choose as *compadre*/godparent a person whom they could not respect.

This rule derives from the nature of the *compadre-compadre* relationship which has respect as its foundation; in the context of the *compadrazgo*, respect is an elaboration of spirituality, and, therefore, the regulation implies that the *compadrazgo* is a spiritual relationship. In practice the rule means that a prospective godparent must be at least eleven or twelve years of age, for a younger child would not know how to respect sufficiently. A potential *compadre* cannot be an enemy; and close, joking friends cannot become *compadres* unless their relationship is transformed to one of respect. A close neighbour who can hear bad words being spoken in his godchild's house is not an appropriate choice. The general rule clearly has many applications; some of these are made explicit by the following corollaries, all of which are consciously expressed by the people.

Corollary A: A person should not refuse to be a godparent nor should a parent refuse a would-be godparent.

It is said that the man who refuses to be godparent brings bad luck to his potential godchild. He 'takes away the grace'. A person's refusal means that he does not want the child to have a spiritual or Christian personality or, more broadly, to be a member of society. Similarly, in the rare case when a person asks to be godparent, if the father refuses he harms his own child. Since there are a few persons who, for reasons of their own, do not wish to become *compadres,* the corollary states in effect that they should never be asked.

In addition, some people are said to have a 'hot hand' *(la mano caliente);* often, their godchildren die. Such a person also has bad luck, for his godchildren not only die, but he spends money for nothing, and when old he has no godchildren to whom he can look for aid. It is considered better not to choose one with a hot hand, or for him to explain his bad luck and to refuse.[5]

Corollary B: It is best not to choose as godparent a person who lives outside the community.

Although it is permissible to choose someone from outside the community, it is considered better if the godparent lives in or near the village, for he will be more able to engage in the requisite relationships. If the prospective *compadre* is from the community, it is also easier to know if he respects and is respected by others.

Corollary C: It is not always wise to choose a wealthy person as *compadre.*

The people consider themselves to be poor, and only outsiders are truly wealthy. This corollary, therefore, is related to Corollary B in that it, too, helps keep *compadre* selection within the community. Wealthy outsiders should not be chosen because they frequently do not greet or respect their poorer *compadres,* and sometimes do not pay attention to their godchildren. Also, if a rich individual is chosen, people in the community may think a man has selected his *compadre* on the basis of financial prospects rather than spirituality.[6]

Corollary D: It is better not to choose the oft-chosen.

Since it is important to have a godparent who will give attention to one's child, it is unwise to select a frequently chosen person, for his loyalties will be divided and he will be unable to respect all his godchildren and *compadres.* This corollary has the effect of spreading *compadre* choice throughout the community.

Rule 2:   Parents may not be godparents to their own children; parents may not be their own *compadres.*

This rule is basic to the complex and is related to the ecclesiastical regulations which specify that neither father nor mother may sponsor his own offspring. The regulation ensures that parents do share their child with others and codifies the fundamental conceptual and actual separation of natural and spiritual paternity.

Corollary A: Parents may not choose as *compadres* persons with whom either has had or is having sexual relations.

Since having sexual relations is tantamount to saying that a man considers the woman to be a possible spouse and since this means that the woman could become step-mother to the child, the corollary reduces to saying that parents cannot choose themselves. In addition, the corollary follows from Rule 1, for sinful sexual relationships are incompatible with respect and spirituality. Compliance with the corollary sometimes causes household disruptions, for when the conjugal pair are deciding who shall be *compadres,* if one hesitates at a suggested name but does not explain why, the other will deduce what has happened and this leads to a row. Even if a spouse says nothing, the prospective *compadre* may refuse if he has had sexual relations with one of the pair.

Rule 3: Parents should not choose their own children as *compadres;* one sibling should not become godparent to another.

This norm has no theological basis. The people justify it by pointing out that the relations set up would be impossible to maintain. Parents, godparent and child/godchild would all be living in the same household. One sibling would become godparent to another, and the respect required of the relationship would be incompatible with the fact that brothers and sisters often fight. The parents would become *compadres* with a child, and this respect relationship would be incompatible with the fact that a parent has to discipline his child as he raises him.

Contradiction A: A child may choose a parent to be *compadre:* parents may become godparents to their grandchildren.

The situation of a child selecting a parent to be *compadre* is not the same as a parent choosing his offspring. When a child selects his parent, the godchild is grandchild to his godparent. The parent becomes godfather-*compadre* to his child rather than the reverse, and one sibling does not become godparent to another. In addition, the parent-child relation as *compadre-compadre* occurs when the child is grown and living in a separate household, as specified by the co-residential couples prohibition; therefore, there is little likelihood that the parent will have to discipline his *compadre*-child, and by this time a child knows if the relationship with his parent is respectful or stressful. Similarly, the godparent and godchild live in separate homes. Although the situation is less strainful than that prohibited by Rule 3, it is still sufficiently full of tension to be seldom practised. There were only two cases of a child selecting a parent as *compadre,* and in both a daughter chose her mother to be godmother. If a parent becomes godparent to his grandchild, the godchild/grandchild refers to his grandparent as grandparent. The godparent is called father or mother by the offspring but uses the term *compadre* or *comadre* in return.

Contradiction B: Siblings may choose each other to be *compadres.*

Although two siblings do not become godparent and godchild, they may become *compadres.* An uncle or aunt, therefore, may become godparent to his or her nephew or niece. This set of relations is less strainful than that proscribed by Rule 3, for it does not impose respect relationships on the immediate domestic group. When it occurs, one, if not both, of the siblings is grown and lives in a separate residence from his family of orientation as dictated by the co-residential couples prohibition. In fact, siblings are fairly frequently chosen as *compadres.* But, unless there is deep respect between the two, it is considered unwise for one to choose the other as *compadre.* If a sibling becomes a *compadre*, in address the title *'compadre'* replaces the proper name or sibling term. The godparent-godchild terms replace those of parent's sibling-sibling's child.

Aside from the nuclear family, there are no explicit rules concerning the selection of kin as godparents. If parents frequently choose their own kin it may be a sign that they have no other acquaintances to select, and this may lead to some loss of respect for them. When more distant kinsmen are selected as godparents, *compadrazgo* terms replace those of the family.

Rule 4:   A person may not reverse the direction of choice and choose the parent of his godchild to be godparent to his child.

The people say that one cannot 'return the *peón*'. 'It is like a debt repaid, both remain without anything.' Should the direction of choice be reversed, the child would revert to an unbaptized state and the adults would cease to be *compadres.* This is not a rule of the church but of the people. One woman claims that many years ago she asked a priest about the rule, and upon receiving no confirmation of it reversed the direction of *compadre* choice with no ill effects. Although others are aware of her example, no one has yet copied it.

Related Rule A: A parent may choose the same person any number of times to be godparent for the same child or for different children, although it is better not to do so.

It is permissible for a parent to choose the same person as the god-parent for different offspring, but as one person said, 'it is not the custom for one to take all or even some of the same house'. Selecting different godparents for each child, it is recognized, creates a greater sense of community. If the parents die, and there is no one but the godparents to take the children in, then all will have to go to one house. With a plurality of godparents, both parents and children feel more secure and valuable. In addition, it is thought to be nearly an absolute norm that different godparents should be selected for different cere-monies for the same child; this rule is considered to be more inflexible than the immediately preceding.

Related Rule B: A godchild may choose his godparent to be godparent to his own child.

If a person chooses his godparent as *compadre,* then the godparent addresses him as *compadre,* but he continues to call his godparent *padrino.*

Rule 5: Parents may not choose as godparents for the same child two persons who are living together in a civil or common-law union; the chosen *compadres* must be church-married or living in separate homes.

Since the godfather and godmother are spiritual guardians to the child, the church prohibits the choice of persons who are living in a common-law or sinful union. The church prohibition, however, is interpreted by the countrymen to mean only that two godparents to the same child may not live in an unlawful union with one another. Each may be in an unrecognized union with someone else. From the perspective of the godparents the rule means that common-law mates must each have different godchildren but church-married spouses need not. It might be added that if this interpretation were not applied to the church rule, the system would collapse, for too few people would qualify as *compadres.*

There is little difference, however, among choosing a person who is single, in a common-law union, or church-married. It is sometimes said that since church-married couples 'live better in God's eyes', selecting a married pair as godparents is nicer; however, there is no marked tendency to do so. If a married pair are chosen, the woman becomes the *madrina de pila,* the principal godmother.

In spite of Rule 5, however, and the cultural idea that engaging in sexual relations implies that a pair could be united, there is no prohibition upon choosing two persons who are known to have had sexual relations, or upon the godparents becoming a common-law pair after the baptism.

Analytically these rules may be considered from several perspectives. In the first place, they are connected to the current and historical church norms (Gudeman, 1972). From a different perspective the regulations are related to universal cross-cultural rules of the *compadrazgo.* For example, from one viewpoint the basic rule in the complex is that which prohibits parents from choosing themselves; the norm creates an exchange between parents and godparents. A regulation which sometimes follows this rule is that which prohibits return of choice from godparent to parent (Gudeman, 1975; Hammel, 1968: 73). But here I wish to consider the people's rules from a different perspective: what is the impact of these five rules of choice upon the system of *compadrazgo* relationships within Los Boquerones itself? In what respect are the norms themselves systematically interrelated?

Rule 1, with its corollaries concerning respect in the selection of *compadres,* essentially delimits the range of persons who may be chosen. Only people who are known to respect others and who are willing to participate in sacred and respectful relationships should be selected. The rule expresses a bias against choosing townspeople or others of a higher social status. In effect only other countrymen are qualified to be selected. The rule places the *compadrazgo* system within the community as a spiritual and moral entity.

Rules 2 and 3 are the basic ones. They force *compadre* choice to be made from without the household. Rule 2, by prohibiting parents from choosing each other, impels them to choose other adults. The *compadrazgo* cannot be superimposed on the co-residential parental pair. Rule 3 also forces the *compadrazgo* out of the household, and with its two contradictions illustrates perfectly the extra-residential nature of the *compadrazgo.* The rule states that parents may not choose their own children to be *compadres,* but the contradictions state that children may choose their parents, and siblings may choose each other. The discrepancy is resolved when interpreted as resulting from a ban on the choice of co-residents. Thus, parents may not choose one child to be godfather to another, but when children bear their own offspring, they are separately domiciled and, therefore, it is possible for them to choose their parents. Similarly, if a sibling has offspring, he must, by the co-residential couples prohibition, have his own home. Hence, one sibling may choose another to be godfather/*compadre*. Thus rules 2 and 3 together force the *compadrazgo* to be extra-residential, but they do not force it to be extra-familial, for family may be chosen, if they are not co-resident.

Both Rules 2 and 3, are compatible with Rule 1. Because the *compadre-compadre* and godparent-godchild ties are sacred, it is difficult to choose a co-resident. Everyday relations within the household are_ incompatible with the absolute respect one must have for a *compadre* partner. The co-residential parent-child link, in particular, is antipathetic to respect equality. Further, sexual relations between the parents or between parent and would-be godparent (Rule 2) are incompatible with the respect that must exist between them.

Rule 4, which prohibits choice reversal, has an interesting sanction. If choice is reversed, the first child becomes unbaptized. The people express this as the closing or paying off of a debt; since having a debt outstanding implies trust and social recognition between the partners, the closing of a debt must symbolize the severance of the relationship. Thus, the rule prohibits the exchange from becoming direct and closed. It does not simply prohibit certain *compadre* partners, it forces the people continuously to forge fresh links with different households. In a situation of bilateral kinship with 'neolocal' residence and relative fluidity, the rule leads to greater cohesion within the community, whether or not this was its intended purpose. This cohesion, incidentally, is strengthened by the regulations which specify that people should not be selected repeatedly either by the same parents or by different individuals.

Rule 5, the prohibition stating that godparents to the same child who are in common-law unions must be from different homes is a way of circumventing church regulations. Intended or not, it too has the effect of spreading choice among households.

To summarize, the rules of choosing *compadres* delimit a field of choice. First, they define an inner circle. No co-residents may be chosen. Second, two households may not have reciprocal links and form a closed unit. Many individuals must be brought into the network. Third, the rules impose outer limits on who may be selected. Usually, the godparents must be community members or other countrymen who live nearby.

The 'compadrazgo' in relation to the individual, the family and the household

Within the community the *compadrazgo* has an impact on the levels of the individual, the family and the household. As a reflection of the spiritual character of the person, it is first a system of sacred links among persons. When an individual acquires *compadres* as godparents to his own children and as parents to his godchildren, he becomes embedded in enduring bonds of respect and committed to the village and its environs as a spiritual community. Having *compadres*, godparents, and godchildren helps identify the individual to himself and to the community by giving and reminding him, and reaffirming to others, that he has an assured social place, just as the rites of baptism and confirmation in themselves give the individual an enduring jural position. As the people themselves suggest, a person with *compadres* feels more valuable, significant and secure.

This personal aspect of the system may be related to the emphasis placed on using proper forms of address. The frequency of address is partly an indication of the importance of the ties. The *compadrazgo* has no perpetuity beyond one generation nor continuing observable duties, and the obligatory address forms also may help compensate for this lack of material expression. In addition, the greetings imply that the receiver is a respected person who is a part of the community, for he is either a household head responsible for offspring or a godparent responsible for a godchild. *Compadrazgo* bonds, unlike family ties, are community links, and they may be expressed publicly partly because they are social and not private ties. But finally the address forms show that a greeted individual occupies a total social position. The terminology implies that the addressed has both a spiritual and a natural position in the community and stands for both.

The 'compadrazgo' in relation to the family

In addition to its importance on the individual level, the *compadrazgo* is linked to the family, for just as the person is born to natural parents he is reborn to spiritual parents. Ideologically, the same three-member structure underlies both sets of relationships. In the family the parents and child are contrasted on the basis of age, while the parents themselves are contrasted on the basis of sex; in the *compadrazgo* parent and godparent are united in contrast to godchild by a generational difference, whereas they are differentiated by choice, as are the natural parents.

Although the model for the *compadrazgo* and the family is the same, the two are contrasted as the spiritual to the natural, and, as deployed in Panama, the relationships are not only opposed but complementary. In some respects each is an inversion of the other, and an understanding of one is gained by viewing it within the total set of relationships that includes the other. I turn now to an examination of this opposition which is expressed in language, ideology and ritual behaviour.

In the family a birth normally follows formation of the conjugal tie. In the *compadrazgo* a baptism precedes or is the reason for founding the *compadre-compadre* bond. The parents bring the child into the physical world and household; the godparents initiate him into the spiritual world and community. One is ritually unmarked, the other marked.

In the family the mother-child bond is thought to be unbreakable; a mother is rarely renounced. An individual, however, may have several fathers or his recognized father may not be his genetic father. The family presents a system of one mother but possibly several fathers. In the *compadrazgo* of baptism, by contrast, there is only one godfather but two godmothers, and the godfather is more important. In the family the parent-child bond is more important than the conjugal tie, but in the *compadrazgo* the *compadre-compadre* tie is more important than the godparent-godchild one; that is, in one the vertical bond predominates over the horizontal tie, whereas in the other the reverse is true. In the family, also, a child is like his sibling in that he shares the same set of parents. In the *compadrazgo* each child in a given family is individuated by having a different set of godparents.

Kinship originates in birth and is founded on blood and residence. The *compadrazgo* begins in baptism (or confirmation or marriage) — the counterpart to birth — and is based on spiritual affinity. But where the household and material goods provide the cohesion for kinship, it is respect, that is expressive actions, that cements the *compadrazgo*. Both are types of property in the broadest sense, but they are opposed as the concrete to the abstract.

This same contrast is reflected linguistically. In both systems special words of address are used, and as in English, the terms denoting the comparable roles are related linguistically:

father	:	godfather	::	*padre*	:	*padrino*
mother	:	godmother	::	*madre*	:	*madrina*
son	:	godson	::	*hijo*	:	*ahijado*
daughter	:	goddaughter	::	*hija*	:	*ahijada*

A different linguistic usage is more interesting. The term 'hot hand', as noted, is used for a man whose godchildren die. He has bad luck and is seldom chosen to be a godfather. But the same expression, 'hot hand', can refer to a man's sexual potency. Jokingly it is a way of saying that a man is very masculine. The one expression, then, is used in the two spheres but in contrasting ways. In the context of familial relations 'hot hand' refers to a man's sexual power and life-giving force. In the context of the *compadrazgo* 'hot hand' refers to a destructive role, the killing of a child. In each case a man is the agent and a child is the object, but in the family hot produces life, while in the *compadrazgo* hot produces death. A categorical separation is made between natural and spiritual relations. When they intrude upon spiritual bonds, natural ties are reversed and become destructive.

The three uses of the term 'political' also present some contrasts. The previous children of two adults who form a conjugal union are termed 'political brothers' or 'political sisters'. The spouse of a parental sibling is a 'political' aunt or uncle, and the child is a 'political' nephew or niece. A godchild and the offspring of his godparents are 'political' brothers or sisters. The word 'political' is used only in these contexts. In all three cases the individuals classed as political relations are in an unusual category. In the first two situations they are neither kin nor non-kin. Their bond is made up of kinship and affinal links. In the third they are neither fully in the *compadrazgo* network nor fully out of it. Their bond is constructed from kinship and *compadrazgo* ties. And although persons in a political relationship are close to being prohibited partners, sexual relations are not proscribed between them. In the 'political' domain the *compadrazgo* shares features with both kinship and affinity.

A look at the terms used when individuals become *compadres* over a rice spigot is also of interest. The spigot is cut at its base, then pulled by one person from its sheath which is held by the other. The expression used to describe this process is 'to draw out' or 'obtain' a godchild, the same as that used in ordinary baptism. Is there an analogy between these two forms of baptism and the process of birth when a child is pulled from the womb? More significant the rice itself — the symbolic child and staff of life — forms the basis for a different series of associations. Rice is hulled in a mortar called a *pilón*; the process of hulling is *pilar*; the baptismal font is a *pila*. The substitution of rice for child is congruent with linguistic categories.

Conceptually, the godparent-godchild and *compadre-compadre* bonds are spiritual ties, and this spirituality is underscored by the heavy emphasis placed upon maintaining respect among the partners. The bonds amount principally to positive assurances of mutual esteem and prohibitions on profane elements entering. *Compadres* do not contract debts nor have sexual relations. The prohibitions of respect separate the bonds and assure their sacredness. From this perspective, a man with a hot hand, a godfather who retains in his hand the *bolo* coins, or a person who refuses to sponsor a child, are alike in that they represent an intrusion of the natural into the spiritual and take away the child's grace. Their behaviour is antithetical to spirituality — although in the realm of the natural, their actions are of value. Conversely, having *compadres* brings a person good luck, and a godparent can help protect a natural child against dangerous forces.

Through the *compadrazgo* the people come closest to reaching God during life on earth. The complex is an expression of discipline and good. The *compadrazgo* is formed over church rites, and through it the people carry into their lives something of the church.

The *compadrazgo* provides a means of placing all persons in the ideal order and gives them an enduring position in society. The godparent-godchild tie is complementary to that of parent and child. Godparents are linked to the moral aspect of their godchild's personality, and through the mediation of his godparents an infant enters the spiritual world. Godparents should counsel and teach their godchildren, and through this process children are individuated from their siblings. Yet, this complementary link is not laden with material obligations; a godparent gives gifts to his godchild out of his own free will and to receive the affection of his godchild. Conversely, a godchild feels free to ask of his godparent what he would not of others.

Compadres themselves have a mutual moral bond. A *compadre,* whether parent or godparent, is always assured of being respected and respecting, thereby lifting him to a spiritual level. *Compadres* are eternal: they greet one in heaven and intercede with God on one's behalf. The *compadrazgo* implants a perpetual sacred obligation between persons.

In contrast the family is primarily a material and sexual organization. Coition is shameful, and just as *compadres* do not contract debts, conjugal partners avoid a sacred tie. Through his parents a child enters the natural world, and his parents are the guardians of his material and physical life. The jural obligations of kinship are immutable; yet, from a different perspective, kinship bonds themselves, unlike *compadrazgo* ties, lack permanence. Sexual freedom on the part of men is permitted, and paternity may be denied. When an individual enters a household he nearly always assumes the role of a nuclear kinsman with the existing members, regardless of his original link, and kinship bonds sometimes are renounced.

Ties of kinship extend through time; the person is an offspring of his parents and a genitor of others. The *compadrazgo* has no temporal dimension. Nature regenerates itself, but the spirit must be imposed. Yet, the family is an impermanent unit in the continuous chain of kinship, for family ties cease at death. *Compadrazgo* bonds do not themselves generate further relationships, but they continue in the hereafter. As a natural being, man is part of the diachronic procession on earth, as symbolized by his last name which is collective and which continues. As a spiritual being his position on earth is 'fixed' as symbolized by his unique first name which cross-cuts the flow of surnames. Yet, this same name classifies him with others in the continuing spiritual order.

Birth gives a child the entitlement to a social position; baptism allots and implants the position. Each human can pass on the entitlement, but not the legitimation, for this can only be accorded by society as represented by the godparents. Baptism and confirmation are symbolic ventures whereby the child acquires an increasingly communal focus and personality outside his family. The godparent, then, like the parents, is connected to the growth of his godchild. But he stands outside the family and represents the society. The *compadrazgo,* in this respect, has a time dimension, but it is that of the individual life cycle, and this cycle, legitimated by the godparent, eventuates in the breakup of the family.

Elaborate ritual and public marking accompany the formation of the *compadrazgo.*   Long before a *compadrazgo* rite takes place it is announced, and representatives of the community are invited to attend. Family formation, be it by birth or non-church union, occurs without ritual and privately. Planned conjugal unions (and even pregnancies) are kept secret until the physical fact of co-residence (or motherhood) makes them obvious to the community. Family bonds are natural and private; *compadrazgo* ties are sacred and public.

The 'compadrazgo' and family in relation to the household

Family and *compadrazgo* bonds are deployed not only in relation to each other but with respect to the household. This brings me to the final stage of my argument: the interdigitation of kinship, residence and the *compadrazgo*. The elementary family provides the model for the household group, the *compadrazgo* is formed between these units.

Household groups are the basic units of organization in the community. They exploit the environment, undertake the sexual, reproductive and affective functions, and are independent, largely self-sufficient and based upon material ties. Kinship and conjugal unions are ways of recruiting members to and organizing households, and any new resident regardless of this true link may become a member of the family.

Kinship and affinal bonds link different households, but such ties are relatively weak. They are optative, and tend not to be utilized.

Suspiciousness and stealing exist between households. Children are kept at home to play, and houses are always set apart from one another. One's primary allegiance is to the household, and this group is set in opposition to other like groups.

The *compadrazgo* establishes safe links between households, for the mistrust normally encountered between them is eliminated by the spiritual bond. It is perfectly safe for a child to play at the house of his godparent. *Compadres* are always trusted, and they do not steal from one. Since *compadres* are sexually prohibited partners, a man will always trust his spouse to be alone with the godfather of their child or the father of one of her godchildren. He will trust no other men. *Compadres* are a different order of people but trust in them is achieved by eliminating them from the sphere of life in which sex, stealing and mistrust occur.

The people's rules for choosing godparents ensure that the ties be formed between household groups. Parents and child occupy one home; the godparent/*compadre* must live in a different one. Also, the fact that the children of the godfather become political brothers with the godson illustrates that the godfather's household has a unity with respect to the group composed of the godchild and his parents. When a young adult becomes a *compadre*/godparent and the term *compadre* is extended to his co-resident same-sex parent, this too is indicative of the unity of the godparental house in relation to the parent-child home. And when a young person is selected as godparent, it is often his co-resident parent who pays his godparental expenses. Furthermore, it sometimes happens that when a chosen young person cannot become the godparent, one of his co-resident siblings is selected in his place. Finally, the people's interpretation of the church dogma concerning married sponsors is itself influenced by the concept of the household: two individuals in common-law unions may be selected as sponsors so long as they are not themselves co-resident. Thus, the *compadrazgo* links households yet emphasizes the integrity and unity of each.

The countrymen themselves say that a household does not become a full unit nor have the appropriate internal organization until children are born. This event makes it a complete group. (Childless couples cast about to find a youngster to raise.) And until the children are baptized the household has no external ties which link it as a group to other such units. *Compadrazgo* bonds between the man or woman and others may exist, but these are individual bonds of the two adults and are different for each. The kin of each adult also are dissimilar. Only when it has baptized children does a household group have links as a unit to other such groups. Birth, which contributes to the internal organization and stability of the group, is always followed by baptism which results in the inter-household ties of the *compadrazgo*. Just as children cement a conjugal union and hence the group by the fact of their birth, so also they help establish its unity, validate its position and connect it to other households through baptism and the *compadrazgo*. The *compadrazgo* anchors the father-mother-child unit into the broader society by setting up diffuse links emanating from it in many directions. Thus, although households are not perpetual entities, for their duration the *compadrazgo* provides a system of spiritual links between them, and this lends a cohesion to the community it otherwise might not have. This cohesiveness is strengthened by replication of the institution over church marriage and by the prohibitions upon reversal of choice and repeated selection of the same sponsor.

Compadrazgo ties within a household, comparable to weak family bonds between households, have a minor function. Co-residents may not be selected as *compadres*. Following the church dogma the people say that a godparent should raise or be responsible for his godchild if the parents are unable to do so or die. At the least a godparent should act as if he were a parent when he sees his godchild. But in only two cases were godchildren raised by godparents, despite the many occasions when children need care. Significantly, in one, although the child was taken in at a young age, he did not become a 'raised' son but remained a godson. In the other, godmother and godson were also half-siblings. They confessed to their spiritual relationship with some embarrassment and pointed out that the godson, along with two of his siblings, was taken in on the basis of his kinship and not his spiritual link. It is not in the domain of the *compadrazgo* to recruit members to a household. Just as natural parents may not become spiritual parents to their natural child, so spiritual parents do not become natural parents to their spiritual child. And, just as family links between households are unemphasized, so the functions of *compadrazgo* ties within a household are minimized.

Thus, the family and *compadrazgo* are in a relation of complementary opposition; one is concerned primarily with intra-household ties, the other pertains to inter-household links. The kinship system is bilateral and fractionates the people into households; the *compadrazgo* cuts across these units. One entails physical and material exchanges, the other consists of spiritual and respectful bonds. Each intrudes in the sphere of the other, but their polarization minimizes the importance of the *compadrazgo* within the household and the family between households. There is a disjunction of these two relationship systems, but through their ideological opposition and complementary natures they also are united.

14 Relationships, residence, religion and the individual

The Panamanian countryside is somewhat unusual in that a distinctive *campesino* culture has been able to develop over the years with but subdued outside influences. Furthermore, no Panamanian village is average or normal; Los Boquerones is unique. Yet, the primary themes of my study are only variations of broader Hispanic ones, and Los Boquerones itself represents a local working out of certain Latin American values and institutions.[1] One contribution of my study has been to show both some of the diverse forms which these patterns may take and how they are woven together in a local setting. By way of conclusion I shall first summarize some of the important aspects of 'social structure' in Los Boquerones in order to underline the place of my study within this broader context.

The individual, a culturally defined entity, is composed of nature and spirit, is conceptualized in terms of his sex, and is classified according to his age. As a spiritual creature the person engages in spiritual relationships with God, the saints and other men. As a natural being the individual participates in earthly relationships with others and is engaged in practical affairs of the world. The natural character of the individual in turn provides one conceptual justification for the dichotomy of the sexes in that women are thought to be hot while men are cold. This opposition defines the person as a sexual being and sets the pattern for male-female relationships in all domains of the culture.

Religious conceptions provide an ultimate legitimation for these ideas about the individual and his systems of relationship. The uniqueness of the individual in relation to God, the devil and the saints is stressed. The natural and spiritual sides of the person are linked in that his destiny, which emanates from God, provides the framework and explanation for his everyday actions. All individuals are born in sin to a natural family. All must be cleansed of this sin, and at baptism the person is reborn to God and a spiritual family. But the individual carries a weight of sin through his life, and the entire age cycle of the person is partially conceptualized in terms of the religious formulations. The natural dichotomy of and asymmetric relationship between the sexes also receive religious validation in that Eve and Mary provide the models for females as sexual partners and as mothers.

The system of respect and shame links the individual to God and the social order. To have shame and respect, a person must be raised by others, and shame partially represents the ideals of society bred into the individual. Like a currency, respect cuts across all relationships, positions and characteristics of the individual, expressing and summarizing his total social standing while defining him as a complete but unique entity.

The domain of locality has been considered from several perspectives. On the broadest level, the community itself is a geo-political entity, although its boundaries are imprecise. Within the village and its environs a person is normally, though not prescriptively, kin with one or more persons, a result of the fact that mobility is low and that kin look for one another.

The household has been viewed as both concept and object. As entities, household groups are the principal functioning units in the community, while through the household as a concept ideas emanating from other domains receive expression. To be raised means that the individual is brought up in a house, and the complete life cycle of the person is thought out and expressed in terms of his changing relationship to the household, from his initial confinement in the bedroom after birth, to his restriction to play at the household while young, to his freedom in the street during young adulthood, to his movement to a new household at a conjugal union, to the physical restructuring of the house after his death. The male/female contrast also is most fully worked out in relation to the home, as seen in the precisely enumerated division of labour and epitomized in the expression: 'The man is in the fields, the woman is at home.'

The link between the household and kinship is an intricate one. In part, the kinship system is moulded by the concepts of the household and the individual. Ideas about the complementary natures of men and women, concepts about the relation between adults and children, and the co-residential couples prohibition (a codification of these same ideas about humans) ensure that at least one but no more than one conjugal family occupy a home. Furthermore, the specific characteristics of the spouse-spouse bond, the sibling-sibling tie and the parent-offspring relation. are themselves a function of ideas about the person and his growth cycle, as these are expressed through the household. Kinship ties among elementary family members are shaped by the definition of the individual and the concept of the household, and both these complexes of ideas are broader than the domain of kinship itself.

Choice among conjugal forms also is influenced by the ideals which individuals hold about themselves as independent persons and by whether or not the relationship is co-residential. Conjugal separations are motivated mostly by the strains which are inherent in the asymmetric relationship of the sexes. Thus, the conjugal sphere, too, is shaped by ideas which derive from non-familial domains.

But the family system also is partly defined by or composed of residence. The concept of raising links not only the individual and the household but also these two with kinship, for a raising relationship creates a tie of kinship. Furthermore, conjugal unions are differentiated from all other heterosexual but non-conjugal bonds on the basis that they alone are co-residential relationships. In these respects kinship is not simply genealogical nor does it compose a discrete domain; it includes the concept of the household.

Finally, the *compadrazgo,* the system of spiritual relationships, is founded on religious ideas about the individual. Based on the opposition of spiritual and natural paternity, in many respects the *compadrazgo* is an inversion of the natural family. But like kinship, the godparenthood system is worked out in relation to the household, as seen in its reciprocal relation to the household family. The *compadrazgo* can be fully understood only by first examining the religious formulations, and ideas about the individual, the household and the family.

In sum, I have tried to delineate an orderliness in the culture and social structure of Los Boquerones — a pattern not previously described by anthropologists working in cognate Latin American communities. Specifically, in terms of other Hispano-American studies I suggest the value of my work lies in its focus on the interwoven dimensions of the religious conceptions, the concept of the individual, the idea of the household, and the relationship systems. Los Boquerones is indeed unique, but I would hope that other analytical studies will emerge to prove my contention that something of the general may be seen in the particular.

Viewed more broadly this book also may be compared to the many family studies which have recently been conducted in the Caribbean area.[2] From this perspective I see three important levels where further comparative work might be carried out. At the most narrow, Caribbean investigators have been concerned with a number of problems, such as the form of the family, variability and instability in mating relations, forms of parent-child legitimacy, and the role of extra-domestic kinship ties. At the 'middle-level' they have considered such themes as the distinction between kinship and domestic group, the developmental cycle in the household, and domestic variations between different cultural groups within the same society. Finally, Caribbean anthropologists also have broached broader problems of 'explanation'. Are Caribbean systems best understood in terms of their history, either African or colonial, as units within plural societies, or as entities existing within particular economic, ecological and demographic conditions? The problems and arguments on the different levels raised by the Caribbean anthropologists may not yet be resolved, but their sophisticated analyses have scarcely been matched in the Latin American ethnography. My study, then, may also be considered in these comparative terms in that many of the ethnographic problems I have focused upon have been raised for the circum-Caribbean area, yet the approach I offer — emphasizing the analysis of a total set of interrelated cultural categories — is a new one.

I have intended for my exposition, however, to fit into an even broader framework concerning the theoretical study of a relationship system, and let me conclude by returning briefly to this larger issue. Anthropologists often have observed that persons in distant cultures are related or bound together by many-stranded ties. But from here there is a divergence in their methods of analysis. One line of argument starts with the observation that most of these multi-stranded ties have a kinship component. The kinship system next is abstracted from the diverse and multiplex actions in which it is manifested, and then an explanation of what is perceived to be kinship behaviour is given in purely kinship terms. In one final step of the argument 'action, belief, and practice, as well as the natural environment' are said to be simply the situations in which the social relations are expressed (Fortes, 1969: 307). In this argument analytical abstractions such as 'patrilineality' and 'matrifiliation' become moral imperatives and axioms of behaviour. Descriptive statements are given explanatory value.

Against this form of analysis a number of objections have been raised. To cite one example, Worsley (1956), in his re-analysis of Fortes's account of the Tallensi, has stressed that a kinship system exists within an ecological and economic context. Yet, at times his argument seems to waiver between saying that kinship may be reduced to economics and stating that much of what is said to be kinship motivated is in fact to be explained by economic facts. A careful reading of Worsley, however, shows that he does not demonstrate how economic practices themselves are translated into kinship relationships. He only elucidates the ways in which the Tale system is shaped by the mode of production. Worsley attacks the empty analytical concepts of the observer, but he does not offer anything in their place. It follows quite logically that in his argument kinship is seen to be only an idiom for other relations and its distinctive nature is denied.

The Worsley-Fortes controversy is an instructive one, but neither side, it seems to me, does full justice to the anthropological endeavour. Both omit the cultural dimension of social institutions – Fortes by his emphasis on abstract principles of social structure, Worsley by his assumption that economics, as in capitalistic societies, encompasses kinship. Both arguments are posited on the idea that the task of the anthropologist is to translate from one culture to another. I am in agreement that it is useful to employ words like kinship, residence and religion in order to direct attention to some facet of social life, but these words, derived from our own culture, do not necessarily represent an isolable entity in the ethnographic material. Rather than translate, the more interesting endeavour is to try to be sceptical about our own ideas and to attempt to assimilate the people's notions. The first question, then, is not what is the patterning of kinship in Panama, but does kinship exist and of what is it composed? What the countrymen mean by kinship is not what we mean by the term, although the two referents partially overlap, and to understand what the social institution of kinship is in rural Panama requires an examination of the ideas, beliefs and values which define the relationship and make it significant for the people. A kinship system cannot be treated as a discrete domain at the beginning of an inquiry, for what a people symbolize and mean by kinship – what it is – may link it to other domains from which it is useless, even incorrect, to abstract it. Rather than translating from one society to another, it is more valuable to confront distant systems of thought in order to understand these systems, our own, and our way of describing these systems. With this approach we come closer to the elusive goal of understanding, and anthropology truly becomes the study of relationships, both within and between cultures.

Appendix: household and population statistics

In this appendix, I am concerned primarily with the relation between the statistics on household organization and the principles outlined in the body of the book. From Table A.2 (Frequency distribution of household sizes) it is clear that the great proportion of houses contain from one to five persons; only 22 per cent of the groups are larger. In Table A.3 (Household heads classified by age and sex) the term 'household head' is introduced. The word refers to the person who holds ultimate authority over and responsibility for the group. In houses containing a conjugal couple the male is the head. Females are household heads only when they do not have a male partner, and an aged parent who joins the home of an offspring is not the head. In ambiguous cases headship was determined by asking villagers whom they considered the head to be. From Table A.3, then, it is apparent that over 85 per cent of the houses are headed by males, and among them the largest proportion of heads are aged between thirty-five and fifty-four. Female headship is not so bunched age-wise, but the numbers are too few for drawing conclusions.

In Table A.4 households are classified by sex and age of head and number of inhabitants. Of the larger households, most are headed by males. Females usually head households with four or fewer persons; it is more difficult for females than males to provision a group.

A summary of the relationship of members to heads of households is presented in Table A.5. Listed here are the original relationships between members and head. (As noted, more distant kin links often are converted into elementary family ties when fostering occurs.) These figures illustrate more clearly a fact which is hidden in Table A.4. There is an exactly equal number of single male and female heads; yet, the females have more than four times as many other persons within their households than the single males. Thus, while it is true that males in general head the larger households, (single) females head larger households than single males. The males in a conjugal union have an average of 3.5 (225/65) other persons within their homes; the single male has 0.5 (6/13) other persons; the single female has 2.2 (28/13) persons in addition to herself. Similarly, ten times as many children live with single females as with single males. Thus, females tend to keep the domestic group intact. Finally, it should be noted that only a few aged parents are affiliated with households of their children.

In Table A.6 (Household types classified by sex and age of head) are contained the figures of most relevance. The table divides household types into three 'categories': Conjugal male head of household; Single male head of household; Single female head of household. Each of these categories is divided into 'classes' which are labelled consecutively from A to J. An examination of the Table shows that a very large proportion of the households reflects the rules of domestic organization described.

Class A, numbering 32 per cent of the total households, consists of true nuclear families. Fourteen per cent of the households, class B, are made up of a conjugal pair plus fostered, adopted and/or step-children to one of the parents. Class C, listing those households with full offspring plus recruited children, contains 5 per cent of the households. In class D conjugal couples with children (recruited by any method) plus others, such as aged parents and children of the resident children, are listed. This class has 4 per cent of the households. Classes E and F contain conjugal couples without children, but these, too, reflect the basic pattern. The one couple in class F joined together during field-work and therefore have not had time to have children. The head's semi-incapacitated parents live in a home on the house site. The reasons for the couples of class E being childless are various. Most of those with the head more than fifty years of age are too old to bear children, have done so previously, and/or are at the end of the developmental cycle. Of those heads between forty and forty-nine years old, two have spouses more than fifty who are not their first mates. The third is church-married to a woman who has two grown daughters living else-where. Therefore, allowing for the effect of the developmental cycle, all the childless couples are living in households that follow the basic plan.

All of category I, therefore, or 71 per cent of the households, directly reflect the pattern of the elementary family household.

The households headed by a single individual present a more complex picture, but most of these also reflect the basic scheme of organization. Single male and female heads exist in equal numbers, but when their households are classified by whether or not they have other members in them an important difference emerges. Ten of the men live alone while only three have other persons in their households. In contrast, only four women live alone while nine have other members. Of these nine heads at least six have members who help provision the households. Two of the nine women were recently separated or widowed and one is a grandmother who takes care of her daughter's children but receives aid for doing so. This contrast in the composition of households headed by single male and female heads is illustrative both of the greater difficulty women have in living singly than men, and of the closer tie between mother and child than father and child.

If the households of categories II and III are closely examined it becomes apparent that only a few do not conform to the rules.

Of the single males who head households:

5 are bachelors;
2 were recently separated from their spouses;
1 is a young man looking for a spouse;
1 is a 'renounced' old man;
1 lives next door to a son who feeds him.

Thus, except for the five bachelors, all find themselves in their unusual positions as the result of old age, young age or a recent separation.

Of the single males who head households which include other members:

1 lives with his mother and a fostered child;
1 lives with his mother and a sibling;
1 lives with some of his children and was recently separated − his daughter is seventeen and tends the house.

In two of the cases, then, a female does live in the house. The third had his mate stolen from him and his daughter takes care of the domestic activities.

Of the single females who head households all have been in unions and are older women:

1 lives next door to a son who supports her;
1 farms by herself;
1 lives next door to a sibling;
1 is a prostitute and sells raffle tickets.

All have been in unions and are at the end of the developmental cycle or are still looking for spouses.

Of the females who head households which include other members:

1 is in an extra-residential union and lives with her son, mother and mother's mother;

1 is a prostitute who lives with her children and has never had a spouse;

1 lives with her mother and children;

1 lives with a step-father and is a prostitute;

3 live with their children and were recently separated or widowed;

1 who lives with her children has been widowed for several years; her eldest son drives a passenger bus and provides important material support;

1 older woman raises her daughter's children.

Except for the first three all are in their positions due to uncontrollable circumstances or have a working male in the house.

In sum, all the households of category I (65) plus all but five of category II (8) and all but three of category III (10) are a reflection of the rules outlined in the body of the book. The composition of 83, or 91 per cent, of the houses is an image of the basic plan of household organization. The other households follow permissible, but not so practicable, alternative modes of organization. Thus, household groups statistically reflect in one way or another the plan of a single conjugal couple living with children.

TABLE A.1   *Population, by age and sex*

	Number			Percentage		
Age	*Male*	*Female*	*Total*	*Male*	*Female*	*Total*
0 – 4	33	21	54	9·4	6·0	15·4
5 – 9	27	21	48	7·7	6·0	13·7
10 – 14	23	16	39	6·57	4·57	11·1
15 – 19	17	11	28	4·9	3·1	8·0
20 – 4	14	9	23	4·0	2·6	6·6
25 – 9	8	10	18	2·3	2·8	5·1
30 – 4	9	6	15	2·6	1·7	4·3
35 – 9	11	10	21	3·1	2·9	6·0
40 – 4	12	9	21	3·4	2·6	6·0
45 – 9	4	14	18	1·1	4·0	5·1
50 – 4	14	6	20	4·0	1·7	5·7
55 – 9	9	6	15	2·6	1·7	4·3
60 – 4	9	6	15	2·6	1·7	4·3
65 – 9	5	3	8	1·4	0·9	2·3
70 – 4	2	1	3	0·6	0·3	0·9
75+	1	3	4	0·3	0·9	1·2
Total	198	152	350	56·6	43·4	100·0

TABLE A.2   *Frequency distribution of household sizes*

No. of persons	*No. of households*	*Percentage of households*
1	14	15·4
2	14	15·4
3	18	19·8
4	12	13·2
5	13	14·3
6	9	9·9
7	5	5·5
8	3	3·3
9	2	2·2
10	1	1·1
Total	91	100·1

Mean household size = 3·8 persons.

TABLE A.3   *Household heads classified by age and sex*

	Number				Percentage		
Age	*Male*	*Female*	*Total*		*Male*	*Female*	*Total*
20 – 4	4	2	6		4·4	2·2	6·6
25 – 9	5	1	6		5·5	1·1	6·6
30 – 4	7	–	7		7·7	–	7·7
35 – 9	10	1	11		11·0	1·1	12·1
40 – 4	12	1	13		13·2	1·1	14·3
45 – 9	4	3	7		4·4	3·3	7·7
50 – 4	13	–	13		14·3	–	14·3
55 – 9	9	2	11		9·9	2·2	12·1
60 – 4	8	1	9		8·8	1·1	9·9
65 – 9	4	2	6		4·4	2·2	6·6
70+	2	–	2		2·2	–	2·2
Total	78	13	91		85·8	14·3	100·1

TABLE A.4   *Households classified by sex and age of head and number of persons*

Male head

Total no. of persons within house

Age of head	1	2	3	4	5	6	7	8	9	10	*Total*
20 – 4	1	–	1	1	1	–	–	–	–	–	4
25 – 9	1	–	2	1	1	–	–	–	–	–	5
30 – 4	1	–	–	1	3	2	–	–	–	–	7
35 – 9	1	–	4	–	1	1	1	1	1	–	10
40 – 4	2	2	2	–	2	2	1	1	–	–	12
45 – 9	–	1	–	–	2	–	–	–	–	1	4
50 – 4	1	1	3	1	2	2	2	1	–	–	13
55 – 9	1	4	2	1	–	1	–	–	–	–	9
60 – 4	1	2	3	2	–	–	–	–	–	–	8
65 – 9	1	–	1	–	1	–	–	–	1	–	4
70 – 4	–	1	–	–	–	–	–	–	–	–	1
75+	–	1	–	–	–	–	–	–	–	–	1
Total	10	12	18	7	13	8	4	3	2	1	78

TABLE A.4 (continued)

Female head				Total no. of persons within house							
Age of head	1	2	3	4	5	6	7	8	9	10	*Total*
20 – 4	–	–	–	2	–	–	–	–	–	–	2
25 – 9	–	–	–	1	–	–	–	–	–	–	1
30 – 4	–	–	–	–	–	–	–	–	–	–	–
35 – 9	–	–	–	–	–	1	–	–	–	–	1
40 – 4	–	–	–	–	–	–	1	–	–	–	1
45 – 9	1	1	–	1	–	–	–	–	–	–	3
50 – 4	–	–	–	–	–	–	–	–	–	–	–
55 – 9	1	1	–	–	–	–	–	–	–	–	2
60 – 4	1	–	–	–	–	–	–	–	–	–	1
65 – 9	1	–	–	1	–	–	–	–	–	–	2
70 – 4	–	–	–	–	–	–	–	–	–	–	–
75+	–	–	–	–	–	–	–	–	–	–	–
Total	4	2	0	5	0	1	1	0	0	0	13

TABLE A.5   *Relationship of members to heads of households*

Member	Conjugal male	Single male	Single female
Spouse	63	X	X
Children:			
Son of conjugal pair	83	X	X
Daughter of conjugal pair	49	X	X
Head's son	3	1	10
Head's daughter	0	1	10
Spouse's son	5	X	X
Spouse's daughter	2	X	X
Son's son	3*	0	0
Son's daughter	0	0	0
Daughter's son	3*	0	2
Daughter's daughter	4*	0	1
Sister's son	1	0	0
Spouse's siblings	3	0	0
Godchild	1	0	0
Distant kin	1	0	0
No kin relation	0	1	0
Legally adopted child	1	0	0
Head's father	2	0	1
Head's mother	1	2	2
Sibling	0	1	0
Head's step-father	0	0	1
Head's mother's mother	0	0	1
Total 259	225	6	28

* May be grandchild to one or both of conjugal pair. In three of these cases the parent of the child also is living in the home.

TABLE A.6   *Household types classified by sex and age of head*

I   Conjugal male head of household

   (A)   Conjugal couple with offspring of both only

Age of head	No.	% within class	% within category	% total
20 – 9	4	13	6	4
30 – 9	10	33	15	11
40 – 9	7	23	11	8
50 – 9	8	27	12	9
60 – 9	1	3	2	1
70+	0	0	0	0
Class total	30	100	46	32

   (B)   Conjugal couple with fostered, adopted and/or step-children (to one of pair) only

Age of head	No.	% within class	% within category	% total
20 – 9	2	15	3	2
30 – 9	3	23	5	3
40 – 9	2	15	3	2
50 – 9	4	31	6	4
60 – 9	2	15	3	2
70+	0	0	0	0
Class total	13	100	20	14

   (C)   Conjugal couple with own offspring plus fostered, adopted and/or step-children

Age of head	No.	% within class	% within category	% total
20 – 9	0	0	0	0
30 – 9	0	0	0	0
40 – 9	2	40	3	2
50 – 9	1	20	2	1
60 – 9	2	40	3	2
70+	0	0	0	0
Class total	5	100	8	5

TABLE A.6 (continued)

(D)   Conjugal couple with children (own, adopted, fostered or step-) plus others (e.g. aged parent, daughter or son with child)

Age of head	No.	% within class	% within category	% total
20 – 9	0	0	0	0
30 – 9	1	25	2	1
40 – 9	0	0	0	0
50 – 9	1	25	2	1
60 – 9	2	50	3	2
70+	0	0	0	0
Class total	4	100	6	4

(E)   Conjugal couple only

Age of head	No.	% within class	% within category	% total
20 – 9	0	0	0	0
30 – 9	0	0	0	0
40 – 9	3	25	5	3
50 – 9	5	42	8	5
60 – 9	2	17	3	2
70+	2	17	3	2
Class total	12	100	18	13

(F)   Conjugal couple (no children) plus others (e.g. aged parents)

Age of head	No.	% within class	% within category	% total
20 – 9	1	100	2	1
30 – 9	0	0	0	0
40 – 9	0	0	0	0
50 – 9	0	0	0	0
60 – 9	0	0	0	0
70+	0	0	0	0
Class total	1	100	2	1
Category total	65		100	71

TABLE A.6 (continued)

II Single male head of household

(G) Alone

Age of head	No.	% within class	% within category	% total
20 – 9	2	20	15	2
30 – 9	2	20	15	2
40 – 9	2	20	15	2
50 – 9	2	20	15	2
60 – 9	2	20	15	2
70+	0	0	0	0
Class total	10	100	77	11

(H) With dependants

Age of head	No.	% within class	% within category	% total
20 – 9	0	0	0	0
30 – 9	1	33	8	1
40 – 9	0	0	0	0
50 – 9	1	33	8	1
60 – 9	1	33	8	1
70+	0	0	0	0
Class total	3	100	23	3
Category total	13		100	14

III Single female head of household

(I) Alone

Age of head	No.	% within class	% within category	% total
20 – 9	0	0	0	0
30 – 9	0	0	0	0
40 – 9	1	25	8	1
50 – 9	1	25	8	1
60 – 9	2	50	15	2
70+	0	0	0	0
Class total	4	100	31	4

TABLE A.6 (continued)

(J)   With dependants

Age of head	No.	% within class	% within category	% total
20 – 9	3	33	23	3
30 – 9	1	11	8	1
40 – 9	3	33	23	3
50 – 9	1	11	8	1
60 – 9	1	11	8	1
70+	0	0	0	0
Class total	9	100	69	9
Category total	13		100	14
Grand total	91			100

Notes

1 **The country, people and problem**

1 A number of histories relating to Panama and the Veraguas area in particular are now available. See Carles (1959), Castillero, C. (1967, 1970), Castillero, R. (1962), Fuson (1958), Guzmán (1956), Lothrop (1950), Mercado, S. (1959), Pereira, J. (1963), and Sauer (1966).

2 According to Carles (1959: 272) the name 'Veragua' was changed to 'Veraguas' in 1739.

3 See Castillero C. (1967: 126; 1970: 83) and *Censos Nacionales de 1960,* vol. I, 1966.

4 Robe (1960: 18) remarks: 'Current speech of the central provinces contains a fairly large core of forms which are obsolescent or which in other Spanish-speaking regions have been replaced by other forms. Such terms were apparently introduced into the vocabulary of the Isthmus during the Spanish dominion.' He provides a list of such archaisms, many of which I recorded myself. For example, *asina* (thus) has not been replaced by *así*; *enantes* (formerly) is used where others might now employ *antes.*

5 See also Fuson (1958: 6).

6 *Censos Nacionales de 1960,* vol. IX, 1964.

7 Rubio (1950: 80) suggests that the town dweller is also differentiated from the *campesino* by his 'human type' and by his greater participation in 'Spanish cultural elements', but these are difficult distinctions to maintain, particularly since the countrymen, more than their urban counterparts, have retained elements of sixteenth-century Spanish culture.

8 *Censos Nacionales de 1940,* vol. VI, 1944; *Censos Nacionales de 1950,* 'Lugares Poblados de la Republica', 1954; *Censos Nacionales de 1960,* vol. I, 1966.

9 Kroeber's (1948: 284) well-known observation that peasants constitute part-societies with part-cultures is also relevant to the discussion.

10 See also Barnes (1961, 1964), Beattie (1964, 1965a, 1965b), Gellner (1960, 1963), Needham (1960, 1971), and Schneider (1965b, 1968, 1972).

2 **Village life and ties to the larger society**

1 To receive a *botella* one must have a *palanca* (lit: lever) or go-between who can secure the job.

2 After I left, the 1968 elections took place and Arnulfo Arias, a man popular among some of the *campesinos,* was elected to the presidency. For the third time, however, he was deposed by the National Guard, or police force. Panama has no regular army.

3 Occasionally a person will make a trip to Panama City in the hope of contacting a government official to solicit his aid in solving a problem. The

most dramatic example of this bypassing of channels occurred during the struggle, reported later, the people had to keep their land.
4 The bishopric of Santiago de Veraguas was created in 1963.

3 Economic organization

1 The material which follows is based upon my own research; however, mention should be made of several other studies which are concerned, wholly or in part, with Panamanian rural agriculture: Adams (1957); Biesanz (1950b, 1952); Fuson (1958, 1964b); Guzmán (1956); Hooper (1943, 1945); and Lombardo (1956).
2 Panama uses the currency of the United States.
3 House sites will cost $50.00 per hectare; for agricultural land the people will be charged $30.00 per hectare up to 10 hectares and apparently $1.50 for each hectare after that. Every parcel of land will have to be surveyed at a cost of $50.00 per survey, i.e. if a person buys separate house and farming plots he will be charged $100.00. Paperwork fees will amount to more than $20.00. The terms will be 20 per cent down with up to 20 years to pay, but the survey and paperwork costs will have to be paid in full at the outset.
4 Most authorities refer to this as the *roza* system. Fuson (1958: 189) suggests that the word comes from the Spanish *rozar*, a term he translates as 'to weed', and that in Spain a similar system is *la rozada*. In Los Boquerones the word *la roza* is not commonly used, and the term refers only to a new thick *monte* that is cut down for use.
5 Let me note certain assumptions in the figures: (a) the field is used for one year only; if used in a second year part of the first-year costs should be allocated to the second year; (b) the value of double- and inter-cropping maize, beans and other products, or adding sugar cane is not included; (c) the costs are based on the materials used or upon a rate of $1.00 per day which is the normal wage for such work; however, the latter is not a true 'opportunity foregone' since a man often cannot find wage work in the rice season. The *campesinos* themselves, although fully aware of these different figures, never unite a stream of costs and a revenue to produce a profit, for they do not sell the entire harvest − they are subsistence farmers. I provide these figures, then, to give a sense for the scale of the activity involved.
6 Ten-ton trucks for hauling the cane to the mills are owned by individual growers. Now, four persons in the community have bought trucks on hire-purchase. They make between $200.00 and $300.00 per cane harvesting season.
7 In addition to the general references cited earlier concerning rural agriculture, see Fuson (1959) and Erasmus (1956).
8 A *dicho* (saying, proverb) is a belief; it is said to be a truth because the public has tried it, although a saying is not a matter of law. All such sayings are thought to be old, having been passed down over the generations.
9 Adams (1957: 97) also notes that a distinction between the 'better off' and the 'poorer' is recognized in the countryside, but he adds: 'Within a person's lifetime he may move from a poor status to a better off status or the reverse. The distinction is one primarily of wealth and use of wealth. It is not really a class distinction at all.'

4 God, the devil and the saints

1 It is common and permissible to request a drink of water at another's house;

however, one must request and never serve himself. There is always some fear that an offering at a stranger's home may contain a malignant charm, and this theme is implicit in the story. Rights of the mother as mistress of the house and her antipathy toward a potential son-in-law also are evident.

2   The reasons why the countrymen so avidly play and follow the lottery are complex. As the payoff rate is fairly high, it is, in one respect, a form of savings. However, the notion of continually trying one's luck at the lottery also is fully consistent with the belief in God's unknowable power and the idea that each must seek his fate. The lottery is a prototype of man's life; the outcome of both is unknown, and the person plays the numbers just as he must play his life.

3   In this connection Adams's (1957: 102) comments from the early 1950s are pertinent: 'There were relatively few instances . . . of the priests making much effort to visit the countryside. They remained, for the most part, in the towns and administered to the needs of the townspeople. This has doubtless played a great part in the nature of the contemporary participation in religious activities on the part of the countryman.' But he also noted: 'As between townsmen and countrymen . . . the latter are, generally, more devoted than the former.'

4   For an interesting comparison see Dundes *et al.* (1971).

5   *Rezandores* are *campesinos* who have learned how to recite prayers. Their most frequent task is to lead the congregation who come for a wake. Two males and one female in the community are accomplished *rezandores,* and for their services they often earn money within and outside the village. *Rezandores,* however, are not thought to have special powers, although some also know how to recite over certain classes of illness.

6   The flagrant man and woman, it should be noted, are not simply turned into animals but into male and female horses whose actions they are replicating. The sexual distinction is preserved; the similarity is exact. In commenting upon the story one informant explicitly pointed out that one pair hid like people, while the other like animals did not.

7   As I note in the text my consideration of Eve and Mary has been influenced by Leach's (1961a, 1962, 1967) discussions of them. See also Christian (1972: 153-4).

8   Leach has published two similar articles on Genesis (1961a, 1962). For purposes here either version may be used and I therefore make reference to the latter publication. In the context of a more general critique Nathhorst (1970) attacked Leach's analysis; the material presented here, I think, provides some support for Leach's view.

9   Adams (1957: 104) noted: 'A pregnant woman, it was said, had a glance so strong that she could not only *ojear* [give the evil eye] a child, but make a snake stop moving by staring at it.' I cannot here trace the connection of these customs to the ambiguous power of sight.

10 See, for example, Kenny (1966: 57) and Reichel-Dolmatoff and Reichel-Dolmatoff (1961: 301-2).

11 Various euphemisms are used for coition. Eating and sex often are linked.

12 Two negative female images are presented by the concepts of the *tulivieja* and the female witch. The *tulivieja* is a woman who both aborted and threw away several of her live children. Eventually she confessed her sins to a priest; God condemned her to walk with her feet backwards and to search eternally for her lost offspring. She is said to lurk in the trees and near rivers, and to grab small children. From one perspective the *tulivieja* stands as an inversion of the proper female characteristics. Normal mothers live in a

house, die, raise children and these children have a named genitor. Female witches can fly, like to travel, can enter an unprotected house, can transport people over great distances, and like to attack small children and to suck on the umbilical cord of a newborn.

13 San Martín de Porres (1579-1639) was canonized in 1962. Born in Peru to a Panamanian woman and a Spanish *hidalgo,* he ministered to the sick and beggars, and was, I believe, the first *mestizo* to be canonized. See Attwater (1965: 234-5).

14 'Rarely does the countryman participate in the religious brotherhoods and societies which exist predominantly among the women of the towns; such societies require a church, a saint, and enough people to participate' (Adams, 1957: 101-2).

5 The individual

1 Concerning the concept of the individual see Dumont (1965, 1970a, 1970b, 1971), Schneider (1968), and Gillin (1955).

2 See Rubio (1950: 64).

3 In a fit of anger one man may call another *'cholo'.*

4 According to Robe (1960: 28) *cholo* comes from Aymará and refers to Indians who have recently acquired the manners and language of Europeans.

5 Robe (1960: 28) states that *cimarrones* were those Negroes who fled for the jungle from labour teams at the canal.

6 Cf. Pitt-Rivers (1967), and Wagley (1959). The Panamanian situation has been immensely complicated by the presence of the Canal Zone which both drew West Indians in the days of construction and brought USA racial attitudes to the country. Cf. Biesanz (1950a), Biesanz and Biesanz (1955: 202-35), and Biesanz and Smith (1951).

7 My findings do not accord with Pitt-Rivers's (1967: 548) statement: 'The term *Negro* refers only to the population of Jamaican origins. Imported for the construction of the canal, these people have retained their English tongue and their Protestant faith. Language and religion are the significant qualifiers of color in the definition of *Negro* in Panama.' It is true, however, that attitudes toward Negroes probably have been influenced by feelings toward the low paid West Indian immigrant labourer in the Canal Zone (Biesanz, 1949). See below, the word *'chombo'.*

8 On the other hand, dark-skinned people are thought to be more sensual, whites are cold. Thus, a man may use *mi morena* and even *mi negro* (masculine form) as terms of affection and intimacy for a woman, though *mi negra* (female form) is taken descriptively and considered insulting. The use of such terms in a heterosexual bond seems to indicate that closeness not respect is expected in the relationship. It also seems significant that one class of dog names is drawn from these colour categories: *negro, moreno, canela* (cinnamon) and *chombo.* Dogs are the only named animals. They also are addressed, like children, by the intimate *tú* (you) and not the respectful *usted* (you).

9 The term also may be lexically marked. A *persona particular* is sometimes said to be a non-kinsman, although he may be a *compadre.*

10 The countryman is usually conscious particularly of his own rural community, his friends and relatives in neighboring communities and towns, and only slightly of the entire structure within which he lives. In one region, that of the mountains and backlands of Azuero Peninsula, the countrymen are ·more conscious of their differences from the

townspeople. They are said to . . . call each other, among themselves, *'manos'* or *'manitos'* . . . The writer has received information from diverse sources . . . that the term *manos* refers to 'hands' and stems from the fact that they are supposed to shake hands upon meeting (Adams, 1957: 98).

However, Hooper (1945: 237-8) thinks the term *manos* is derived from brother *(el hermano)*. I did not encounter this expression in Veraguas although Adams's general description fits the ethnography here reported. See also Rubio (1950: 64) who agrees with Hooper's derivation.

11   The period of mourning generally lasts for six months at the end of which time the widow may begin to see other men. As she forms new relationships with males, the term of reference is dropped. The word is used out of respect and 'to distinguish her'. When the widow sees other men, they no longer need to 'keep consideration' for her.

12   For comparison, see Brown (1965: 51-100), Foster (1964), and Nelson (1971: 78-80).

13   See, for example, Reichel-Dolmatoff and Reichel-Dolmatoff (1961: 180-3).

14   By canon 761 it is the cleric's responsibility to see that a child is given a Christian or saint's name, although it is first the parents', then the guardians', and finally the sponsors' right to select the name.

15   See also Robe (1960: 77) and Reichel-Dolmatoff and Reichel-Dolmatoff (1961: 183-4).

16   The hot/cold system of classification has been reported from innumerable societies in Latin America. Several explanations of it have been offered. To my knowledge, however, all such explanations have been formulated with reference to particular social groups; the system has not been considered as a cross-cultural complex with local permutations. Useful historical and contemporary descriptions, and possible explanations, can be found in the following: Currier (1966), Foster (1953b, 1960: 14-15, 20n, 61; 1967: 184-93), Foster and Rowe (1961), Ingham (1970), Lloyd (1962, 1964), Stein (1961: 80-6, 292-5), Taylor (1922).

17   Some items, however, are categorized as neither hot nor cold but 'fresh' *(fresco)*.

18   In Alcalá, Spain, *la naturaleza* means nature, place of birth, and community to which one belongs by origin. It is related to the sense of closeness felt by persons born in the same village (Pitt-Rivers, 1961: 8, 30, 111, 225).

19   Although most countrymen assert that female humours are far stronger than males', others hold that there is little difference between the sexes. Those who say women have stronger humours point to the fact that the sexual passion of a woman is endless while a man's is not. The view that the sexes differ in relation to hot and cold goes back to the Greek philosophers. But it is notable that even these thinkers differed with respect to which sex was hotter, argued from *a priori* considerations, and adduced almost any evidence to support their views (Lloyd, 1964: 102-6).

20   For similar beliefs see Foster (1953b: 205).

21   One man explained that it is possible to cook an egg between a woman's legs, her humour is so hot; egg *(el huevo)* is a common metaphor for testicle.

Some 10-15 years ago one man, who is still in the community, began to grow weak from the strong humour of his newly acquired spouse. As he bent over in the fields air, from her strong humour, would pass from his buttocks. His father prepared a cure which is the only known antidote. He took three eggs and broke them open on a plate without cracking the yolks. The man took down his pants and bent over the eggs. Air passed out and then came rushing back into his buttocks. As it did so one egg was sucked up into his anus; he repeated the act two times. It is said that eventually he would have died without this remedy.

22 For comparative insights I have found the following to be useful: Campbell (1964), Davis (1970), Kenny (1966), Lauria (1964), Lisón-Tolosana (1966), Peristiany (1965), Pitt-Rivers (1961).

23 This dual aspect of respect (and honour) has been noted for a number of societies. See, for example, Lauria (1964: 55) and Pitt-Rivers (1965: 21, 72).

24 Pitt-Rivers (1965: 38) has argued that this semantic confusion preserves social integration. The honour of the ruler is validated and the social code is legitimated when honour as precedence becomes honour as virtue.

25 This definition is similar to that provided by Pitt-Rivers (1961: 113; 1965: 42).

26 This aspect of the notion of respect in Puerto Rico has been well described by Lauria (1964).

27 A related expression as used in Alcalá appears to be *la cara dura* (hard-faced) (Pitt-Rivers, 1961: 114).

28 *La cara limpia* (clean, pure face) is employed almost equivalently. A person who steals or asks for a loan and is refused, and then returns again to ask for help has *la cara limpia* and is shameless.

29 The response is appropriate in that a man's identity is linked to providing his family with produce from the *monte*. Implicit also is an opposition between the safety of the house and the danger of the fields.

30 The patterns of distrust and living without obligations are congruent with the general types of ties that the people form with outsiders. Political, economic and social power, broadly speaking, lie outside the community. The countrymen are distrustful of and try not to be dependent upon these outside forces, just as they distrust others in the community. At the same time to avoid personal affronts in the village they find it easier to let outsiders settle disputes among themselves. The values concerning the independence of the person and power lying in the hands of outsiders are self-supporting patterns.

6 The household

1 A small plot of beans in the field is known as a 'garden of beans', and beans which are planted as a second or double crop in the field are a 'pot garden' *(la huerta de olla)*. If the context requires, the house garden may be distinguished as *la huerta de la casa*.

2 The situation is slightly more complicated than I describe in that combinations of the house types also are found. Fuson (1964a) provides a culture trait study of house types, and some brief information may be found in Rubio (1950: 91-102).

3 To rid the domicile of the 'vapour' of the dead, at the death of a household member the entire room is abandoned or the bedroom walls are reshaped so that the place where the deceased's bed was located falls outside the house.

4 Such potions may be obtained from a sorcerer *(el hechicero)*. They are specific-purpose medicines which may kill an individual, cause a woman to leave her mate, or lead to other deleterious effects.

5 More broadly, a person rarely accepts uncooked food or drink from another; and an individual should offer only cooked food.

6 Garden crops need the 'heat of people', and non-utilitarian fences are often constructed about a house site. People always sleep at a house and not in the *monte*, which is thought to be dangerous at night.

7 Parents frequently voice the fear that their children, unless watched, will take up the habit or vice of eating dirt.

7 The household and the elementary family

1 Concerning domestic groups and the family see Adams (1960), Bender (1967), Berkner (1972), Fortes (1949), Gonzalez (1969), Goody (1958, 1972a, 1972b), Smith, M. G. (1962b), and Smith, R. T. (1956, 1963).

2 As I shall describe in chapter 9 the countrymen distinguish between legal (church and state) marriage and common-law unions. I use the terms 'marriage', 'husband', 'wife', and 'legitimate' only for such official bonds and employ terms like 'conjugal', 'connubial', 'spouse', and 'mate' to refer to non-legal forms *or* in a more general sense to refer to both the legal and non-legal forms together. The referents of these latter terms should be clear from the context.

3 For comparison with similar patterns of the male-female (and spouse-spouse) relationship in Spain and Latin America see Lewis (1951: 98-9, 319-29), Pitt-Rivers (1961), and Reichel-Dolmatoff and Reichel-Dolmatoff (1961: 184-93, 254-7). Lisón-Tolosana (1966: 168) points out that the current division of labour between husband and wife in Belmonte de los Caballeros (Spain) is based upon sixteenth-century prescriptions.

4 Fathers and brothers are not so shamed by the activities of their daughters and sisters, although the household head is always concerned with the behaviour of the junior members of the group.

5. See Campbell (1964: 152), Kenny (1966: 83), and Pitt-Rivers (1961: 116).

6 See Aguilera Patiño (n.d.: 161-2) and Robe (1960: 118).

7 As Pitt-Rivers (1965: 46-7) pointed out, one of the great curiosities is that the man who steals the woman is not labelled nor thought to be injurious of the moral order. In Panama, however, the term *'el picaro'* (rogue) can be used in several senses: (1) a thief; (2) a man who does not repay debts; (3) a man who steals another's mate. Stealing another's spouse, it is said, is not the same as being *facultado* in the street. According to Caro Baroja (1965: 112) in the sixteenth-century the *picaro* was the archetype of the shameless one. The Panamanian usages would appear to have preserved this sense of the term.

8 According to the Santiago mayor all children legally have an equal right to the inheritance. None has a special right or obligation towards his parents. I heard of no cases in which a person had gone to an official to resolve a dispute concerning an inheritance or familial responsibilities.

9 It is considered worst to fight with one's mother, then one's father. Fighting with brothers or *compadres* is almost as bad as with the father. Following them, quarrels with aunts/uncles and nephews/nieces, then cousins, and finally more distant kinsmen, are considered to be wrong.

10 Unlike the practice in other parts of the interior (Hooper, 1945: 240-1), the word is not used for a political boss.

8 From natal to conjugal household

1 In his summary of the Jamaican family system Davenport (1961: 446) notes: 'The rule of household formation, then, is that no single household will contain more than one active conjugal pair.'

2 The *campesinos's* proscriptions are roughly equivalent to the canonical laws concerning matrimonial impediments (canons 1076, 96); however, the countrymen do not recognize affinity as an impediment, which is specified

in the code (canons 1077, 97).

3   By canon law second cousins and first cousins once removed are both related in the third degree (canon 96).

4   Ecclesiastically, until the end of his seventh year a person is termed an infant and is presumed not to have the use of reason; at the end of his seventh year an individual is said to enjoy the use of reason.

5   It is also said that an older person in his dotage who no longer is able to think or act, once again becomes a child or *angelito*. He no longer sins, and his past sins become lighter.

6   For the funeral of an *angelito* candles are not always used, people are not expected to cry and the prayers are shortened. It is said that in the past the death of an *angelito* was celebrated with singing and the provision of food. Adams (1957: 94) reports a similar custom. For comparison see Pitt-Rivers (1958: 425).

7   Although land rights presently are not an important part of the inheritance, when the people do obtain ownership rights through the agrarian reform programme the inheritance system itself may become of much greater import. A glimmering of the impact this change may have on the household is provided by the few cases in which men have accumulated valuable goods. In such instances the fathers have found it more profitable to keep the property together and not part it as their children have left the household. In turn, this has had an effect on the household and family arrangements which the children have worked out. In one case father and non-resident sons pool their labour; in another the sons have remained at home; and in a third sons and sons-in-law work part of the time for the father.

9   Forms of conjugal relations

1   If a common-law union lasts for ten years, the state does recognize it as having the same effects as a civil marriage, although the people are not aware of this law.

2   One test case for my argument would be the following situation. What happens in the case of a legally married couple who separate but do not seek a divorce? Are subsequent children of the mother recognized by her legal husband? In the few examples which I have, the later children were not recognized by the legal husband but by the man who was co-resident with the mother when they were born. Separated but legally married spouses are considered by the people to be married, but from their standpoint the bond would have been dissolved if the state permitted. (By Panama law children born to a legally married but separated couple are considered offspring of both, if born within 300 days following the separation. A child born after 300 days of a *legal* separation is not automatically legitimate. See *Codigo Civil de la Republica de Panama*, 1960, articles 140, 146, 149.)

3   See articles 92, 94, 97, 130, 131 and 205 of the *Codigo Civil* (1960).

4   Civil marriages like *juntado* unions are often robberies in that the father's rights have been usurped. The cost is probably for the right to dispense with the fifteen days of waiting while the marriage proclamation is made public.

5   See articles 88 and 89 of the *Codigo Civil* (1960).

6   In these two Tables only 41 *juntado* unions are included. I was unable to obtain information concerning the duration of one of the common-law bonds.

7   The only other church celebrations of the life cycle, baptism and confirmation, require much smaller *fiestas* and the costs of the celebrations are shared among several persons.

8   Regardless of his legal status a child always bears his mother's surname. If he is legally recognized, then the offspring also carries his father's surname. The issue here was whether or not the father's patronym was inherited. In the past if a woman were an unrecognized offspring and if her children also were unrecognized, then her surname or matronym also became the surname of her children. In this case surnames could and did pass matrilineally.

9   Nevertheless, no children were fatherless, for in cases of renunciation the mother always named someone else. In this respect no persons were natural in the sense of having only a mother. Filiation was either acknowledged by or imputed to a male; it was always bilateral.

10   For example, one of the prostitutes always names a man who lives outside the community, and he apparently has agreed to recognize her children. But he has never been sued by her for child support, and it is pointed out that several of her children bear no resemblance to him.
        Shortly after his child was born in hospital one man told me that he had been in to sign for and recognize his offspring; however, the hospital had been out of the proper forms and so he had been permitted to remove his common-law spouse and child but had to return in a few days to complete the form. He added jokingly that in the meantime the child had no name, but then corrected himself saying that of course it had a name, even if it was not officially recognized. But there was a point to his humour. Although it has been biologically procreated, until a child is recognized it has no kinship status and therefore no right to a name indicative of that status. Mere possession of a name and kinship status within the community, however, does not give a child a full jural position and entitle it to be buried in the cemetery. Only when a child has been baptized, that is has both a recognized natural and spiritual personality, may it be buried in the communal grave-yard.

11   In the following chapter we shall see that the proportion of children who are resident with their mothers only is higher than those who are resident with their fathers only. However, even the matrifilial link, although not denied, may be attenuated. In two cases young women formed relationships with males, bore children, and then returned with their offspring to their own mothers' houses. Both, then, proceeded to live quite free lives, wandering in the street. Neither contributed to her mother's house, and both left over the principal job of raising their children to their mothers. In both cases, then, the matrifilial in addition to the patrifilial link was weakened. But in neither case was the mother-child bond renounced, and in both situations mother and child were co-resident. Moreover, the mother-child tie was supplanted by the grand-matrifilial bond. Here, then, were functional analogues of the male's freedom in the street; however, neither female had as much freedom as a man would have had, and both were discussed with some scorn by others.

12   According to the Santiago mayor the cost varies in conformity with the resources of the persons and could well be less than this amount.

13   Even if it were argued that the possibility of a civil divorce protects males in a state marriage, it is still true that a man would be legally obliged to support his state-married ex-wife. Moreover, although it was never considered, a man could also seek a civil divorce from his church-married spouse.

14   The term *empeñado* (pawned, obliged, compelled) is sometimes used in reference to church-married persons.

15   Thus, there is a conflict within male values. To exhibit his manliness a male wishes to preserve his sexual freedom; however, he can also demonstrate financial independence by marrying a woman in church. Similarly men want

to have the right to renounce their paternity, but the man who consistently does so is without foundation. With respect to the first conflict a man exhibits his financial manliness simply by entering a conjugal union, but he preserves his freedom by choosing the *juntado* form.

16 A church marriage always includes a civil bond. Therefore, the true total of civil marriages includes both church and civil marriages, or 35 per cent of the conjugal unions had a legal bond. Further, the statistics collected at a particular moment hide the fact that a number of persons had taken out civil marriages, separated and then entered common-law unions with other partners. At least six additional persons, not married to one another, had been civil married and separated. I also suspect that a few others had at one time taken out state marriages. On the other hand, only two women had been separated from their church-married spouses. Because a church marriage is public and cases of separated, religiously married partners are always well known, I doubt that other examples escaped my attention. Thus, the statistics understate the total number of persons who have entered a civil marriage and the people's comparative acceptance of this form of union.

17 The conflict between the male value of preserving freedom and the church value of entering sacred, monogamous, permanent bonds is certainly not confined to Panama. It is possible to envisage other solutions. One would be to practise church marriage along with concubinage and keeping mistresses, but several factors militate against this pattern. Keeping a mistress or concubine is expensive, and except in a few instances, most men are unable to do so, while a church marriage diminishes rather than enhances a man's rights in the street. Also, it is not necessary to preserve a paternal name or estate and therefore unnecessary to contract a legitimate marriage. Finally, unlike many areas, common-law unions may be contracted. Therefore, instead of practising official marriage plus keeping mistresses, the people normally keep open the possibility of serial mating.

10 Conjugal instability

1 Of the twelve separations, eleven were between *juntado* partners; one separation was between a church-married pair. After a few months they re-united.

2 Other women made clear that Eufemia either had acted quite purposely or had not shown a good understanding of the relations between the sexes. Strategically a woman should not have on a long face when her drunken mate returns. She should feed him and humour him, otherwise it is likely that he will hit her.

3 A 'junior household member' is one who is under the authority of the household head and has not yet assumed the full adult role. This analytic category does not include spouses or aged persons who live with their offspring.

4 If there were no 'double recognition' fostering would reduce to adoption and would amount only to the switching of a child from one kinship position to another.

5 It is always the recognized parents who become *compadres* with the child's godparents. Thus, even though a raising father, in place of the recognized father, may accompany the child to his baptism or select the godparents, he is not integrated into the network of spiritual ties which surround the child. The basic kinship position of the child is preserved with respect to the *compadrazgo*.

6 Such are the people's conceptions. In present times a one-year-old offspring

of a common-law union would already have been legally recognized by a male.

7   The term 'political brother' is never applied between the offspring of a prostitute and the offspring of her lover. The ambiguity of kin relation only holds between the lover and the prostitute's offspring or between the prostitute and the lover's offspring.

11   Extra-domestic kinship and affinity

1   Males of the community carry the coffin and dig the grave. Both men and women of the village attend the nine nights of the wake.

2   For example, the night the widow began to have her miscarriage, a neighbour came to find out what the problem was and then went to notify the sister-in-law.

3   A brief contrast to this example is afforded by the case of a man and woman who have an epileptic son. All their other children have separated and established their own households. The epileptic son, although he is now fully grown and capable of doing some work, is kept at home, fully supported, and supplied with medicine, much to the financial hardship of his parents. So long as he is at home their obligations continue. I never heard them suggest that he might move elsewhere.

4   Whether or not a couple is legally married has no effect upon the use of the term *'politico'*.

5   Some of these issues have been cogently discussed by Fortes (1962: 5-7), although I believe he underestimates the impact of low mobility.

12   Forming the 'compadrazgo'

1   By canon laws 759 and 742 non-solemn, private baptisms are permitted to be held in danger of death. Laymen are allowed to perform such rites. However, if a layman performs the ritual only the acts essential to the baptism may be discharged. If the child lives, those ceremonies which were omitted should then be conferred in church. For a private baptism the church requires that at least one, if not two, witnesses be present. What follows in the text is the people's version of this rite.

2   By canon 742 for non-solemn baptism a priest is preferred to other lower-order religious functionaries and to a layman; a man is preferred to a woman. A father or mother is not allowed to baptize, unless in danger of death there is no one else to do so.

3   By canon law 745 baptism may be conferred only upon living persons; however, the rules governing the baptism of a foetus (canons 746-8) are more complicated. Under certain conditions, for example, baptism in the womb is permitted.

4   When baptism is performed a second time conditionally, the same sponsor should be used; a new sponsor does not contract spiritual relationships (canon law 763).

5   According to canon law 770, infants should be baptized as promptly as possible. Some authorities seem to indicate that baptism should occur within fifteen days following birth (Abbo and Hannan, 1960a: 769).

6   Although exceptions are allowed, canon law (canons 773 and 774) specifies that a baptism should be performed at the baptismal font of the parish church.

7   This of course is the people's idea, although it coincides with general church views. As we shall see the *madrina de pila* also stands up for and holds the

child at the font. Theologically this is the most important act.

8   The saying does not fit the practice in that it implies that the godmother of the church door takes the child from the house (lodging = *posada*) to the church. The people explain that the park is the *posada;* however, I have some indications that in other parts of the countryside the godmother of the church door comes to the infant's house, puts on street clothes she has purchased, and takes the child from the house to the church door. At the park the *madrina de pila* puts on the new suit of clothes, and takes the child. After the baptism the *madrina de la puerta de iglesia* sometimes carries the child from the font to the church door. In these cases the people think that the godmother of the church door is the most important godmother as she protects the child from the devil during the journey to the church, even though she does not present the infant at the font. The fact that in Los Boquerones the godmother of the church door occasionally buys clothes in addition to the godmother of the font may be the result of the intrusion of the one set of customs upon the other.

9   Theologically sponsors bind themselves to answer for another. They bring the child to the church; in his name they ask for the gift of faith, make a profession of faith and renounce Satan. Sponsors pledge to have an enduring spiritual interest in their spiritual child and to ensure that he leads a Christian life.

10   By canon 761 pastors should see to it that the baptized person is given a Christian name. If he does not have a Christian name the pastor should add a saint's name to the name selected by the parents and record both in the register of baptisms.

11   In Nocorá, Puerto Rico, the child is not bathed for twenty-four hours following his baptism (Padilla Seda, 1956: 295).

12   The father is the one who invites the guests and therefore controls the size of the *fiesta*. The food costs may not represent actual expenditures if household chickens and rice are used. The cooks are not paid. They eat at the *fiesta* and take some food home.

13   According to canon law the preferred age for reception of confirmation is seven years. Confirmation may be conferred before then if there is danger of death, or good and serious reasons exist. A child should be confirmed before he has been admitted to his first Holy Communion.

        The church qualifications for the lawful and valid reception of confirmation are that the child be baptized, be in a state of grace and be sufficiently instructed in the faith if the age of reason has not been reached.

14   By canon 787 the sacrament of confirmation is not deemed to be absolutely necessary for salvation; however, if the opportunity to be confirmed exists, it cannot be bypassed. Refusal to be confirmed is a grave sin.

15   According to canon 794 no more than one confirmation sponsor is permitted. By canon 795 a sponsor must be used, if possible.

16   According to canon 791 the appropriate place for confirmation is a church, but for good and sufficient reasons it may be conferred in other 'worthy' places.

        By canon 782 the ordinary minister of confirmation is a bishop; the extraordinary minister is a priest to whom that power has been granted by the common law or special indult of the Apostolic See.

17   In discussing his conception of life (and reincarnation) one person stated:
        'The spirit is just like a rice seed. You plant the seed in the earth and a rice stalk grows. The rice stalk is like the body, the new seeds that form are like the spirit. When the rice stalk is cut this is like the body's death. Now, the body-stalk is worth nothing, but one takes the seeds and

guards them to plant next year. The same as the spirit roams freely for a year or so before being planted in the womb of a woman.'

18   The word *moro,* of course, was brought to Panama by the Spanish settlers. Use of the term for the unbaptized is not restricted to Panama; it is commonly employed in Spain and Spanish America.

19   Canon law 1239 specifies that the unbaptized, including the unbaptized children of Catholic parents, may not have a Christian burial. They may not be interred in a sacred place nor have the sacred rites performed over them.

20   Cross-culturally the blessing of animals is not uncommon. Sometimes the *compadre-compadre* relationship may be formed over the rite 'baptizing' them. See, for example, Romney and Romney (1966: 56).

21   As animals, dogs occupy a special position. They are kept at the house to guard the human inhabitants. Unlike all other animals they should be fed from a dish, otherwise they will have to eat the dirty earth with their food. Often, dogs are given the leftovers of human food. They are scolded in the same tones of voice, sometimes the same words, that are used for a child. Dogs are said to be more intelligent than other animals. Unlike horses they 'understand' rather than just 'recognize' their masters. Chickens do not even recognize their owners.

22   Change of dress is, of course, a common theme in many transition rites; but the obligation of the godparents to purchase baptismal clothes is quite widespread among those societies which practise the *compadrazgo.* For example, animals, houses or idols which are blessed are often first 'dressed' by the godparents. See Romney and Romney (1966: 56).

23   It is common for one segment of a transition rite to be more emphasized than another. The journey to Santiago is considered to be more dangerous and important than the trip back home. This is undoubtedly linked to the unintegrated, unspecified position which the unbaptized occupies. The custom of employing two godmothers may be connected to the importance of this first journey. As noted, there is some disagreement concerning which godmother is more important, although everyone agrees that the one who carries the child to the church is the most important. It could be argued that the maternal sponsor has two important functions: to carry the child to Santiago and to hold the child at the font. These two duties, in many communities of the countryside, are stressed by separating the functions between two different godmothers: the *madrina* of the font and the *madrina* of the church door. Perhaps for this reason the *campesino* populace has replicated the godmother role from the more ordinary core structure. In Los Boquerones, however, as in neighbouring villages, these two functions have been coalesced back into one and are carried out by the *madrina de pila.* The godmother of the church door, therefore, has only residual duties. Finally, it may be that a godmother rather than the godfather carries the child precisely because baptism is a rebirth.

24   *El bolo:* dunce, stupid fellow.

25   The godfather holds the baby's head which is baptized directly.

26   In discussing luck in Mitla, E. C. Parsons (1936: 322) refers to 'the *peso bautisado* which is one the godmother puts into the clothes of her godchild where the padre will not see it and which gets baptized along with the child. This baptized piece is called by the child's name. If the woman pays it out, on her way home she will call it by name and it will return to the place where she carries her money'. Parsons identified this custom as being of Spanish origin. The *bolo* also is practised in Mitla in variant forms (Parsons, E. C., 1936: 90 n. 61).

27 This choice between baby and money also is made evident by the expressions which the children shout at the godfather as he emerges from the church.

28 Funerals also are public; an individual is expected to attend the funerals of his *compadres,* godparents and godchildren.

13 The structure of 'compadrazgo'

1 This type of salutation appears to have cross-cultural consistency. See, for example, Hammel (1968: 80), E. C. Parsons (1936: 198, 384, 458), Pierson (1951: 121, 142), and Ravicz (1967: 240).

2 When one man was complaining that much of his rice and yuca were being stolen from his field, I asked who worked in the adjoining area. He replied with great surety that it could not be his neighbour since that man was his *compadre.*

3 For an examination of this term in relation to respect see Lauria (1964).

4 Foster (1953a: 6) reports that midwives in Spain occasionally are called *'comadres'.* I recorded no such use of the term in Panama, where a midwife is termed *'la comadrona'* or *'la partera'.*

5 Like the man who refuses outright, the person with a hot hand also takes away the child's grace. In Yugoslavia, too, a sponsor whose godchildren die is often replaced. 'Injury or slight to the sponsor brings ill luck, and an angered sponsor may curse either the family of the godchild or the new relationships formed without his permission. The curse of the *kum* . . . is dreaded more than that of a father' (Hammel, 1968: 42).

6 Similar views about rich *compadres* are found elsewhere. 'A man who seeks a wealthy *compadre* in Poyal is held in some contempt by his fellows; a wealthy *compadre* would not visit him nor invite him to his house' (Mintz and Wolf, 1950: 359). A number of folk tales which I cannot detail here concern the ambivalent relationship between 'rich *compadre*' and 'poor *compadre*'.

14 Relationships, residence, religion and the individual

1 See, for example, Beals (1946), Doughty (1968), Fals-Borda (1955), Foster (1967), Gillin (1945), Harris (1965), Lewis (1951). Pierson (1951), Redfield and Villa Rojas (1962), Reichel-Dolmatoff and Reichel-Dolmatoff (1961), Richardson (1970), Service and Service (1954), Stein (1961), Steward (1956), Wagley (1949, 1953), and Whitten (1965).

2 For some of the works relevant to the discussion see: Clarke (1966), Davenport (1961), Frazier (1937), Gonzalez (1969), Henriques (1953), Herskovits (1941), Horowitz (1967), Mintz and Davenport (1961), M. G. Smith (1962a, 1962b, 1966), R. T. Smith (1956, 1957, 1963).

Bibliography

ABBO, J. A. and HANNAN, J. D. (1960a), *The Sacred Canons: A Concise Presentation of the Current Disciplinary Norms of the Church,* vol. I (2nd rev. ed.), St Louis: B. Herder Book Co.

ABBO, J. A. and HANNAN, J. D. (1960b), *The Sacred Canons: A Concise Presentation of the Current Disciplinary Norms of the Church,* vol. II (2nd rev. ed.), St Louis: B. Herder Book Co.

ADAMS, RICHARD N. (1957), *Cultural Surveys of Panama – Nicaragua – Guatemala – El Salvador – Honduras* (Scientific Publications No. 33), Washington: Pan American Sanitary Bureau.

ADAMS, RICHARD N. (1960), 'An Inquiry into the Nature of the Family', in *Essays in the Science of Culture* (ed. G. E. Dole and R. L. Carneiro), New York: Thomas Y. Crowell Co.

AGUILERA PATIÑO, L. (n.d.), *El Panameño Visto a Traves de su Lenguaje,* Panamá: Ferguson y Ferguson.

ATTWATER, D. (1965), *The Penguin Dictionary of Saints,* Harmondsworth: Penguin Books.

BARNES, J. A. (1961), 'Physical and Social Kinship', *Philosophy of Science,* vol. 28, no. 3, pp. 296-99.

BARNES, J. A. (1964), 'Physical and Social Facts in Anthropology', *Philosophy of Science,* vol. 31, no. 3, pp. 294-97.

BARNES, J. A. (1973), 'Genetrix: Genitor:: Nature: Culture?', in *The Character of Kinship* (ed. J. Goody), Cambridge University Press.

BEALS, R. L. (1946), *Cherán: a Sierra Tarascan Village* (Publ. Inst. Social Anthrop. Smithsonian Inst. 2). Washington: Smithsonian Institution.

BEATTIE, J. H. M. (1964), 'Kinship and Social Anthropology', *Man* 130: 101-3.

BEATTIE, J. H. M. (1965a), 'The Content of Kinship', *Man* 38: 51-2.

BEATTIE, J. H. M. (1965b), Letter to *Man, Man* 109: 123.

BENDER, D. R. (1967), 'A Refinement of the Concept of Household: Families, Co-residence, and Domestic Functions', *American Anthropologist,* vol. 69, no. 5, pp. 493-504.

BERKNER, L. K. (1972), 'The Stem Family and the Developmental Cycle of the Peasant Household: An Eighteenth-Century Austrian Example', *American Historical Review,* vol. 2, no. 2, pp. 398-418.

THE HOLY BIBLE: DOUAY VERSION (1914), New York: P. J. Kennedy.

BIESANZ, J. (1949), 'Cultural and Economic Factors in Panamanian Race Relations', *American Sociological Review*, vol. 14, no. 6, pp. 772-9.

BIESANZ, J. (1950a), 'Race Relations in the Canal Zone', *Phylon*, vol. XI, no. 1, pp. 23-30.

BIESANZ, J. (1950b), 'Social Forces Retarding Development of Panama's Agricultural Resources', *Rural Sociology*, vol. 15, no. 2, pp. 148-55.

BIESANZ, J. (1952), 'The Economy of Panama', *Inter-American Economic Affairs*, vol. VI, no. 1, pp. 3-28.

BIESANZ, J. and BIESANZ, M. (1955), *The People of Panama*, New York: Columbia University Press.

BIESANZ, J. and SMITH, L. M. (1951), 'Race Relations in Panama and the Canal Zone', *American Journal of Sociology*, vol. LVII, no. 1, pp. 7-14.

BROWN, R. (1965), *Social Psychology*, New York: The Free Press.

CAMPBELL, J. K. (1964), *Honour, Family and Patronage*, Oxford: Clarendon Press.

CARLES, R. D. (1959), *220 Años del Periodo Colonial en Panama* (2nd ed.), Panama City: Ministerio de Educación.

CARO BAROJA, J. (1965), 'Honour and Shame: A Historical Account of Several Conflicts', in *Honour and Shame: The Values of Mediterranean Society* (ed. J. G. Peristiany), London: Weidenfeld & Nicolson.

CASTILLERO C., A. (1967), *Estructuras Sociales y Económicas de Veragua desde sus orígenes históricos, Siglos XVI y XVII*, Panama City: Editora Panamá.

CASTILLERO C., A. (1970), *La Sociedad Panameña: Historia de su Formacion e Integracion*, Panama City: Direccion General de Planificacion y Administracion de la Presidencia.

CASTILLERO R., E. J. (1962), *Historia de Panama* (7th ed.), Panama City: Impresora Panama.

CENSOS NACIONALES DE 1940 (1944), vol. VI, Panama.

CENSOS NACIONALES DE 1950 (1954), 'Lugares Poblados de la Republica', Panama.

CENSOS NACIONALES DE 1960 (1961), vol. III, Panama.

CENSOS NACIONALES DE 1960 (1964), vol. IX, Panama.

CENSOS NACIONALES DE 1960 (1966), vol. I, Panama.

CHRISTIAN, W. A. (1972), *Person and God in a Spanish Valley*, New York: Seminar Press.

CLARKE, E. (1966), *My Mother Who Fathered Me* (2nd ed.), London: Allen & Unwin.

CODIGO CIVIL DE LA REPUBLICA DE PANAMA (1960), Panama City: Universidad de Panama.

CURRIER, R. L. (1966), 'The Hot-Cold Syndrome and Symbolic Balance in Mexican and Spanish-American Folk Medicine', *Ethnology*, vol. 5, no. 3, pp. 251-63.

DAVENPORT, W. (1961), 'The Family System of Jamaica', *Social and Economic Studies*, vol. 10, no. 4, pp. 420-54.

DAVIS, J. (1970), 'Honour and Politics in Pisticci', *Proceedings of the Royal Anthropological Institute of Great Britain and Ireland for 1969,* pp. 69-81.

DOUGHTY, P. L. (1968), *Huaylas: An Andean District in Search of Progress,* Ithaca: Cornell University Press.

DUMONT, L. (1965), 'The Modern Conception of the Individual, Notes on its Genesis and that of Concomitant Institutions', *Contributions to Indian Sociology,* vol. VIII, pp. 13-61.

DUMONT, L. (1970a), *Homo Hierarchicus: An Essay on the Caste System* (trans. M. Sainsbury), University of Chicago Press.

DUMONT, L. (1970b), 'The Individual as an Impediment to Sociological Comparison and Indian History', in *Religion/Politics and History in India,* Paris: Mouton.

DUMONT, L. (1971), 'Religion, Politics, and Society in the Individualistic Universe', *Proceedings of the Royal Anthropological Institute of Great Britain and Ireland for 1970,* pp. 31-41.

DUNDES, A., LEACH, E. R., MARANDA, P. and MAYBURY-LEWIS, D. (1971), 'An Experiment: Suggestions and Queries from the Desk, with a Reply from the Ethnographer', in *Structural Analysis of Oral Tradition* (eds P. Maranda and E. K. Maranda) (University of Pennsylvania Publications in Folklore and Folklife, no. 3), Philadelphia: University of Pennsylvania Press.

ERASMUS, C. J. (1956), 'Culture Structure and Process: The Occurrence and Disappearance of Reciprocal Farm Labor', *Southwestern Journal of Anthropology,* vol. 12, no. 4, pp. 444-69.

FALS-BORDA, O. (1955), *Peasant Society in the Colombian Andes: A Sociological Study of Saucio,* Gainesville: University of Florida Press.

FORTES, M. (1949), 'Time and Social Structure: An Ashanti Case Study', in *Social Structure: Studies Presented to A. R. Radcliffe-Brown* (ed. M. Fortes), Oxford: Clarendon Press.

FORTES, M. (1958), 'Introduction', in *The Developmental Cycle in Domestic Groups* (ed. J. Goody) (Cambridge Papers in Social Anthropology, no. 1), Cambridge University Press.

FORTES, M. (1962), 'Introduction', in *Marriage in Tribal Societies* (ed. M. Fortes) (Cambridge Papers in Social Anthropology, no. 3), Cambridge University Press.

FORTES, M. (1969), *Kinship and the Social Order,* Chicago: Aldine Publishing Co.

FOSTER, G. M. (1953a), 'Cofradía and Compadrazgo in Spain and Spanish America', *Southwestern Journal of Anthropology,* vol. 9, no. 1, pp. 1-28.

FOSTER, G. M. (1953b), 'Relationships Between Spanish and Spanish-American Folk Medicine', *Journal of American Folklore,* vol. 66, no. 261, pp. 201-17.

FOSTER, G. M. (1960), *Culture and Conquest: America's Spanish Heritage,* (Viking Fund Publication in Anthropology, no. 27), Chicago: Quadrangle Books.

FOSTER, G. M. (1964), 'Speech Forms and Perception of Social Distance in a Spanish-Speaking Mexican Village', *Southwestern Journal of Anthropology,* vol. 20, no. 2, pp. 107-22.

FOSTER, G. M. (1967), *Tzintzuntzan: Mexican Peasants in a Changing World,* Boston: Little, Brown & Co.

FOSTER, G. M. and ROWE, J. H. (1961), 'Suggestions for Field Recording of Information on the Hippocratic Classification of Diseases and Remedies', *Kroeber Anthropological Society Papers,* no. 5, pp. 1-5.

FRAZIER, E. F. (1937), *The Negro Family in the United States,* University of Chicago Press.

FUSON, R. H. (1958), *The Savanna of Central Panama: A Study of Cultural Geography,* Dissertation, Louisiana State University, Ann Arbor: University Microfilms.

FUSON, R. H. (1959), 'Communal Labor in Central Panama', *Rural Sociology,* vol. 24, no. 1, pp. 57-9.

FUSON, R. H. (1964a), 'House Types of Central Panama', *Annals of the Association of American Geographers,* vol. 54, no. 2, pp. 190-208.

FUSON, R. H. (1964b), 'Land Tenure in Central Panama', *Journal of Geography,* vol. LXIII, no. 4, pp. 161-8.

GELLNER, E. (1957), 'Ideal Language and Kinship Structure', *Philosophy of Science,* vol. 24, no. 3, pp. 235-42.

GELLNER, E. (1960) 'The Concept of Kinship', *Philosophy of Science,* vol. 27, no. 2, pp. 187-204.

GELLNER, E. (1963), 'Nature and Society in Social Anthropology', *Philosophy of Science,* vol. 30, no. 3, pp. 236-51.

GILLIN, J. (1945), *Moche: A Peruvian Coastal Community* (Inst. of Soc. Anth. Pub. 3), Washington: Smithsonian Institution.

GILLIN, J. (1955), 'Ethos Components in Modern Latin American Culture', *American Anthropologist,* vol. 57, no. 3, part 1, pp. 488-500.

GONZALES, N. L. (1969), *Black Carib Household Structure: A Study of Migration and Modernization* (American Ethnological Society monograph 48), Seattle: University of Washington Press.

GOODY, J. (ed.) (1958), *The Developmental Cycle in Domestic Groups* (Cambridge Papers in Social Anthropology, no. 1), Cambridge University Press.

GOODY, J. (1972a), 'Domestic Groups' (Addison-Wesley Module no. 28), Reading, Mass.: Addison-Wesley.

GOODY, J. (1972b), 'The Evolution of the Family', in *Household and Family in Past Time* (ed. P. Laslett), Cambridge University Press.

GOUGH, E. K. (1959), 'The Nayars and the Definition of Marriage', *Journal of the Royal Anthropological Institute,* vol. 89, part I, pp. 23-34.

GUDEMAN, S. (1972), 'The *Compadrazgo* as a Reflection of the Natural and Spiritual Person', *Proceedings of the Royal Anthropological Institute for 1971,* pp. 45-71.

GUDEMAN, S. (1975), 'Spiritual Relationships and Selecting a Godparent', *Man* (N.S.), vol. 10, no. 2, pp. 221-37.

GUZMÁN, L. E. (1956), *Farming and Farmlands in Panama* (University of Chicago, Dept of Geography, Research Paper no. 44), University of Chicago Press.

HAMMEL, E. A. (1968), *Alternative Social Structures and Ritual Relations in the Balkans,* Englewood Cliffs: Prentice-Hall.

HARRIS, M. (1965), *Town and Country in Brazil,* New York: Columbia University Press.

HENRIQUES, F. (1953), *Family and Colour in Jamaica,* London: Eyre & Spottiswoode.

HERSKOVITS, M. J. (1941), *The Myth of the Negro Past,* New York: Harpers.

HOOPER, O. (1943), 'Rural Panama: Its Needs and Prospects', *Rural Sociology,* vol. 8, no. 3, pp. 247-53.

HOOPER, O. (1945), 'Aspectos de la Vida Social Rural de Panama', *Boletín del Instituto de Investigaciones Sociales y Económicas* (Universidad Inter-Americana, Panama), vol. II, no. 3, pp. 67-315.

HOROWITZ, M. M. (1967), *Morne-Paysan: Peasant Village in Martinique,* New York: Holt, Rinehart & Winston.

INGHAM, J. M. (1970), 'On Mexican Folk Medicine', *American Anthropologist,* vol. 72, no. 1, pp. 76-87.

KENNY, M. (1966), *A Spanish Tapestry: Town and Country in Castile,* New York: Harper and Row.

KROEBER, A. (1948), *Anthropology: Race-Language-Culture-Psychology-Prehistory* (rev ed.), New York: Harcourt, Brace & Co.

LAURIA, A. (1964), ' "Respeto", "Relajo" and Inter-personal Relations in Puerto Rico', *Anthropological Quarterly,* vol. 37, no. 2, pp. 53-67.

LEACH, E. R. (1955), 'Polyandry, Inheritance and the Definition of Marriage with particular reference to Sinhalese customary law', *Man,* vol. LV, no. 199.

LEACH, E. R. (1961a), 'Lévi-Strauss in the Garden of Eden: An Examination of Some Recent Developments in the Analysis of Myth', *New York Academy of Sciences: Transactions,* series II, vol. 23, no. 4, pp. 386-96.

LEACH, E. R. (1961b), *Pul Eliya: A Village in Ceylon,* Cambridge University Press.

LEACH, E. R. (1962), 'Genesis as Myth', *Discovery,* vol. XXIII, no. 5, pp. 30-5.

LEACH, E. R. (1967), 'Virgin Birth', *Proceedings of the Royal Anthropological Institute for 1966,* pp. 39-49.

LEACH, E. R. (1968), 'Introduction', in *Dialectic in Practical Religion* (ed. E. R. Leach) (Cambridge Papers in Social Anthropology, no. 5), Cambridge University Press.

LEWIS, O. (1951), *Life in a Mexican Village: Tepoztlán Restudied,* Urbana: University of Illinois Press.

LISÓN-TOLOSANA, C. (1966), *Belmonte de los Caballeros: A Sociological Study of a Spanish Town,* Oxford: Clarendon Press.

LLOYD, G. E. R. (1962), 'Right and Left in Greek Philosophy', *Journal of Hellenic Studies,* vol. 82, pp. 56-66.

LLOYD, G. E. R. (1964), 'The Hot and the Cold, the Dry and the Wet in Greek Philosophy', *Journal of Hellenic Studies,* vol. 84, pp. 92-106.

LOMBARDO, H. A. (1956), 'Costos de Producción de arroz: coa y machete; Provincia de Veraguas, Rep. de Panamá' (Mimeo.), Panama: Ministry of Agriculture.

LOTHROP, S. K. (1950), *Archaeology of Southern Veraguas, Panama* (Peabody Museum Memoir, vol. IX, no. 3), Cambridge: Peabody Museum.

MERCADO, S. E. (1959), *El Hombre y La Tierra en Panama (S. XVI): Segun Las Primeras Fuentes,* Madrid: La Universidad de Madrid.

MINTZ, S. W. and DAVENPORT, W. (ed.) (1961), *Working Papers in Caribbean Social Organization, Soc. and Eco. Studies,* vol. 10, no. 4.

MINTZ, S. W. and WOLF, E. R. (1950), 'An Analysis of Ritual Co-Parenthood (Compadrazgo)', *Southwestern Journal of Anthropology,* vol. 6, no. 4, pp. 341-68.

NATHHORST, B. (1970), *Formal or Structural Studies of Traditional Tales* (2nd ed.) (Stockholm Studies in Comparative Religion, 9), Stockholm: Kungl Boktryckeriet P. A. Norstedt & Söner.

NEEDHAM, R. (1960), 'Descent Systems and Ideal Language', *Philosophy of Science,* vol. 27, no. 1, pp. 96-101.

NEEDHAM, R. (ed.) (1971), *Rethinking Kinship and Marriage* (ASA vol. 11), London: Tavistock.

NELSON, C. (1971), *The Waiting Village: Social Change in Rural Mexico,* Boston: Little, Brown & Co.

PADILLA SEDA, E. (1956), 'Nocorá: The Subculture of Workers on a Government-Owned Sugar Plantation', in *The People of Puerto Rico* (J. H. Steward et al.), Urbana: University of Illinois Press.

PARSONS, E. C. (1936), *Mitla: Town of the Souls,* University of Chicago Press.

PARSONS, T. (1972), 'Culture and Social System Revisited', *Social Science Quarterly,* vol. 53, no. 2, pp. 253-66.

PEREIRA, J. B. (1963), *Historia de Panamá* (2nd ed.), Panama City: Agencia Internacional de Publicaciones, S.A.

PERISTIANY, J. G. (ed.) (1965), *Honour and Shame: The Values of Mediterranean Society,* London: Weidenfeld & Nicolson.

PIERSON, D. (1951), *Cruz Das Almas: A Brazilian Village* (Institute of Social Anthropology, 12), Washington: Smithsonian Institution.

PITT-RIVERS, J. A. (1958), 'Ritual Kinship in Spain', *New York Academy of Sciences: Transactions,* series II, vol. 20, no. 5, pp. 424-31.

PITT-RIVERS, J. A. (1961), *The People of the Sierra,* University of Chicago Press.

PITT-RIVERS, J. A. (1965), 'Honour and Social Status', in *Honour and Shame: The Values of Mediterranean Society* (ed. J. G. Peristiany), London: Weidenfeld & Nicolson.

PITT-RIVERS, J. A. (1967), 'Race, Color, and Class in Central America and the Andes', *Daedalus,* vol. 96, no. 2, pp. 542-59.

RAVICZ, R. (1967), 'Compadrinazgo', in *Handbook of Middle American Indians,* 6 (ed. R. Wauchope), Austin: University of Texas Press.

REDFIELD, R. and VILLA ROJAS, A. (1962), *Chan Kom: A Maya Village* (Phoenix ed., abridged), University of Chicago Press.

REICHEL-DOLMATOFF, G. and REICHEL-DOLMATOFF, A. (1961), *The People of Aritama: The Cultural Personality of a Colombian Mestizo Village,* London: Routledge & Kegan Paul.

RICHARDSON, J. (1970), *San Pedro, Colombia: Small Town in a Developing Society,* New York: Holt, Rinehart & Winston.

ROBE, S. L. (1960), *The Spanish of Rural Panama: Major Dialectal Features* (University of California Publications in Linguistics, vol. 20), Berkeley: University of California Press.

ROMNEY, K. and ROMNEY, R. (1966), *The Mixtecans of Juxtlahuaca, Mexico* (Six Cultures Series, vol. IV), New York: Wiley.

ROYAL ANTHROPOLOGICAL INSTITUTE OF GREAT BRITAIN AND IRELAND (1951), *Notes and Queries on Anthropology* (sixth edition), London: Routledge & Kegan Paul.

RUBIO, A. (1950), *La Vivienda Rural Panameña* (Publicación No. 18), Panama: Banco de Urbanización y Rehabilitación.

SAUER, C. O. (1966), *The Early Spanish Main,* Berkeley: University of California Press.

SCHEFFLER, H. W. and LOUNSBURY, F. G. (1971), *A Study in Structural Semantics: The Siriono Kinship System,* Englewood Cliffs: Prentice-Hall.

SCHNEIDER, D. M. (1964), 'The Nature of Kinship', *Man,* 217: 180-1.

SCHNEIDER, D. M. (1965a), 'The Content of Kinship', *Man* 108: 122-3.

SCHNEIDER, D. M. (1965b), 'Kinship and Biology', in *Aspects of the Analysis of Family Structure* (A. J. Coale et al.), Princeton University Press.

SCHNEIDER, D. M. (1968), *American Kinship: A Cultural Account,* Englewood Cliffs: Prentice-Hall.

SCHNEIDER, D. M. (1969), 'Kinship, Nationality and Religion in American Culture: Toward a Definition of Kinship', in *Forms of Symbolic Action* (ed. R. F. Spencer), Seattle: University of Washington Press.

SCHNEIDER, D. M. (1972), 'What is Kinship all About? ', in *Kinship Studies in the Morgan Centennial Year* (ed. P. Reining), Washington: Anthropological Society of Washington.

SERVICE, E. R. and SERVICE, H. S. (1954), *Tobatí: Paraguayan Town,* University of Chicago Press.

SMITH, M. G. (1962a), *Kinship and Community in Carriacou,* New Haven: Yale University Press.

SMITH, M. G. (1962b), *West Indian Family Structure,* Seattle: University of Washington Press.

SMITH, M. G. (1966), 'Introduction', to *My Mother Who Fathered Me* (2nd ed.) (E. Clarke), London: Allen & Unwin.

SMITH, R. T. (1956), *The Negro Family in British Guiana,* London: Routledge & Kegan Paul.

SMITH, R. T. (1957), 'The Family in the Caribbean', in *Caribbean Studies: A Symposium* (ed. V. Rubin), Jamaica: Inst. of Soc. and Eco. Res., Univ. of the West Indies.

SMITH, R. T. (1963), 'Culture and Social Structure in the Caribbean: Some Recent Work on Family and Kinship Studies', *Comparative Studies in Society and History*, vol. VI, no. 1, pp. 24-46.

STEIN, W. W. (1961), *Hualcan: Life in the Highlands of Peru*, Ithaca: Cornell University Press.

STEWARD, J. H. (1956), *The People of Puerto Rico: A Study in Social Anthropology*, Urbana: University of Illinois Press.

TAYLOR, H. O. (1922), *Greek Biology and Medicine*, Boston: Marshall Jones Co.

THOMAS AQUINAS, SAINT (1947), *Summa Theologica*, vol. II (trans. Fathers of the English Dominican Province), New York: Benziger Brothers.

WAGLEY, C. (1949), *The Social and Religious Life of a Guatemalan Village* (American Anthropological Association Memoir 71).

WAGLEY, C. (1953), *Amazon Town: A Study of Man in the Tropics*, New York: Macmillan.

WAGLEY, C. (1959), 'On the Concept of Social Race in the Americas', in *Actas del 33 Congreso Internacional de Americanistas*, vol. I, San José: Lehmann.

WHITTEN, N. E. (1965), *Class, Kinship, and Power in an Ecuadorian Town: The Negroes of San Lorenzo*, Stanford University Press.

WORSLEY, P. M. (1956), 'The Kinship System of the Tallensi: A Revaluation', *Journal of the Royal Anthropological Institute*, vol. 86, part 1, pp. 37-75.

Index

Abortions, 49, 108, 194
Address in *compadrazgo*, 208, 211, 212-13, 214, 216, 220, 224; *see also* Terminology
Adoption, 164-5; *see also* Fostering
Affines, 176-7
Age, 70, 241; *see also* Life cycle
Agrarian reform agency, 18, 28, 29-30; *see also* Land
Agriculture, 30-2
All Souls' Day, 48, 72
Amarillo (yellow), 67
Angelito (little angel), 58, 119-20, 164, 204, 255n.5,6
Animals, 49, 79, 260n.21; and children, 109, 200-1, 204; and dirt, 91; and respect, 81; concepts about, 46; *see also* Dogs

Baptism, 119, 120, 190-205, 223, 225, 226, 228, 230; of animals, 201
Baptismal clothes, 195, 196-7
Blanco (white), 67
Blood, 75
Bolo, 196, 202-4, 227, 260n.24
Bordón, 112-13, 115, 116, 181
Borrowing, 37, 38; and *compadrazgo,* 210, 213, 227
Botella, 17
Bravo (angry), 68, 81; *see also* Fighting

Cabecera (head), 115
Cabrón, see Cuckold
Cacique, 116, 254n.10
Campesino (countryman), xi, 4, 64; and civilization, 65-8, 139; and government organizations, 16-21, 188-9, 253n.30; and larger society, 22, 25, 41, 80-1, 212-13, 222; and national market, 35, 41; and Panama City, 158; and Panama law, 132, 135, 140-2, 162, 164-5; and political participation, 16-18, 21, 28; and Santiago, 22, 35; and sugarcane mills, 32, 33, 41; as squatter, 8, 27-30; communities, 4, 8, 9-10; evaluation of, 38, 65-8; *see also* Spanish culture
Canal Zone, 1, 18, 158
Capitolino, 64-5
Caribbean area, 10, 234-5
Caserío, 7
Chapel, 6, 24, 63
Children, 62, 108-10, 162-3, 200-1, 204; *see also Criar,* Life cycle, Parent-child bond
Chivas (buses), 23
Cholo, 65, 67, 73, 81, 251n.2,3
Chombo, 67, 251n.8
Christ, 42, 43, 52, 62, 63
Chulo, 106-7
Church marriage, 136-46 *passim,* 154, 190, 198, 205, 221-2; and *compadrazgo,* 221-2, 227
Cimarrón, 66
Civil marriage, 135-46 *passim,* 153-4
Civilization, 65-8, 81
Climate, 26
Cochino, see Pigs
Colour terms, 66-7
Common-law union, *see Juntado*
Community, 69, 83-4, 85, 95; *see also* Los Boquerones
Compadrazgo: and respect, 81; and sin, 58, 62; and wealth, *see* Economy and *compadrazgo;* costs, 194, 195-7; in relation to other domains, 224-31, 234; nature of, 190, 225; network, 206, 217, 223, 224; terms, 70, 73
Compadre, 145, 190, 194, 198, 199; at death, 48; bond, 210-15; fighting with, 49; power of, 216-17; selection, 217-23

Compromiso, 83, 101, 126, 145

Confirmation, 120, 190, 198

Conjugal separations, 143, 144, 156-61, 162-3; and baptism, 197; statistics on, 155, 157-8, 163, 257n.1

Conjugal unions, 101-3, 233-4, 254n.2; and *compadrazgo*, 218-19, 222, 224-31; and love, 99; and prostitutes, 149-51; and social status, 139; and wealth, 99, 139-40; compared, 151-4; in relation to other domains, 99-101, 140-2, 154, 168, 187-8; stability of, 138; statistics on, 131, 136-8, 145-6, 154, 257n.16

Corporate groups, 10

Council of Trent, 191

Countryman, *see* Campesino

Criar (to raise), 79, 83, 126, 165-8, 233-4; and *compadrazgo*, 230-1; and kinship, 97, 108-10, 156, 171-4, 177

Cuckold, 106, 147, 157, 158, 160

Culture, 13

Death, 44, 252n.11, 253n.3; and *compadrazgo*, 209, 212; family at, 178-81; *see also* Funerals

Defend the self, 79, 83, 106

Destiny, 44-5, 50-1

Developmental cycle, 112, 114-15, 117, 126-8, 137

Devil, 60, 144, 164, 192, 195; and *angelitos*, 58; and households, 95; and sexual relations, 57

Dicho (saying, proverb), 249n.8

Dirt, 49, 58, 254n.7

Distrust, 83-4, 95, 103, 109-10, 213, 229, 253n.30, 261n.2

Divorce, *see* Conjugal separations

Dogs, 46, 201, 251n.8, 260n.21; *see also* Animals

Easter, 60-1

Ecology, 26, 28, 31, 32, 42

Economy, 30-42; and *compadrazgo*, 194, 195-7, 202-3, 209-10, 214, 218; and conjugal separations, 156, 158, 162-3; and conjugal unions, 139, 143, 147, 148, 151, 154; and kinship, 176, 177, 179-81, 186, 188; capital, 37, 38, 41

Elderly persons, 176, 181-2

Elopement, 134, 135

Eve, 51-3, 58, 76-7, 191, 233

Evil eye, 54, 192-3, 250n.9

Extra-residential liaisons, 146, 147-8, 153

Fábrega family, 27, 28

Faith, 45, 46, 51

Family, 182

Father-child bond, 97-8, 111-15, 132, 134, 141, 161, 225, 256n.9

Female, *see* Male-female, Man, Women

Fictive *compadrazgo*, 198, 199, 215-17

Fictive kinship, 171, 183

Fighting, 84, 115, 156-7, 177, 178, 219, 254n.9

First name, 190, 196, 200, 204, 228

Fortes, M., 11, 12, 117, 184, 235-6

Foster, G., 10, 202

Fostering, 58, 164-5, 168, 174, 184, 257n.4; *see also* Adoption

Friends, 34, 68-9, 80

Fruit trees, 53, 57

Fundamento, 126

Funerals: attendance at, 69, 209, 212, 258n.1, 261n.28; of *angelitos*, 120, 255n.6; of unbaptized, 200-1; *see also* Death

Gardens, 54, 58, 87

Genealogy, 175, 183-4, 186

Genesis, 52-8

Getting an interest, 46, 111-13, 115, 121, 128, 164

God, 99, 221, 232; and destiny, 44-5; and devil, 47-8; and faith, 46; and man, 43-7, 129; and respect, 80; and social order, 85; at death, 48-9, 72, 118, 144, 214, 227; power of, 44, 47-8

Godmother, 195-7, 259n.8, 260n.23

Godparents, 190; and godchildren, 206-10; power of, 203, 204, 217-18, 226, 227; selection of, 217-23

Gough, K., 131-2

Honour, 77, 78, 101, 213; *see also* Respect

Hot and cold, 74-5, 87, 218, 226, 227, 232

Household, 94-6, 98, 233-4; and *compadrazgo*, 219-23, 228-31; and conjugal separations, 163-4; and economy, 26, 34-6, 38-41, 94-5, 100-1;

and family, 86; and fields, 61, 90; and kinship, 228-31; and male-female relationship, 91-4; and street, 68; authority, 102-3, 111, 113, 115-16, 122; concept, 86, 90; headship, 101, 111-13, 237, 242-3; labour, 91-4, 111; property, 89-90, 111-13, 127-8; statistics, 237, 241, 243; *see also Criar,* Residence
Houses, 87-9
Huevo (egg), 107, 252n.21
Humours, 74-6, 252n.19

Incest, 118-19, 124, 150, 172-4
Indians, 1, 65, 193
Individual, 85, 232-4, 253n.30; and *compadrazgo,* 191, 199-205, 224; and conjugal separations, 63-4; and conjugal unions, 141, 142, 144-8, 154; and household, 90-4, 96, 118-30 *passim*; and kinship, 116; and respect, 77-85; and social order, 83-4; concept of, 64; nature/spirit of, 218; responsibility, 92; *see also* Male-female, Man
Inheritance, 111-13

Joseph, Saint, 52
Junior household member, 257n.3
Junta, 34, 180
Juntado (common-law union), 132, 134-5, 136-54 *passim,* 156, 161, 162, 170

Kinship: amity, 184, 188-9; and *compadrazgo,* 219-20, 222-3; and conjugal unions, 187-8; genetics, 11, 108, 156; and household, 97-8, 118, 124, 155-6, 164-74, 233-4, 237, 243; and labour, 34; and locality, 175, 183-9; and respect, 81; explanations, 11-14, 235-6; extra-domestic obligations of, 175-6, 177-81; in relation to other domains, 116, 129, 142, 170, 171-2, 233-4; nature of, 11-14, 97-8, 132-3, 141-2, 174, 225, 234; network, 178-81, 182-9; obligations, 186-8; optative nature of, 175-81, 187, 189; *see also Criar,* Economy, Father-child bond, Legitimacy, Mother-child bond, Parent-child bond, Recognition, Sibling bond
Knowing, 46

Labour, 33-4, 91-4, 100-3, 160
Land, 8, 26-30, 213, 249n.3; *see also* Agrarian reform agency
Leach, E., 12, 52-3, 131, 133
Legitimacy, 131-2, 140-2, 154, 254n.2
Life cycle, 119-24, 166, 181-2, 228, 232-4, 253n.3; and *compadrazgo,* 192-205 *passim*; and conjugal unions, 137-9; and household, 94, 117-18, 120-2, 233-4; and kinship, 170; and respect, 81, 82; and step-parenthood, 150-1, 170, 173; names for, 70, 73-4, 119-20
Little angel, *see Angelito*
Locality, 178, 186-8, 233
Los Boquerones, 4, 6-10, 19, 23-5
Lottery, 250n.2
Luck, 44-5

Male-female, 33-4, 123-4, 233-4; and animals, 94; and conjugal separations, 158-61, 174; and conjugal unions, 99-101, 139, 141-2, 144-5; and eating, 76; and hot/cold, 75-6; and household, 61, 91-4, 102-3, 129; and religion, 52-8, 61; and respect, 81, 100-1; and sexual relations, 52, 76; contrast, 119-22, 126-7, 237-9, 241-3, 246-7; in-equivalence of, 57, 58, 70; *see also* Conjugal unions, Men, Women
Man: and animals, 46, 49, 50, 79, 90-1, 94; and devil, 47; and respect, 81; as natural being, 75, 77, 191, 228, 232, 234; as spiritual being, 76-7, 191, 224, 228, 232, 234; *see also* Individual
Manda, see Vows to saints
Marriage, 131-3, 254n.2; *see also* Church marriage, Civil marriage
Martín de Porres, San, 24, 43, 59-60, 63, 251n.13
Mary, (Virgin), 44, 51-2, 58, 76-7, 233
Mayor, 143
Men: and conjugal separations, 157, 158, 160-1; and conjugal unions, 145-6, 154; and polygyny, 147; and respect, 81, 100-1; and the street, 104; financial independence of, 113; sexual freedom of, 104-5; work of, 92-4; *see also* Individual
Midwife, 261n.4
Monte, 84, 90, 134, 163, 253n.29
Montuno, 65

Moreno (dark), 66
Moro (Moor), 192, 200, 260n.18
Mother-child bond, 113-14, 142, 161, 170, 180; and genetics, 97-8, 132; as basic tie, 52, 108, 225

Names: of animals, 201, 251n.8; of persons, 71-3; *see also* First name, Surnames
Nature (*la naturaleza*), 75
Negro, 3, 66
Neolocal, 118, 188
Novios (sweethearts), 123-4

Padres de Familia (Family heads), 23
Panama, 1, 4, 6, 16, 21; *see also* Campesino and larger society
pesino and larger society
Panama City, 1, 33, 158, 159, 161, 179, 180
Parent-child bond, 99-100, 108-10, 175-6, 233-4; and *compadrazgo*, 219-20, 222-3; and conjugal separations, 161; and conjugal unions, 140-2, 147, 153-4; and residence, 147-8, 167-8; statistics on, 162; tensions in, 113-15
Patron saint, *see* Martín de Porres, San
Peasant, *see* Campesino
Pena (penalty), 78
Pendejo, 107, 145
Peón, 34, 220
Peonada, 34
Peter, Saint, 45-6, 48, 49-50, 72, 92, 129
Pigs, 47, 48, 66
Political relationships, 170-2, 215, 226, 258n.4,7
Polygyny, 146-7, 153
Population, 6, 28-9, 241
Potions, 76, 89, 160, 253n.4
Pregnancy, *see* Women
Prestige, 82
Prostitutes, 104, 123, 149-53
Proverb, *see* Dicho

Raising, *see* Criar
Reciprocity, 37, 69, 176, 177-8, 188
Recognition (*reconocer*), 140-2, 153, 166, 169-70, 172, 176, 255n.2, 256n.9,10
Regidor, 17, 19-21, 113
Regimiento, 6, 8, 17
Religion, 250n.3; and *compadrazgo*, 190-200 *passim*, 204, 206-8, 210,
218-19, 221-3, 230; and conjugal unions, 139, 143-6; and household, 50-1, 94, 95; and political organization, 48, 59; and sexual relations, 61; and social organization, 58, 63; liturgical calendar of, 60
Renouncing kinship, 113-14, 132-3, 141, 142, 176, 178, 181, 189
Residence: and *compadrazgo*, 206, 216; and conjugal unions, 133-5, 142, 146, 147, 149, 151-4; and incest, 172-4; and kinship, 97-8, 155-6, 165-8, 174; and siblings, 171-2; and step-parenthood, 168-70; rules, 118-19, 128-9; transition at conjugal union, 127; *see also* Criar, Household
Respect, 103, 123, 126, 170-1, 177, 182, 204, 233; and behaviour, 80, 82-3; and church marriage, 139; and *compadrazgo*, 208-19 *passim*, 222, 223; and conjugal unions, 144, 145; and friendship, 80; and God, 46, 80; and household, 129; and individual, 83-4; and prestige, 82; and responsibility, 82; and social order, 78-9, 80-2; and wealth, 38, 82; as currency, 85; defined, 77-8; terms of, 70-1, 73-4
Responsibility, 45, 46, 69-70, 82, 83-4, 92
Rezandor (prayer), 193, 250n.5
Rice, 30, 102, 190, 199, 215, 226, 259n.17

Saints, 43, 63, 72-3; as intermediaries, 48, 58-9, 62; vows to, 24, 59, 61-2
Santiago, 3, 4, 21, 193, 194-6, 201, 213; marketplace, 35; mayor, 19-21, 113; political organization, 17
Schneider, D., 11, 12
Settlement patterns, 41
Sexual relations, 120-1, 144-5, 171, 173; among young people, 122-4; and children, 109; and *compadrazgo*, 208, 212, 215, 219, 223, 227; and conjugal unions, 104-7, 150-1; and devil, 57; and eating, 50, 55, 106, 154, 173; and hot/cold, 75-6; and household, 87, 129; and kinship, 149; and passion, 52; and religious prohibitions, 61; and respect, 80; and sin, 49-50, 57-8;

prohibited, 124; public/private, 49-50
Shame, 77-9, 81, 82-3, 106; *see also* Respect
Sibling bond, 115-16, 170-2, 174, 177-81, 220, 222-3, 233-4
Sin, 48-50, 118, 120, 129, 144, 204; and dirt, 49, 58, 91; at death, 57; original, 55, 76, 191
Snakes, 53-5, 57-8
Social structure, 10, 13, 30, 85
Soul, 44, 48
Spanish *compadrazgo,* and culture, 199-200
Spanish conquerors, 1, 3
Spanish culture, 3, 9, 74, 77, 190-1, 222, 232, 234, 248n.4, 254n.7
Spirit, 44, 75, 259n.17
Spiritual relationship, 191, 206, 208, 210, 214
Spouse selection, 124-6
Stealing, 84
Step-parenthood, 150-1, 159-60, 168-70, 173, 174, 184
Stores, 35, 37
Sugar-cane mills, 32, 41, 213
Suicide, 114
Surnames, 71, 141-2, 165, 166, 190, 204, 228, 256n.8

Synchronic description, 10

Terminology, 70-4, 225 *compadrazgo,* 207, 211, 220-1; kinship, 70, 73, 166, 168, 170-1, 176-7, 182-3; *see also* Address in *compadrazgo*
Town dweller, 4; *see also Capitolino*
Trigueño (dark), 67
Tulivieja, 110, 250n.12

Veraguas, 3, 4, 16
Vergüenza, see Shame
Vice, 49-50
Vows to saints (*manda*), 59, 61-2, 79

Wealth, 37-40, 51, 82, 89-90
Witches, 192-3, 216-17, 250n.12
Women: and conjugal separations, 157, 158, 160-1; and conjugal unions, 145-6, 154; and cooking, 102; and extra-residential liaisons, 148; and nature, 75-6, 81, 106; and polygyny, 147; and respect, 100-1; and shame, 81; and snakes, 53-8; as prostitutes, 81-2, 149-50; concepts about, 51-2, 60, 62; pregnant, 54; sexual role of, 105-7; work of, 92-4; *see also* Individual
Worsley, P., 12, 235-6